W9-DBT-036

Unless Recalled Earlier

DATE DUE

DEMCO, INC. 38-2931

The Allure of the Foreign

Linking Levels of Analysis
Emilio F. Moran, Series Editor

Covering Ground: Communal Water Management and the State in the Peruvian Highlands
David W. Guillet

The Coca Boom and Rural Social Change in Bolivia
Harry Sanabria

Diagnosing America: Anthropology and Public Engagement
Shepard Forman, editor

The Social Causes of Environmental Destruction in Latin America
Michael Painter and William H. Durham, editors

Culture and Global Change: Social Perceptions of Deforestation in the Lacandona Rain Forest in Mexico
Lourdes Arizpe, Fernanda Paz, and Margarita Velázquez

Transforming Societies, Transforming Anthropology
Emilio F. Moran, editor

The Allure of the Foreign: Imported Goods in Postcolonial Latin America
Benjamin Orlove, editor

The Allure of the Foreign

Imported Goods in Postcolonial Latin America

EDITED BY BENJAMIN ORLOVE

Ann Arbor

THE UNIVERSITY OF MICHIGAN PRESS

Copyright © by the University of Michigan 1997
All rights reserved
Published in the United States of America by
The University of Michigan Press
Manufactured in the United States of America
⊗ Printed on acid-free paper

2000   1999   1998   1997   4   3   2   1

A CIP catalog record for this book is available from the British Library

Library of Congress Cataloging-in-Publication Data

The allure of the foreign : imported goods in postcolonial Latin
   America / edited by Benjamin Orlove.
        p.   cm. — (Linking levels of analysis)
     Includes bibliographical references and index.
     ISBN 0-472-10664-3 (acid-free paper)
     1. Consumption (Economics)—Latin America—History.   2. Imports—
Latin America—History.   3. Consumer goods—Latin America—History.
I. Orlove, Benjamin S.   II. Series.
HC130.C6A43   1997
382'.5'0948—dc21   96-45899
                                                                   CIP

Acknowledgments

As is so often the case with edited volumes, this book has had a long history. The overall notion of this book developed in a seminar on anthropological and historical approaches to consumption that Arnold Bauer and I offered in 1990. It first took recognizable form at a symposium at the 1993 Annual Spring Meeting of the American Ethnological Society with the special theme "Goods and Objects." Early drafts of several of the chapters in the volume (Fletcher, Heyman, Langer, and Orlove and Bauer) were presented at that symposium, entitled "Giving Importance to Imports." Mary Weismantel was the discussant at that symposium, and her thoughtful comments have had a strong influence on all of the papers. Two of the individuals initially scheduled in that session (Leedom Lefferts and Richard Wilk) have not continued through to this volume, while two new individuals (Krüggeler and Vega) have joined it.

Of the many people who have offered comments and other sorts of assistance, I would particularly like to thank those at three stages: Ward Stavig, whose collaboration at the earliest point of the book encouraged me to continue; Peter Hunter and Susan Wilcox, who, halfway through, reassured me that the combination of quantitative and qualitative research was indeed a possibility; Shelly Diaz and James Hafner, whose efforts near the end convinced me that it would be feasible to assemble the numerous different drafts into a single manuscript.

I wish also to thank the anonymous reviewers for their suggestions, and Susan Whitlock, of the University of Michigan Press, for her thoughtful guidance and steady encouragement.

Series Introduction

The series Linking Levels of Analysis focuses on studies that deal with the relationships between local-level systems and larger, more inclusive systems. While we know a great deal about how local and larger systems operate, we know a great deal less about how these levels articulate with each other. It is this kind of research, in all its variety, that Linking Levels of Analysis is designed to publish. Works should contribute to the theoretical understanding of such articulations, create or refine methods appropriate to interlevel analysis, and represent substantive contributions to the social sciences.

The volume before you, *The Allure of the Foreign,* is the product of thoughtful analysis by authors noted for their expertise in the study of consumption. They bring this expertise to the subject of consumption in Latin America. The materials are rich in historical detail, as they construct a complex narrative of how the allure of the foreign leads to the neglect of the local and the reification of imported goods. That this should be the case should come as no surprise to anyone, since we all recognize that with the acquisition of greater capital, or aspirations for upward mobility, populations everywhere engage in display behavior of their goods and capital to accentuate their achievement, superiority, or supralocal aspirations. There is hardly any more noticeable display than goods that are foreign and thus exotic enough to distinguish one from those yet unable to command such purchases. Why and how such a process unfolds has hardly ever been analyzed with the kind of detail provided by the authors in this volume. This book will constitute an important intellectual "beachhead" on the topic of consumption. A recent National Academy of Sciences expert panel met to discuss this topic and outlined an agenda for research that will influence social science research on this topic for some time to come. It is no surprise that the organizers of this volume were among that group of experts and that their counsel, here and in that panel, provides important directions for this emerging field of research. *The Allure of the Foreign* fits into this series because it tries to link anthropology's traditional focus on economic anthropology and the study of production to the urgent need to expand this interest to the consumption side of human behavior. The volume is concerned with intergenerational wealth flows, and with processes that link local communities to global flows of capital and material production.

This volume not only sets a challenge and an agenda for the next generation of social scientists but also informs other social scientists on the ways in which the combined efforts of historians, anthropologists, sociologists, and experts in other human sciences provide a distinctive voice about the problems of the past, the present, and the future. It has been common to blame the problems of the contemporary world on population growth. Efforts to point out that our consumption is part of the problem have been muffled. This volume provides one of many needed correctives to that view. It offers a cautionary set of historical tales about how local communities are linked to global processes of material consumption that have costs unimaginable when the process begins. In so doing, the volume serves to relink anthropology to the other policy sciences, and highlights the fact that one of the contributions of the social sciences is its capacity to speak to different temporal and spatial levels of analysis.

It is my hope that this volume will not only be a major contribution to our understanding of how consumption is tied to the processes of production and accumulation, but that it will also inspire readers to submit their work to the series. Please contact the series editor, or other members of the editorial board, to discuss your proposed work and our possible interest in publishing it.

Editor

Emilio F. Moran, Department of Anthropology, University of Indiana

Editorial Board

John Bowen, Department of Anthropology, Washington University, St. Louis

Conrad Kottak, Department of Anthropology, University of Michigan, Ann Arbor

Kathleen Newman, Department of Anthropology, Columbia University, New York

Douglas White, Department of Anthropology, University of California, Irvine

Contents

Chapter

1. Giving Importance to Imports 1
Benjamin Orlove and Arnold J. Bauer

2. Changing Consumption Patterns and Everyday
Life in Two Peruvian Regions: Food, Dress, and
Housing in the Central and Southern Highlands
(1820–1920) 31
Thomas Krüggeler

3. From Benches to Sofas: Diversification of Patterns
of Consumption in San José (1857–1861) 67
Patricia Vega Jiménez

4. Foreign Cloth in the Lowland Frontier: Commerce
and Consumption of Textiles in Bolivia, 1830–1930 93
Erick D. Langer

5. Chile in the Belle Epoque: Primitive Producers,
Civilized Consumers 113
Benjamin Orlove and Arnold J. Bauer

6. Imports and Standards of Justice on the
Mexico–United States Border 151
Josiah McC. Heyman

7. Building from Migration: Imported Design and
Everyday Use of Migrant Houses in Mexico 185
Peri L. Fletcher

Bibliography 203

Contributors 215

Index 217

Chapter 1

Giving Importance to Imports

Benjamin Orlove and Arnold J. Bauer

This book is centered on a single phenomenon: the vast expansion of imported goods in Latin America in the nineteenth and twentieth centuries. By tracing the demand for these goods and their patterns of use, the authors in this volume offer an account of the origins and consequences of this expansion of imports. Summarized in a single sentence, the contributions of this volume to Latin American studies, to economic history, and to social scientific studies of the international order at large lie in its emphasis on the internal social factors that created a strong appeal for foreign goods among many sectors of the independent Latin American nations in the nineteenth and twentieth centuries. This view contrasts sharply with the few earlier studies on the topic, which have stressed external economic factors, particularly shifts in global trade, as the principal forces shaping the importation of foreign goods into Latin America. As we show later in this chapter, this attention to internal social factors helps explain the varied responses to European goods in other parts of the preindustrial world: their avid acceptance in Eastern Europe, their rejection in China, and a mixed, ambivalent reception in the Middle East.

Like a distant cousin who appears each year at Thanksgiving but whom nobody ever talks to very much, the theme of imports in Latin America has a familiar look, despite the lack of acquaintance with its personal character. Some tendencies within the social sciences and history have contributed to making imports a long-known but little-examined topic within Latin American studies. By emphasizing production over consumption and by stressing industrial capitalism as a key dynamic force in world history, many writers have directed attention toward the exports of raw materials from Latin America and away from the imports of goods into Latin America. The standard treatment of imports within many works on Latin American studies reflects these tendencies. For example, the fourth volume of the *Cambridge History of Latin America,* covering the period 1870–1930, contains two chapters, simply titled "Economy, 1870–1914" (Glade 1986) and "Economy, 1914–1930" (Thorp 1986). These chapters explore the development of different economic sectors through their relations to the production of exports, and allocate little space to the discussion of imports. Glade states

> What happened in Latin America between 1870 and 1914 is . . . indisputable. The principal engine of growth in this period was the industrial production in countries of the economic centre [Europe and the United States], with its concomitant social and economic changes. The aggregate growth rate in these advanced countries was largely determined by the rate of growth of industrial output, which in turn determined the rate of increase in the demand for exports from the peripheral economies, including those of Latin America. (1986, 7)

Thorp's analysis of later decades is similar; she writes of "the countries of Latin America, which were still almost exclusively primary producers and exporters" (1986, 63).

In their popular text *Modern Latin America,* Thomas Skidmore and Peter Smith describe "export-import growth" (1992, 44) as the key motor of change from the stagnation that occurred immediately after Latin American independence in the 1820s and the key source of the region's current difficulties in consolidating economic development and participatory democracy. Throughout their discussion, Skidmore and Smith often replace the terms *export-import growth* with phrases such as *export economies* (45) and *export-oriented economic growth* (47), suggesting the greater importance that they give to exports than to imports. As exports of raw materials grew during the long cycle of European and North American industrial expansion between 1880 and 1930, forms of production such as plantations, mines, and ranches also expanded, and the consequent shifts in class structure led to a reorganization of political relations. The authors mention briefly that this export-based growth allowed the wealthy to import many luxuries and the masses to replace local crafts such as textiles and pottery with cheap manufactured items from Europe and North America. The authors also note that some machinery was imported. Imports receive central attention, though, only after the depression of 1930 caused global demand for Latin American products to plummet. With its links to world trade greatly diminished, the region was forced to expand its manufacturing sector in order to produce the items it had formerly obtained from Europe and North America. This import-substitution industrialization marked the 1930s and 1940s, leaving a legacy (of strong state participation in the economy and centralized populist regimes that drew support from new urban working classes) that in turn has shaped Latin America to the present. In this "export-centered view," then, levels of imports are shaped by the availability and affordability of foreign goods, which in turn depend largely on external economic factors such as transport costs, terms of trade, and exchange rates.[1]

Bulmer-Thomas's more recent review, *The Economic History of Latin America since Independence* (1995), offers essentially the same perspective. He seeks to explain why Latin America, potentially a rich area, continues to be poor and to face great inequality of wealth and income. He emphasizes "three basic ideas" (14) to explain this situation, all connected directly with exports. For the first, he introduces the term *commodity lottery* (15)—the features that lead particular raw materials to encounter higher or lower rates of growth of demand and to promote greater or lesser expansion in other economic sectors. In the second, he examines the "mechanisms of export-led growth"—the transfer of export-generated capital to nonexport sectors, the growth of a skilled and monetarized labor force in the export sector, and the establishment of state policies to transfer revenues, especially taxes on foreign trade, in order to promote development (16–17). The third basic idea overlaps with the final element of the second: the "economic-policy environment" (17), again concerned with "transferring productivity gains from the export to the non-export sector" (17). Though the book pays very close attention to the structure and dynamic of export sectors, it grants imports only the most cursory treatment—a brief analysis of the distribution of imports according to the countries from which they originated (76–78), occasional reference to the influence of state policies on import levels (138, 251, 262–63, 379–80). Even the explanation of import-substitution industrialization—what Bulmer-Thomas terms *inward-looking development* (276)—centers on disruptions in export economies during depressions and wars.

Though the export of primary products clearly has been one of the fundamental forces that have shaped Latin America's history, Bulmer-Thomas exaggerates the role of these exports by underplaying the significance of the demand for imports as an autonomous factor. He fails to note the strong preference for imports as one of the factors that slowed the development of textile manufacturing in the mid-nineteenth century (42–43) and of domestic agriculture in later decades (121–30), and he does not attempt to explain the puzzling fact that the wealthy in Latin America have invested less, and consumed more, than their counterparts in other regions of the world where income and wealth are also unevenly distributed (423, 428). An item in the index captures the perspective of the entire book: "boom and slumps, *see* exports, cycles" (477).

To take one concrete example of this emphasis on exports—this export-centered view, as it might be termed—we turn to a recent book *Coffee, Society, and Power in Latin America* (Roseberry, Gudmundson, and Samper 1995), an edited volume which contains nine studies of the expansion of coffee economies in the nineteenth and twentieth centuries in Central and South America and the Spanish-speaking Caribbean. Of these, eight focus exclusively on coffee production: the shifts in patterns of land tenures, labor systems, and power relations that accompanied the expansion of the trade in coffee. To mention only one of several possible topics of research on coffee consumption, the development of the taste for instant coffee merits discussion. There are two major species of coffee raised commercially in the world. The beans of *Coffea arabica*—a more delicate tree, often grown at higher elevations and under shade—are usually sold to make brewed coffee, while most of those from the tougher *Coffea robusta* are processed industrially for instant coffee powder. Most Latin American and Asian producers raise the former, though there are some areas in Latin America, especially in Brazil, where the latter (the dominant species in Africa) is cultivated. Though there are some agronomic and botanical differences between the two species—the bean of *robusta* contains more bitter substances—the history of the consumption of brewed and instant coffee reflects social and cultural factors that remain less studied than the production. The comparative study with other tropical crops consumed as hot beverages is evident: much cocoa is prepared in the form of instant powders, while tea, with the exception of some inexpensive iced teas, is always made fresh from leaves. Nonetheless, this edited volume contains only one chapter (Jiménez 1995) that examines demand, and even this study centers on the "coffee interest" within the United States, the large-scale traders and processors who mounted campaigns to expand the demand for coffee—for example by pushing the notion of "the coffee break" (49). Even in this case, North American consumers are passive. Apparently unable to develop new patterns of consumption on their own, their behavior changes only as a response to price stimuli and to advertising. Latin American consumers are entirely absent in this description, although they also accounted for a significant portion of global coffee demand. They even formed part of the international coffee trade, since some Latin American countries were not self-sufficient in coffee production. Though the individual chapters of this work possess considerable solidity, merit, and interest, the volume as a whole excludes questions of Latin American consumption and Latin American imports.

The export-centered framework of the *Cambridge History of Latin America,* of Skidmore and Smith's text, of the coffee volume, and many other similar works provides a minor position for imports. This framework does not permanently remove imports from view, although it does often set them aside. It usually accords them a brief mention and a position of distinctly secondary importance. In this way, it complements the purely anecdotal comments on consumption in many historical works on the Latin American belle epoque. A number of writers notice the construction boom of the last third of the nineteenth century when the low-lying, patio-centered houses inherited from the Spanish regime gave way to two- or three-storied mansions, inevitably modeled on the mansard-roofed style of the Second Empire, with fancy staircases and gates displayed to the street. A few sources provide greater detail. In Mexico City in the 1880s, French cuisine became "all the rage" and the city's most elegant restaurants, such as the Maison Dorée and the Fonda de Recamier, "did not dare open their doors without a French chef" (MacLachlan and Beezley, 1994, 132–33). Lima's upper class, estimated at only 18,000 people in 1895, fell over itself to join private golf courses and horse-racing clubs while the "highest ambition of a Limeño" was to dress in the Parisian style (Burga and Flores Galindo 1980, 14). The Parisian *Revue des Deux Mondes* lay half open in several hundred salons and even perhaps read by those with a taste for fin-de-siècle literary and political discussion and ideas. The elite, from Mexico through Lima to Buenos Aires and Santiago, "imported grand pianos, European wines and liquors," traveled abroad, and sent their children to European schools—and believed that in doing so, they were "sharing the same activities and attitudes of the international gentry" (Beezley 1987, 14). These observations are acute, but remain little developed. They suggest the opulence of the newly rich and their separation from the poor working masses, but do not explore consumption as a key theme in Latin American economy and society.

Recently, a few writers have focused more closely on the role of domestic and foreign goods within the sphere of consumption in Latin America. Even their books, though, do not move very far in challenging the framework that treats imports as a secondary, derivative phenomenon, a consequence imposed on Latin America by external economic forces. Two works focus on these patterns of fashion in this period at the height of Europeanization. *A Tropical Belle Epoque: Elite Culture and Society in Turn-of-the-Century Rio de Janeiro* (Needell 1987) examines the daily lives and social institutions of the wealthy in Brazil's capital in the last decades of the nineteenth century and the first decades of the twentieth, focusing on this group's "profoundly Europhile culture" (236). The book's central themes include the development of new avenues and neighborhoods in the city, the modernization of urban services, the emergence of elite clubs, and the development of new patterns of family life and social visits within the new salon society, though a variety of other themes are also discussed—the anxieties apparent in society newspaper columns, the difficulties in adopting radical and avant-garde literary movements from France and Germany, the great appeal of European prostitutes, chiefly of French and of Eastern European Jewish backgrounds.

The essays in *Judas at the Jockey Club and Other Episodes of Porfirian Mexico* (Beezley 1987) offer a nuanced view of the eager adoption of foreign luxury goods by the urban elites in Mexico during the Porfiriato (1876–1910) and the general opposition to imported tools and machines by the urban and rural working poor of this period. He shows that the Jockey Club in Mexico City was not simply a refuge in which the wealthy could play at being like their European counterparts, but rather a place in which the elites also met opposition to their efforts to combine European and national traditions: visiting Frenchmen expressed their disdain of Mexican-style rodeos, and, in the events which gave the book its title, the local newspapers and working-class crowds alike were angered by the efforts of club members to adapt into these new surroundings the folk custom of burning effigies of Judas on the day before Easter. In an essay on rural workers, Beezley explains their loyalty to such local goods as sandals, the one-handled plow, and the fermented drink called pulque through their commitment to the steady, familiar, and integrated world of tradition—a commitment which grew not so much from habit as from active opposition to the pressures for change and modernization emanating from the government and capital-owning classes.

These two books offer fascinating details, but they remain largely within the parameters of the export-centered model. They suggest that the Europeanization of Latin American consumption patterns is limited to certain classes, places, and times: the wealthy in the capital cities from the late nineteenth century to the Depression. In the view suggested in these books, then, export earnings supported a boom of luxury imports among the wealthiest groups in the capital cities—a narrow and deep market, in economic terms, because it was confined to a small sector of the society and included many items. These earnings also supported an expansion of basic commodities, particularly cloth and simple metal items, among the majority of the population—a wide and shallow market, in economic terms. Both of these arose with the growth of exports, generally between the 1850s and 1880s, and came to a halt with the depression of the 1930s. These books thus fit closely with the export-centered model, at most offering minor adjustments through their recognition of the influences on the development of capital cities that stem from the specific political histories of each country (Mexico with its early and profound revolution, Brazil with its unique path to independence and to republican status), and through their occasional acknowledgment of some ambivalence or uncertainty on the part of the elites.

Our goal in this volume is not to invert the relations between exports and imports and between production and consumption by proposing an economic and social history based entirely on "import economies." Instead, we seek to establish a balance in which imports and consumption can receive attention as partially autonomous phenomena. More concretely, we wish to examine closely the temporal patterning and social dimensions of the consumption of imports, rather than assuming that these follow directly upon the dynamic of the export economies. We seek to complement, rather than to displace, the hypotheses of the export-centered model that stress the importance of export economies in shaping the consumption of imports. If the export-centered model emphasizes the economic affordability of imports, we seek to understand their social cachet and cultural appeal. In other words, we argue that foreignness is an attribute of the imported goods that merits consideration, like their availability and cost.

In particular, we note two sets of forces that have influenced this demand and use of goods. The first stems from the questions of social identity in the postcolonial context of Latin American nations after independence. The consumption of goods played a central role in the working out of a key question: how could individuals, families, groups, and classes resolve the tension between the evident hierarchies within their societies on the one hand and the impulse toward equivalence as fellow citizens on the other, implied in their new national identities, in their membership in what Anderson (1983) has famously termed *imagined communities?* No longer part of European empires, Latin Americans had to redefine their relationship with the European world. It is the difficulty of this redefinition that leads us to use the term *postcolonial* to refer to this period of Latin American history, rather than the alternative terms of *Independence Period* and *Republican Period,* which, in emphasizing formal political discontinuities, imply a cleaner break than the one we observe (Mallon 1995a). We propose that the sphere of consumption, and in particular the use of domestic and imported goods, is one of the key contexts in which national identities were stated, contested, and affirmed in postcolonial Latin America. (We note that a great deal of research at present is engaged in an exploration of other such contexts: shifting patterns of political suffrage [Borja y Borja 1988]; the development of national literary traditions [Sommer 1991]; responses to foreign invasions of Latin America in the nineteenth century [Mallon 1995b]; participation in world's fairs [Tenorio 1996].)

The second stems from questions of modernity in the global context that Latin America entered after independence. Where Skidmore and Smith speak confidently, in their book's title, of *Modern Latin America,* we raise the question of Latin American modernities. Rather than seeing modernity as a stage of human history which may be noted in Latin America as in other areas, we suggestion that there are multiple types of modernity, which may contrast with one another. (In this regard, Calderón [1988] suggests that the Latin American modernities may be incomplete, and combined with pre- and postmodern conditions as well—a point very much like the one that Breckenridge [1995] has made for Asia and Mbembe [1997] for Africa.) There were many notions of modernity in Latin America, as there were in Europe and the United States, yet they shared at least some common characteristics: a break from the traditions of the past, a valuation of the present, an openness toward experimentation in seeking to construct a future different from both. Modernity appears almost always as an international movement, but Latin American participation in it was problematic, since the centers of modernity lay in Europe and the United States. As Sergio Villalobos, one of Chile's distinguished historians, remarks, the journeys to Europe and the avid consumption of European goods on the part of the elite was something more than "vain posturing or following the latest fashions. It was to place oneself at the peak of the historical moment or perhaps—it might be imagined—at the center of history." They could enjoy the opera, for example, "with all its truculence and tenderness" in similar and familiar circumstances in Santiago as in Paris or Milan (1987, 78–79). This example captures the sense of modernity as something that is at once accessible and distant.

Villalobos's choice of a musical example of modernity is not surprising, since modernity is often associated with cultural trends. It is also linked to social change and political transformations of many sorts and to economic innovation, especially in realms connected with production and distribution—factories, electrical networks, railroads, airplanes. We propose that the sphere of consumption, and in particular the use of domestic and imported goods, is one of the key contexts in which images of modernity were stated, contested, and affirmed in postcolonial Latin America. (We note that a great deal of research at present is engaged in an exploration of other such contexts, though many of these involved visual and literary culture [Poole 1997], or high and low versions of popular culture [Rowe and Schelling 1991].)

These themes of national identity and modernity have become very timely, within Latin American studies and within the social sciences more broadly. (In particular, Bhabha's notion of mimicry [1977] has attracted a great deal of attention; see also Dirlik 1994, Mallon 1994, Jacoby 1995, and Parama 1997.) Rather than offering a summary of this and other writings on these topics, however, we will shift instead to a text that illustrates them directly, by quoting a paragraph from a short story, "El Zahir," by Jorge Luís Borges.[2] This story, set in Buenos Aires, is written in the first person, narrated by a person who, like the narrator in many other stories by this author, identifies himself as Borges. In the second paragraph, he presents a character whose death sets in motion a tangled plot involving a coin that creates obsessions in those who possess it.

On the sixth of June, Teodelina Villar died. Around 1930, pictures of her were clogging society magazines; this plethora might have contributed to the judgment that she was very pretty, though not all the portraits unconditionally supported this hypothesis. Moreover, Teodelina Villar concerned herself less with beauty than with perfection. The Hebrews and the Chinese codified every human eventuality; in the Mishnah it is written that, once the Sabbath twilight has begun, a tailor should not go out into the street with a needle; in the Book of Rites that a guest, on receiving the first cup of tea, should adopt a serious air and, on receiving the second, a respectfully contented air. Something of this sort, though in much greater detail, was to be discerned in the uncompromising strictness which Teodelina Villar demanded of herself. Like the Confucian adept or the Talmudist, she sought irreproachable perfection in each act, but her zeal was more admirable and more difficult, because the rules of her creed were not eternal, but rather yielded to the fates of Paris or Hollywood. Teodelina Villar appeared in orthodox places, at the orthodox moment with orthodox attributes, with orthodox disinclination, but the disinclination, the attributes, the moments, and the places became out of date almost immediately and served (in Teodelina Villar's words) to define that which was vulgar. Like Flaubert, she sought the Absolute, only hers was an Absolute of a moment's duration. Her life was exemplary and, nonetheless, an interior despair gnawed at her without ever letting up. She was forever experimenting with new metamorphoses as if to flee from herself; the shade of her hair and the form of her coiffure were famously unstable. She also changed her smile, her complexion, the angle of her glance. After 1932 she was studiously thin . . . the war gave her a great deal to think about. With Paris occupied by the Germans, how was one to follow fashion? A foreigner whom she had always distrusted presumed so far on her good faith as to sell her some cylindrical hats; a year later, it was disclosed that this rubbish *had never been worn in Paris* and consequently was not hats, but arbitrary and unauthorized fads. These disgraces did not come one at a time; Dr. Villar had to move to Calle Araoz and the picture of his daughter appeared on ads for cold creams and automobiles. (The creams that she applied in great quantities, the automobiles that he *no longer* owned!) She knew that to exercise her art well required a great fortune; she preferred retiring to abandoning her principles. Besides, it pained her to compete with giddy little nobodies. The gloomy apartment on Araoz was too much to bear; on the sixth of June, Teodelina Villar committed the solecism of dying in the middle of the South Side. Shall I confess that, moved by that most sincere of Argentine passions, snobbism, I had been in love with her and that her death moved me to tears? Perhaps the reader has already suspected as much.

It would be possible to read Teodelina Villar's life entirely within the framework of the export-centered approach. A wealthy socialite in a capital city, she oriented her life around the latest European fashions until the economic collapse of the 1930s made her unable to continue her patterns of consumption. She recognized, after all, that she "required a great fortune."

Such a reading would be, not incorrect, but very limited. Borges's evocative prose brings a number of other points to mind. He suggests that Latin America can be considered as a civilization. Displaying, as he often does, his erudition, he compares Latin America to Hebrew and Chinese civilization, repeating such terms as *orthodox, creed,* and *principles* to suggest that these civilizations contain codes for human behavior. Unlike the emblematic Jewish tailor and Chinese guest, Latin America is represented by a woman, one of indeterminable race (her skin and hair color keep changing, her mother is never named)—emphasizing her relations to several different others, and leaving uncertain her connections to her past and to different places.

He locates Teodelina Villar—and therefore Latin American civilization—within a framework of modernity. Freed from any tradition, she bases her life on change; she pursues perfection in the form of the momentary. She is a public person: her image is printed in such transitory forms of expression as society magazines and advertisements, she simply "appears" in public places, and she is spoken of (Borges mentions the fame with which her hair color and styles changed, the judgment that she is pretty). This public quality is also suggested in the fact that she is urban. Even her surname Villar suggests this urbanity, since she is of the *villa,* the town.

This Latin American modernity is a difficult one. It overcomes great obstacles, since the great width of the Atlantic Ocean makes it harder for Latin Americans than for Europeans to follow European fashions. Indeed, Latin America is defined in relation to that which is outside, especially the city of Paris, mentioned three times in the paragraph. This external source of fashion makes it impossible to establish secure connections with it. Seeking perfection, Teodelina Villar began her downfall when she no longer could judge foreigners correctly and bought the hats which turned out not to be hats, but rubbish.

The difficulties in following foreign fashions create many social divisions. When Teodelina Villar appeared in public, she displayed a disinclination (*desgano*), as if no place—in Buenos Aires, at least—were good enough for her. She insisted on separating herself from vulgarity, and suffered when she appeared in ads or competed with "giddy little nobodies" (*chicuelas insustanciales*). These social divisions corresponded to divisions within Teodelina Villar herself, creating not only a self-consciousness ("she was studiously thin") but a profound alienation: she is gnawed away by an "interior despair," she seeks to "flee from herself."

This portrait is complex and ironic. The qualities that create her artificiality and anxiety are also the ones that make her appealing. An educated and cosmopolitan man, Borges is able to compare Teodelina Villar to representatives of other civilizations and to find "her effort more difficult and more admirable." He had fallen in love with her, "moved by that most sincere of Argentine passions, snobbism." Defined by her search for "irreproachable perfection in each act," centered on something distant from her, Teodelina Villar is absolute, ideal, changing, doomed.

Borges's brief portrait of one exemplar of Latin American civilization provides many lines of inquiry. In our examination of imports into Latin America, we speak of concrete objects (creams and automobiles appear in these chapters), of the social relations of snobbism and the avoidance of vulgarity. We find that many Latin Americans, like Teodelina Villar, found foreign goods to possess a great allure, though the basis and nature of this allure, and the consequences of this allure for their lives, were often very different. And we note that this allure extends far beyond the limits of wealthy households (such as that of Dr. Villar's) in capital cities in times of prosperity.

The different cases in this book point toward several patternings of imports that contrast with this export-led view in five major ways, all of which, oddly enough, echo with the themes of Teodelina Villar's life. Firstly, in temporal terms, the timing of imports does not always follow the growth of exports. The first large import boom of the late nineteenth and early twentieth century is evident in case after case, as is a second import boom in recent years. However, in a number of cases, imported goods became very attractive well before the exports of commodities allowed them to be imported on a large scale. In other cases, the appeal of foreign goods continued after a downturn in exports made importation difficult—much as Teodelina Villar lived well past the stock market crash of 1929 and into World War II.

Secondly, in social terms, the patterning of imports shows more complex divisions than the bifurcation between a small elite heavily committed to foreign goods and the masses of the population, consuming only a few basic imported goods. There were a number of intermediate strata (urban middle classes strongly oriented toward imports appear again and again). Other lines of separation also distinguish individuals by their patterning of imports—at times between men and women, at others between different regions or ethnic groups.

Thirdly, in terms of national identity, we note that there is a certain, though limited, degree of flexibility in the definition of *foreignness*—and hence a similar degree of flexibility in the complementary notion of *nation-alness*. At the level of everyday cultural habits, as at the level of foreign trade policy, there seems to be a core definition of what objects may be classified as an "import," though the boundaries of this category are much harder to draw precisely. We note a range of cases: "foreignness" can be associated with a piano, manufactured in Germany; with a suit, made in Peru from British cloth; with wine, made in Chile from grapes of French rootstock; with a house, built in Mexico of Mexican materials from blueprints brought back from the United States. The first of these consists entirely of foreign materials assembled in a foreign country; the last consists entirely of domestic materials assembled in Latin America, but still being seen as foreign. Rather than emphasizing the breadth of this range, though, we are struck by the proximity of the cases to a central core. We initially expected "foreignness" to be an almost infinitely plastic concept in the usage of the diverse groups discussed in this book—wealthy families in capital cities, provincial merchants, peasants, miners, even "unpacified" Indians apparently beyond the limits of national society like the Chiriguano in Bolivia. In this sense, national identities and nationalist ideologies seem to have spread quite broadly, engendering the corresponding sense of "foreignness," often eagerly sought, on other occasions rejected in favor of a kind of mestizo nationalism in such diverse realms as folklore revivals (García Canclini 1993), a concern for national cuisines (Pereira Salas 1977), an appreciation of distinctively national music (Savigliano 1995), and even in the consumption of home-brew beer (Orlove and Schmidt 1995).

Fourthly, in narrative terms, the association between foreignness and progress comes up again and again. Many different groups hold a belief in the possibilities of creating a local version of modernity, in the sense of joining a universal human march toward a future which is different from, and superior to, a custom-bound past. Foreign goods often are tokens of such modernity, because of their association with Europe, the center of modernity, and because of their evident contrast with local practices. We anticipated that these beliefs would be limited to the wealthy and the well-educated in cities; instead, such beliefs occur many times, among working-class groups such as peasants, miners, and factory workers, and even among ethnically distinct groups such as Indians in Peru and Bolivia. As with the definitions of "foreignness," so too there is both a common core and certain range of definitions of "modernity."

We note that this theme of progress contrasts with elements of the underlying ideologies of colonial rule in Latin America. The people who admire new foreign objects have a kind of subjectivity oriented toward recognizing newness. Without proposing a simple or mechanical contrast between colonial and postcolonial subjectivities, we suggest that this orientation toward the continuous development of new tastes differs from a more rule-bound colonial consuming self, in which there may be a greater emphasis on group-appropriate public symbols and on spectacles: a colonial self that rested on notions of Christian legitimacy rather than modernity, a self perhaps more based on pleasure than on desire, on excess rather than on want. These questions—outside the scope of this volume—remain speculations, and we return to our last element of the patterning of imports in the postcolonial period.

Finally, in cultural terms, imported goods are more enmeshed in a complex web of social relations than many views seem to suggest. Few writers have examined this "social life of things," to borrow Appadurai's phrase (1986), since they often treat imported goods in two simple ways. On the one hand, these goods are sometimes taken as signs—as if they were mere badges that proclaimed an individual to be a sophisticated participant in European civilization. (This view was often attributed to the elite.) On the other hand, they are sometimes taken as objects that serve material needs, as in the case of clothing and tools. (This view was often attributed to the workers and peasants.) By contrast, we note the complexity of patterns of production, distribution, and consumption that distinguish these goods. For example, Orlove and Bauer point out that *yerba mate,* an herb tea widely consumed in Chile, differs from coffee, also widely consumed, not only because the former stands for local customs, the latter for European fashion, or because one or the other serves the need of providing warm liquids and stimulants more effectively than the other. The social habits of drinking them are also different, as shown by the contrasting etiquettes of pouring out servings of these hot drinks and by the distinct social practices of the public urban coffeehouses and the domestic places where *yerba mate* is drunk. Similarly, Fletcher describes villagers in central Mexico who, in selecting between the older-style roofs made of local clay tiles or the United States–style ones of reinforced concrete, choose not only between visible signs of different cultural orientations and between materials that differ in their ability to protect people and goods from extreme temperatures and rainfall. They also, for complex reasons laid out in the chapter, choose between different patterns of storing maize and between different locations of kitchens within the house—thus affecting the relations between husbands and wives, and between mothers and daughters.

It is worth noting that the chapters of this book, apparently quite different in theme and approach, all coincide in supporting this type of revision of the export-centered approach, rather than accepting it in its standard form, as most anthropologists and historians of Latin America still seem to, or rejecting it altogether. Since the chapters may appear to differ considerably, it is worth discussing this agreement in greater detail. A few of the chapters might seem very close to the export-centered view. Krügeller's contrast between two Peruvian regions during the period 1820–1920, for example, could be read as stating that the early and extensive development of mineral exports from the central highlands led to large-scale consumption of European goods across a wide social spectrum in that region, while the later and more restricted development of wool exports from the southern highlands engendered smaller levels of imports there, limited to a narrower set of elites. However, his analysis grants a certain autonomy to local and regional social patterns, especially through the documentation of the ways that provincial urban life shaped the reception and use of imported goods. Krügeller shows how regional specificities in social settings—homes, social clubs, and public spaces such as streets and plazas—allowed individuals, families, and entire towns to establish, maintain, and display their reputations in different ways through the ownership and display of goods. Vega stresses the close overlap between the expansion of exports of coffee from Costa Rica in the middle of the nineteenth century and the growth of the imports of European goods into the capital city at the same time. Rather than merely noting the increase of imports, though, she traces the ways in which class and gender divisions shaped the demand for certain goods over others.

Other chapters might be seen simply as refining the export-centered view through an examination of unusual local patterns of exports, often at variance with broader regional or national trends. Heyman's account of the effects of export-oriented mines on consumption in northern Mexico, though, does more than demonstrate that proximity to an international border shapes the patterning of the flow of goods. He also documents the ways in which purchasing and consumption become arenas of contestation of class identities and relations, especially in the context of company towns. Fletcher's chapter centers on a village in central Mexico that obtains revenue, not from the export of raw materials, but from the export of labor itself in the form of migration. In this setting, the contrasting

Mexican and United States styles of housing influence as well as reflect this export of labor, as the pressure to obtain money for foreign-style houses leads men to migrate, and as the use of space in these houses alters the possibilities of employment for both men and women.

Moreover, even the chapters that might appear to reject the export-centered approach most thoroughly still grant it considerable importance. Langer traces the demand for English cloth among the Chiriguano Indians of eastern Bolivia. As a scarce item that indicated contact with external powers, this cloth was prized as a symbol of chiefly authority even before the group's subjugation and incorporation into national society. Following lines of social distinction that developed from both indigenous and national cultures, this cloth gradually became used by wider segments of Chiriguano society. Nonetheless, even in this remote portion of a particularly poor country, the cycles of expansion and decline of export economies influenced the overall prosperity of the Chiriguano and their ability to purchase this cloth. In a similar vein, Orlove and Bauer show that contradictory aspects of the national identity of Chileans, especially the elites, in the early and middle of the nineteenth century rendered them particularly eager to obtain foreign goods, well before the expansion of mineral exports. However, their account also stresses the ways in which overall levels of imports, and the preferences for different goods, were shaped by the growth and later contraction of foreign revenue from this source.

Most broadly, then, these studies support the claims for a revision of the export-centered approach. The demand for imports is shaped by social dynamics within Latin American nations, as well as by external economic forces at a global scale. Foreign goods arrived in countries that had complex social divisions along lines of class, region, gender, and race, and whose attitudes toward their national identities were frequently ambivalent. In many instances, these goods offered the possibility of altering or redressing these divisions, of changing or resolving these attitudes. In large part, it is this sense of possibility that gave them this allure—and in turn gave this book its title.

We note that this consumption of foreign goods is by no means unique to Latin America. Indeed, Philip Curtin's *Cross-Cultural Trade in World History* (1984) looks very broadly at the exchange of goods across cultural boundaries. He includes dozens of examples, stretching over the last four or five millennia, in which there were steady flows of goods from areas of relative abundance to others of relative scarcity. His principal conclusion is that "trade diasporas"—ethnically distinct groups of traders who reside in several different societies—are a virtually ubiquitous phenomenon, favored by their abilities to speak many languages, to overcome information blockages, to maintain value orientations which favored commerce, and to negotiate with rulers. These trade diasporas, whose origins seem coterminous with large-scale state-organized societies, have only reached their "twilight" (230) with the Industrial Revolution, when the flows of goods increased. Curtin takes the desire for imported goods as an unproblematic response to "differing resource endowments"; whenever possible, human societies will specialize in the goods that they can produce most efficiently, and import the others.

Another broad comparative study, with a more explicit emphasis on consumption, is Jack Goody's *Cooking, Cuisine and Class* (1982). He argues that imported foodstuffs, particularly spices and seasonings brought from long distances, are a common characteristic of the elite cuisines within the stratified societies of Europe and Asia, whose economic bases rest on plow agriculture and private land tenure. Sub-Saharan African societies, by contrast, depend on hoe agriculture and collective land tenure; the meals at which high status individuals demonstrate their position are marked by the greater abundance of local foods, rather than by the presence of imported foods—even in the cases of more commercialized and monetarized societies.

Others carry this comparative research even more broadly. In part because goods produced in distant areas can often be easily identified in archeological sites, the question of cross-cultural trade has attracted a good deal of attention from prehistorians (Flannery 1976; Earle and Ericson 1977). Its importance in the origin of early states continues to be debated (Cohen and Service 1978; Haas 1982; Haas, Pozorski, and Pozorski 1987).

Indeed, imported goods play an important role in many small-scale societies—a topic which has been researched at least since Malinowski's foundational research on the Kula ring in the Trobriand Islands (1922), in which he showed that in that Melanesian society, certain ritual objects are more highly valued when they come from distant islands. More recent work among small-scale societies in the southwestern Pacific have also showed this preference for imported valuables; Hoskins's account (1993) of the Kodi of eastern Indonesia shows the importance in ritual of exotic goods from distant places (porcelain bowls, copies of the Koran), since they indicate specific sorts of connections with distant powers that balance and compete with local bases of power.

Studies that compare wide range of human societies can document what might be termed *the appeal of the exotic.* Whether this appeal is based on practical concerns, social dynamics, or cultural systems of meaning, however, it becomes so broad that it misses the specificities of the Latin America case. Latin Americans were not drawn to all goods that came from distant lands, but primarily to those from Europe. Moreover, in the desire of Latin Americans for foreign goods, there was a fervor, approaching in some cases an insatiability, which contrasts with the more limited appeal of exotic items which is noted in the broader comparative cases. Latin Americans were drawn to these items for reasons beyond those attractive features of trade objects noted in the broad comparative studies: the utility of some of the goods, the simple curiosity elicited by unfamiliar items, the delight which might be taken in novelties, the cachet that came from the wealth and power suggested by the inherent difficulty in acquiring objects from remote places. For Latin Americans, these goods were a means to address specific questions of identity in a postcolonial context. What distinguishes the spatially, temporally, and socially limited allure of the foreign from the much broader appeal of the exotic is this focus on certain sources of goods, this fervor to possess them, and these concerns over identity that they can address.

In seeking comparative cases, we looked to other regions where the three forces noted in Latin America—political economy, nationalism, and modernity—also operate. We turned to three regions of the postcolonial world: Eastern Europe, the Middle East and North Africa, and China, all in the nineteenth and twentieth centuries. In each of these cases, trade relations with the North Atlantic world expanded during this period, and new nations emerged from declining empires (the Habsburg, Romanov, and Ottoman empires in the first case, the Ottoman in the second, the Qing in the third). These societies also had marked social divisions between wealthy urban elites and large rural populations of peasants. To summarize our discussions of these regions (which may strike specialists familiar with them as ludicrous oversimplifications), we note in Eastern Europe an allure of the foreign *similar* to that in Latin America, in the Middle East and North Africa one *more ambivalent* than that in Latin America, and in China one *lesser* than in Latin America.

One of the comparative cases is Eastern Europe, a region that, like Latin America, became more tightly linked with the world economy in recent centuries and experienced growth of nationalist movements. Of our three comparative cases, we find it to be most similar to Latin America.

Many Eastern Europeans in the nineteenth and twentieth centuries felt an "allure of the foreign" quite like what we describe in Latin America, and for many of the same reasons.

Eastern Europe presents a number of challenges to those who wish to offer a brief summary of certain themes. With its complex history, it shows great economic, political, and cultural diversity, as reflected in the debates among specialists whether to treat it as a unit, split it into Central and Eastern Europe, or divide into a larger number of smaller subdivisions. Moreover, any discussion of consumption and the use of goods runs squarely into the question of how to frame the Soviet, or Communist, or centrally planned, or "actually existing socialist" period. We therefore focus principally on Poland and Hungary in the nineteenth and early twentieth centuries.

Daniel Chirot implies a question in the title of his volume *The Origins of Backwardness in Eastern Europe* (1989) and suggests an answer in the subtitle, *Economics and Politics from the Middle Ages until the Early Twentieth Century:* the poverty of the region has deep roots, traceable to the low population densities and lack of urban demand in the medieval period that constrained the development of agricultural and craft production and limited the scope of trade. A number of writers have noted the slow growth of trade with Western Europe, in which Eastern Europe shipped agricultural products in exchange for some manufactured items. In the Eastern European context, where local nobilities faced less competition for power from royal and urban groups than elsewhere on the continent, this trade led to the expansion of great estates and the consolidation of power by aristocratic landowners, whose workers were legally bound to the land in a "second serfdom" (Wallerstein 1979, 197), so-called because it occurred as feudalism had declined in Western Europe. In some places, especially in Hungary and other areas further east, landowners complemented their income derived from agricultural production with fees derived from monopoly control of mills and distilleries (Gunst 1989, 53–91). The second serfdom was established during the sixteenth century in the areas with the strongest trade links, such as Poland, though it was not completed in the most remote zones until the nineteenth century; the timing of these developments is highly varied, differing even over short distances, as shown by studies of neighboring sections of Romania (Chirot 1976; Verdery 1983).

In his *Economic Theory of the Feudal System* (1976), the Polish historian Witold Kula provides a useful model for these aristocratic estates, which dominated social and political as well as economic life for much of the seventeenth and eighteenth century in Poland, Hungary, and elsewhere. Simplifying somewhat, since the estates varied depending on their size and proximity to markets, we may note that each estate formed a relatively closed economic unit, with some production of craft items as well as food-stuffs. Consumption standards were relatively static. The peasants lived close to subsistence, while the landowners channeled some of the surplus, in years of good harvest, into feasts and other ceremonial events on their estates. Some accounts of the period both for Poland (Kochanowicz 1989, 105–6) and Hungary (Janos 1982, 38–40) note that foreign imports and luxury were seen as unnecessary indulgences or as signs of weak moral standards.

This pattern changed around the beginning of the nineteenth century, in both Poland (Kula 1976, 137–40) and Hungary (Janos 1982, 40–48). Agriculture became more commercialized as Prussian, Habsburg, and Romanov imperial rulers, driven partly by imperial competition, pressured landowners to increase their output of grain and other agricultural prod-ucts, either to supply new industrial centers elsewhere in their empires or to sell to Western Europe. Cities grew as trade increased and imperial bureau-cracies expanded; landowners traveled more often into towns and, on occasion, to Vienna or Berlin or further west, and spent more time in con-tact with people from these cities, a process well-described for Poland (Gunst 1989, 73–81; Kochanowicz 1989, 120–22). Landowners began to maintain apartments in cities. One source describe the spread of new tastes in Hungary: "silver, so far seen only in the houses of the rich, now appears in many households, not only on the dining table but in the bedrooms as well. Simple houses are being turned into stately mansions. The watch, beforehand as rare as a white crow, has now turned into an article of neces-sity, so much that even servants wear them" (Janos 1982, 43). These new goods began to spread even to peasants by the mid–nineteenth century, as they began to wear garments made of factory cloth rather than homespun and as they added chimneys and windows to their houses. Though some peasants might have preferred local rather than modern consumption pat-terns, and a few traditionalist landlords argued for the superiority of local wines (48), the shift to what was seen as modern and European patterns of consumption was decisive. The link with Europe might be fragile: civil ser-vants in Hungary in the 1920s, faced with inflation that forced them to cease attending the theater, to wear old clothes, and to sell furniture, phrased this decline as a failure to sustain a "decent" or "European" style of life (38), and an anthropologist who conducted research in Budapest in the 1980s heard local people apologize to her in apartments for messy bedrooms and in restaurants for impolite waiters, both of these named explicitly as signs of deficient Europeanness (Gal 1991, 443). But Europe remained the desired, if not always achieved, icon in the twentieth century that it had become in the nineteenth. Anthropologists have noted this pervasive theme of Europeanness elsewhere in Eastern Europe, as in Verdery's account of Romania (1991).

The "allure of the foreign," or, in the case of Eastern Europe, "the allure of the West," thus seems similar in Eastern Europe to Latin America. The three forces which we have noted for Latin America also seem to be at work in Eastern Europe. The "export economies" of Latin America have their direct parallels in the exports of raw materials—Polish wheat, Hungarian cattle and wine; in Eastern Europe as well they engendered counterflows of imported manufactured goods. The forces of modernity and nationalism were also at play. During the nineteenth century, Poland sought its territorial integrity, briefly reestablished between 1815 and 1830, while Hungary struggled, with more success, to gain greater autonomy within the Habsburg Empire, achieving formal parity in 1867 with the restoration of constitutional monarchy and the conversion of the Austrian Empire into the Austro-Hungarian Monarchy. Despite some engagements in linguistic nationalism and a kind of cultural chauvinism, the road to national independence did not lead toward a return to local lifeways, but rather in the growth of urban life and industry. By becoming more Western and more modern, Hungary and Poland could seek their destinies as independent nations.

Our second case, China, offers a sharp contrast, since its inhabitants were not drawn to foreign goods, especially in the nineteenth and early twentieth centuries. In a general sense, China might be seen as similar to Latin America, Eastern Europe, and the Middle East, since, as it entered the nineteenth century, it had a relatively underdeveloped, preindustrial economy, and it was governed by a declining empire, under heavy pressure from Britain, France, and the United States. Nonetheless, these general circumstances did not lead to the import boom, as they did in Latin America or Eastern Europe, because of a number of features specific to China and its relation to the world economy.

As economic historians have shown, levels of imports into China were lower than those of other parts of the world with comparable incomes (Eastman 1988). The trade imbalance between China and the West became acute in the late eighteenth and early nineteenth centuries, as the West became far more eager to import Chinese tea, silk, and porcelain than the Chinese were to receive Western goods. This imbalance was one of the causes of the Opium War of 1839–42 between Britain and China, which led to the expanded consumption of one of the few goods that created an addiction, and to other consequences as well: the cession of Hong Kong and the opening of five treaty ports where British traders were granted a number of privileges (Spence 1990, 121–22, 153–54). Other nations also pressured China in the late nineteenth century—France sent naval expeditions to coastal zones in order to extract concessions, and Russia and Japan occupied border regions—leading China to lose its influence in the neighboring regions of Burma and Indochina. However, China itself was never fully colonized, and the extensive efforts to force it to increase trade also had limited success. Though foreign pressures played a strong role in the decline and collapse of the last Qing dynasty and the establishment of the Chinese Republic in 1911, the rise of modern republicanism in China did not take the directly anti-colonial form that it did in Latin America, Eastern Europe, and the Middle East. Since China was so transformed by the depression of the 1930s, the Japanese invasions and the Communist Revolution, we will not carry our discussions past the 1920s.

In his article "Chinese Consumption of Foreign Commodities: A Comparative Perspective," Hamilton (1977) provides a thorough review of efforts to explain this low demand for Western goods in China. He rejects what he calls the "faulty merchandise and marketing explanation"—that Western goods were more expensive or of poorer quality than Chinese goods, and that China lacked the necessary transportation networks and market institutions to transport foreign goods—by showing first that there were large numbers of wealthy people in China who could afford many goods and second that the marketing systems in China were efficient and did serve to channel a few foreign imports, such as kerosene, from the ports to the interior. He also rejects a cultural explanation (that the power of Confucianism in China strengthened traditional behavior in the sphere of consumption, as in other spheres of action, thus limiting imports) on the grounds that it fails to explain the high levels of imports in earlier periods of Chinese history, such as the T'ang and Sung dynasties, when Confucianism was also strong. Hamilton prefers an explanation which rests on "status competition": although China was a highly stratified society, it had a high degree of social mobility, and therefore a high degree of status competition, because of partible inheritance of property, which prevented the transmission of large sums of capital across several generations, and because of the relative openness of commerce and the bureaucracy. Individuals, families, and groups that sought to raise their status competed chiefly at the local levels, through lineage associations, secret societies, merchant guilds, and other such organizations. To emphasize their position within these local contexts, they used Chinese goods and avoided foreign goods, which would have marked them as outsiders rather than as locals. In periods of more rigid stratification during earlier dynasties, Hamilton notes, the wealthy made frequent use of imported goods to emphasize their separation from the poor and to mark their participation in wider social networks (885). Hamilton confirms the strategic nature of this choice by noting that the Chinese purchased large quantities of European cloth in the late nineteenth and early twentieth centuries for two sorts of uses: as underclothing and as linings, precisely where they would not be seen (883).

More recent studies support Hamilton's account. Cochran's account (1980) of the cigarette industry in China between 1890 and 1930 shows that Europeans had relative success with an import that—like opium—was unusual because its addictive properties created a physical need. Even so, Chinese preferences for local brands helped local manufacturers stand up to the stiff competition from American and British producers of cigarettes, who had a considerable initial advantage because of their greater capital and access to industrial technology. Anderson's historical study of Chinese diet (1988) shows that the Chinese have maintained the ingredients, cooking techniques, and organization of dishes and meals that developed over a thousand years ago; even specific regional variants are consistent. Though there were some introductions of new food items, such as melons, sorghum, and sugar cane during the T'ang and Sung dynasties (63–64), the food systems have been remarkably stable, especially when compared to the other portions of the world that we discuss.

Though framed in somewhat different terms, Hamilton's explanation fits in closely with the ones in this volume. He shows that political economy issues of price and income, though important, are not sufficient on their own to explain levels of imports and exports. To his discussion of status groups and status competition, we would add issues of nationalism and modernity. The inward-directed gaze of local elites is consonant with the relatively weaker imperialist presence in China, and with a nationalist stance that seeks a major position for China in the modern world. In this sense, consumption patterns and the reliance on local goods forms part of what Jonathan Spence (1990) has recently termed "the search for modern

China." Though Chinese have fought bitterly over the proper forms of economic and political organization in postdynastic China, they have far more often agreed on the importance of maintaining Chinese distinctiveness and assuring Chinese self-sufficiency.

The third set of comparative cases comes from the Middle East and North Africa, a region that, like Latin America, underwent colonization and closer incorporation into the world economy. For many Westerners, it is the region in the world most strongly associated with the rejection of Western commodities. The spread of the *chador* following the Iranian Revolution of 1978 may be the best-known instance of such rejections, though there are parallels in the last two decades in other nations and with other goods: the smashing of bottles of wine in shops in Lebanon, the opposition to European music and film in Algeria. Indeed, it is such rejections that are examined in detail in a recent book, *Jihad vs. McWorld* (Barber 1995), which argues for the mutual dependency rather than the opposition of two forces in the contemporary world, a retrogressive nationalist return to isolation and a forward-looking globalized and electronic integration. To name these interacting forces (which we see as having far deeper historical roots than that book does), the author links Macintosh computers and McDonald's fast food as the globalizing forces, but needs only one source—Middle Eastern Islam—to name the localizing trend.

Though Iran is an extreme and atypical case in many ways, our review of the region does suggest that it demonstrates a widely shared ambivalence toward imported goods. We note—with the uncertainty and tentativeness that come from our relative unfamiliarity with the region—divisions within Middle Eastern and North African societies over the acceptance or rejection of foreign goods. These divisions stand in contrast to the broad allure of foreign goods in Latin America, much as the sharp boundary that separates domestic and foreign goods in some Middle Eastern societies contrasts with the more general spread of foreign goods into many domains of Latin American life.

We focus our examination on two of the larger Middle Eastern nations, Egypt and Turkey, in part because they demonstrate the linguistic, cultural, and historical variation within the Middle East. Some rough parallels can be traced in their histories in the nineteenth and twentieth centuries. They were both portions of the Ottoman Empire (which had its capital and geopolitical core in what is now Turkey). Their indigenous rulers in the early nineteenth century were strong enough to hold off conquest and colonization of the sort that began in Algeria in 1830, but still weak enough to grant broad and unfavorable concessions regarding tariff policies and other economic matters to foreigners. Their foreign trade with Britain and France grew in the nineteenth century, as did their debts to those countries, encouraged by enduring needs of the state for revenue to finance infrastructure and to support military campaigns in a region of endemic conflict. The ensuing bankruptcy led to direct imperial rule in Egypt in 1882 (a country already weakened by the precedent of the Napoleonic Occupation in 1799–1802, by its smaller size, and by the great strategic interest in the Suez Canal site [Tignor 1966, 3–24]), and to considerable indirect foreign control in Turkey after 1881 through the European-run Ottoman Public Debt Administration (Owen 1981, 192). The expanding import-export trade was supported by the foreign communities already present in the multiethnic Ottoman empire, which expanded to include growing populations of Europeans and migrants from other portions of the Mediterranean and Middle East. Independence came to Egypt in 1922, following nationalist rebellions in 1919; out of the defeat of the Ottoman Empire, allied with Germany in World War I, came the Turkish Republic, which emerged between 1919 and 1926. Both countries sought to develop state-supported industries for their domestic markets, but since the 1980s have shifted toward a policy of *intifah* or economic opening, with an increased reliance on the private sector (Richards and Waterbury 1990, 238–49).

Modernity, nationalism, and industrialization were linked in a complex pattern to these nations, which achieved independence as modern nations about a century later than their Latin American counterparts. The Turkish Revolution led by Atatürk set the nation on a path that combined economic independence via industrialization with a firm secularization and westernization—accepting European styles, though hoping to manufacture European goods at home. This new path required the suppression of elite groups, especially clerical sectors, opposed to these changes, as well as the imposition of new patterns of consumption on the largely unwesternized peasant masses. One dramatic gesture was the 1922 expulsion of Greek populations, who had been concentrated in port cities and heavily involved in foreign trade; the replacement of the fez by the hat in 1925 was another (Robinson 1963, 83–85).

The route to such nationalist economic policy was slower in Egypt, where the British retained considerable authority after 1922. Here, too, were tensions between different elite segments, a small group of heavily Europeanized traders committed to the export of Egyptian cotton and the import of European manufactured goods, and other wealthy bankers and commercial interests more eager to develop local industry (Tignor 1984, 246–48). Despite some moves toward industrialization during the Depression, when foreign goods were less available, the major push toward import-substitution industrialization came after Nasser rose to power in 1952 (145–46), soon followed by the Suez Crisis of 1956 and the pressuring of foreigners, concentrated again in coastal cities and the capital, to leave. Egypt, too, had debates over the transformation of local consumption patterns. For example, Egyptian farmers in the 1970s and 1980s were much less willing than their counterparts in other parts of the region to replace their traditional varieties of wheat with the "Green Revolution" high-yielding varieties, despite the availability of necessary inputs and near-ideal growing conditions (Richards and Waterbury 1990, 152–81).

Two recent ethnographic studies document this ambivalence toward foreign goods. Hoodfar's study (1997) of a neighborhood in Cairo in the 1980s and early 1990s documents the economic difficulties of a group of poor families, most of them migrants from rural regions who find work in informal sector jobs. She includes a detailed discussion of consumption patterns in her examination of household organization, gender relations, employment, and education. In this context, kin and neighbors may assume that someone who follows the traditional urban (*baladi*) or rural (*fallahin*) practices is old-fashioned, while they might think that someone who appears to be *afrangi* (literally, Frenchified, or, more generally, westernized) would not meet Islamic standards of moral behavior. Consumption, then, poses problems, both because of the difficult economic circumstances that all the families face and because of the cultural meanings of specific goods. Hoodfar's treatment of women's decisions to wear Islamic scarves—a topic of particularly intense debate in the neighborhood at the time of the study—shows the connection of these factors, since by dressing more modestly women can not only signal their religious orientations, but also save a great deal on clothes and travel far more freely on public transport. Debates over the proper place of Western and Egyptian styles extend beyond clothing to virtually all domains of consumption. Are French rolls to be a part of ordinarily meals, rather than the customary flat bread, or are they to be an occasional luxury, as canned fish and frozen vegetables are (229)? (This concern over types of bread echoes a debate among the wealthiest Egyptians at the turn of the century, when "increasing quantities of high quality foreign flour were required to provide [the] European community [of residents in Egypt] and the well-to-do Egyptian with bread" [Owen 1981, 242].) If a man occasionally drinks a bottle of beer when he meets friends after work, is his expenditure an acceptable form of male public consumption, or should he restrict himself to the more traditional and Islamic beverages of tea and coffee (177, 188)? Are televisions, more common than electric fans or refrigerators, an acceptable form of entertainment for women, or do they introduce scandalous Western images into the household (241)?

Carole Delaney's book (1991) on gender, reproduction, and religion in a village in a hilly interior region of Turkey does not center as directly on economic activity. However, its close focus on the significance of details of daily life presents the reader with discussions of consumption, demonstrating again the split between Western and Turkish styles. The household furnishings and pieces of clothing that prospective husbands must provide to their brides seem neatly bifurcated into Europeanized urban goods and traditional items (119–21). The foods customarily served at festivals are marked as local (296–97, 304–5), rather than foreign, in terms of ingredients or forms of cooking (249–50). The men—few in number—who drink alcoholic beverages do so only in the city (128). A particularly vivid image is that of a young woman, soon to be married, accompanied by her sister, mother, and fiancé ("a thin young man in a pale new suit"), on a trip from the village to Ankara to purchase furniture for her new home. "Halfway down the mountains, the bride calmly removed her *şalvar* [modest baggy pants], under which she had on 'city' clothes, a skirt and sweater, nylons and pumps" (121–22).

The suddenness of her transformation, like the other sudden transformations that occurred at larger scales in the recent history of Egypt and Turkey, suggest the sharpness of the line that separates the local and the foreign. This sharpness may be associated with an ambivalence about foreign goods: at times a strong concern to limit the scope of foreign goods, as in the case of the village woman; at times, as in Turkey under Atatürk, a sharp desire to expand this scope; at times a close attention to the location of this line, as in the urban poor studied by Hoodfar. In this ambivalence we may note, in a general way, the operation of the same forces as in Latin America. In both regions the political economy expanded trade with Europe in the nineteenth and twentieth centuries. However, the postcolonial dilemmas of national identity played out in different ways. Though to some degree modern nationalism in both areas seems paradoxically defined both by separation from the West (as the location of the former colonial powers) and by association with it (as the fountainhead of modernity), the tension between these two seems more acute in the Middle East. Since European colonialism lasted later in the Middle East than in Latin America, and since European religions and languages did not take root with the same force, these dilemmas seem to have played out in a different way in the realm of consumption, making the attraction of foreign goods more ambivalent.

These comparative cases demonstrate two important points: that Latin America was not alone in the nineteenth and twentieth centuries in finding imported goods to be attractive, and that this appeal of foreign goods, though widespread in global terms, was by no means universal. Eastern Europe is the region that most resembles Latin America in its enthusiasm for imported goods, while China, which by and large rejected them, offers the sharpest contrast. The Middle East was marked by greater ambivalence about these goods.

Despite this variety of experiences, these cases show some important commonalities. The potential for import booms is shaped by the political economic forces of world markets and systems of production, through their influence on prices and incomes. However, these forces do not operate in an automatic or mechanical fashion. We note also the importance of nationalism and modernity. It is difficult to disentangle these and to separate them out into independent factors, since in all the regions, the growth of the global economy occurred in the same centuries as older empires collapsed and gave way to new nations, and as the idea that modern history was uniquely dynamic received broad acceptance. Nonetheless, we have seen how nationalism in Eastern Europe was predicated on the close adherence to Western European models of nationhood, an association which reflects the geographical proximity and the historical and religious commonalities of the two halves of the continent. Since imperial rule was far less associated with foreign domination for the Chinese, their transition to republicanism was marked by a number of continuities with their earlier, distinctive cultural patterns, rather than by the strong Europeanization of elites and other groups. For the Middle East, the European conquest and occupation of the declining Ottoman Empire meant that national independence came comparatively late and after comparatively difficult struggles. The length and severity of these conflicts contributed to opposed forces: to some Europeanized consumption patterns similar to those in Latin America and in Eastern Europe on the one hand, and to a strong oppositional nationalism on the other. In a similar vein, Eastern Europe has joined the Western European vision of modernity, while China remains largely with a Sinocentric view of its future; in the Middle East, different nations, and different segments within nations, have formulated a variety of models of modernity and hence have attributed different meanings to the foreign goods that stand so readily as signs of Western modernity.

NOTES

1. In the instances in which Latin American economic policy-making is discussed (in such areas as exchange rates and the convertibility of currency), the interests of the export producers are often seen as critical.

2. This story, first published in book form in *El Aleph* (Buenos Aires: Editorial Losada, 1949), appears also on pages 589–95 of volume 3 of the *Obras Completas* (Buenos Aires: Emecé Editorial, 1966). Our translation is based partly on the one by Dudley Fitts, which was first published in *Partisan Review* in February 1950 (17(2): 143–51) and reprinted in *Labyrinths: Selected stories and other writings,* ed. Donald A. Yates and James E. Irby, 1962, New York: New Directions, 156–64.

Chapter 2

Changing Consumption Patterns and Everyday Life in Two Peruvian Regions: Food, Dress, and Housing in the Central and Southern Highlands (1820–1920)

Thomas Krüggeler

In this chapter I explore how foreign goods and the idea of the consumer society penetrated the Peruvian hinterland during the century following independence. The development of provincial consumer societies in Peru generally lacked the pomp and decadence that characterized the process of adaptation to the modern consumer world in numerous urban centers of Latin America. Provincial societies also became integrated into the consumer world at a slower pace and to a lesser degree. These differences were caused by two major factors: limited cash reserves, geographical isolation, and small markets prevented excessive consumption of foreign goods; and more traditional local societies forced even members of the elites to respect certain limits. Some people (e.g., conservative members of the oligarchy) may have viewed some new fashion trends as immoral, while others (e.g., Indian peasants) did not believe in the civilizing effect of consumption of manufactured goods and demonstrated a more critical attitude toward the consumer world.

I compare how consumer societies emerged in two regions, the central and the southern highlands of Peru, which differed considerably in their economic and social structures and which developed rather differently during the nineteenth century. In the central sierra (Junín, Tarma, Pasco) a relatively dynamic mining industry and the region's geographical proximity to the nation's capital favored economic growth and social change. Mining centers and the city of Lima provided the area's agricultural sector with markets and linked its commerce closely to the capital (Mallon

31

1983; Manrique 1987; Wilson 1982). During the second half of the last century, the increasing amount of cash circulating in the central sierra also favored the gradual development of a domestic market. The departments of Arequipa, Puno, and Cuzco, on the other hand, were considered to form the least developed part of the Peruvian sierra. Only the region's commercial center, the city of Arequipa at the foothills of the sierra, and its immediate surroundings did not exactly fit into this scheme. The relative strength of semiautonomous Indian communities, a poorly developed regional infrastructure, an inefficient hacienda system, and the lack of urban centers hampered economic growth. Increasing integration into the international wool trade during the nineteenth century vitalized the regional economy to a certain extent, but it could not make up for the central highland's structural advantages (Jacobsen 1993; Flores Galindo 1977; Orlove 1977).

People's motives for changing consumption behavior, the meaning they attached to consumer goods, and the way they viewed the consumer society varied greatly from region to region and along class and ethnic lines. Such differences were influenced by economic and social forces. The introduction of the consumer society in the Peruvian sierra was more complex than shipping increasing quantities and larger varieties of goods into the mountains. It reflected social conflicts between provincial elites and their Lima counterparts, revealed the complicated structure of social relations within regional societies, and was accompanied by a lively and changing national discourse about the relation between consumption and national progress. In this debate authors deplore that civilization had not yet reached the interior provinces, make suggestions of how to turn allegedly lazy Indians into hard-working consumers, and blame the backwardness of the hinterland for Peru's lack of national integration. Although the main purpose of this chapter is to demonstrate how the consumer society penetrated the central and southern highlands, I indicate how this process was embedded in this national political debate.

First I present a picture of what kind of foreign goods were available on provincial markets, how merchants organized the distribution of goods, and how the composition of imports changed over time. Were the central and southern highlands equally supplied with foreign goods, or did geographical isolation severely hamper the spread of the consumer society into the southern sierra? In a second step this chapter demonstrates how the elites and an emerging middle class coped with the idea that consumption of foreign goods was an indispensable element of what *Limeños* viewed as the modern and civilized world. I will demonstrate that for the elites of both the southern and the central highlands, consumption of foreign goods required balancing between the desire to imitate Lima consumption behavior and the social restrictions that local societies were able to impose on conspicuous consumption. Since the last quarter of the nineteenth century, the middle class was increasingly pressured to underscore their social status by a moderate "modern" life-style. The problem for shopkeepers, clerks, school teachers, and others was, however, that these people often did not dispose of the necessary means to participate in the consumer world.

Although lower classes were not excluded from the emerging consumer world, they did not participate enough to support the development of more dynamic domestic markets. I discuss why urban poor as well as Indian peasants appreciated the practical value of certain consumer items and why lower classes, particularly Indian peasants, did not share the notion that consumption had some kind of civilizing effect on the consumer. Finally, I attempt to demonstrate how provincial producers reacted toward the challenge of foreign competition and how market conditions of the two regions changed during the century following independence. Were local economies profoundly transformed by the introduction of the consumer world, and were the central and southern highlands ready to absorb American manufactured goods of mass production by the early 1920s?

Availability of Imports

By the mid-1820s, the towns of the central and southern sierra were well supplied and even overstocked with foreign goods, despite the disruptions caused by the war of independence. European merchants, particularly British traders, had begun establishing roots in Peruvian markets during the last quarter of the eighteenth century.[1] Apparently foreign merchants had no doubt that Peruvian as well as other Latin American consumers would dramatically increase their consumption of foreign goods, after having shaken off the yoke of colonial rule. It is likely that cultural prejudices against relatively inexperienced buyers made them believe that Peruvians would celebrate independence and freedom by purchasing foreign goods without paying much attention to quality and selection. Foreign merchants dumped large amounts of all kinds of merchandise on Peruvian markets.[2] What the British traveler Edmond Temple said about the market of La Paz in the early 1830s was also true for Peruvian market places:

English goods are abundant, and are preferred to either French or German manufactures, which seem, however, to have a fair share of the market. Every sort of flimsy, tinsel, gewgaw, and cargoes of divers kinds of worthless articles, unsalable at home, were at first imported by European merchants, in the hope of finding a ready sale here. Whether they did or not is best known to themselves, but now all such articles are duly despised.[3]

European consuls and travelers often complained that European merchants lacked well-planned commercial strategies, a deficit that could hurt long-term business interests of their countries. These comments are combined with suggestions of which goods could actually be sold on different markets. During the 1830s, merchants began to put their businesses on more solid ground, after many of them had suffered substantial losses.[4] The single most important products that European merchants sold on Peruvian markets were cotton and woolen cloth. During the early years of the post-Independence period, textiles counted for around 95 percent of all imports to Peru. However, that share declined gradually until it reached 32 percent in 1872.[5] Particularly during the second half of the nineteenth century, such goods as iron tools, machinery (from sewing machines for tailor workshops to heavy factory equipment), and furniture found an increasing market in Peru (Gootenberg 1990).

The British consul Charles Milner Ricketts estimated that in 1825 around 2.2 million pounds of foreign goods (loaded on eight thousand mules) were transported from Lima to Huaylas and Tarma in the central sierra, and he was confident that sales in these provinces increased significantly over the following years and decades because "prices of these goods are falling [and] the natives are learning to like them."[6] Twenty-five years later, remarks of the American Navy Lieutenant Lewis Herndon confirmed that Rickett's optimism was fully justified. He describes a large variety of foreign goods on the markets of the central highlands and was somewhat surprised to even find British carriages and gigs in the streets of the town of Huánuco.[7] Such bulky and expensive goods may still have been novelties, but English textiles, German hardware, and French perfumes belonged to the inventory of most stores in Cerro de Pasco, Tarma, and Jauja by the early 1850s.[8]

Since the mid-1840s, when increasing sales of guano made many Limeños believe that Peru's splendid future had just begun, the central region's economy felt not only the impact of an expanding Lima market for agricultural products, but landowners and merchants from the Tarma region also supplied surrounding mining areas with *aguardiente* formerly brought in from the coast. During the 1840s landholders had gradually shifted to produce *aguardiente* out of sugar cane they grew in the semi-tropical areas of the eastern slopes of the Andes. Both developments increased the amount of cash available for investment and consumption. Foreign merchant houses that had established their businesses in Lima in the early days of the guano boom opened branches in Cerro de Pasco and Tarma by the 1860s in order to directly take advantage of expanding markets. From these regional centers they also supplied local merchants and retailers in other towns and villages (Mallon 1983). Foreign goods found in small-town stores ranged from silk and cotton handkerchiefs to heavy agricultural equipment.[9]

By contrast, patterns in the southern highlands were very different. Although English pianos and desks and French billiard tables could be found in the geographically isolated southern city of Cuzco as early as in the 1840s, the consumption capacities of southern markets remained far below those of the much more dynamic central highlands. Most foreign goods entered the southern sierra through the small ports of Arica and Islay. From there they were transported to the nearby city of Arequipa, at the foothills of the Andes. Beginning during the second half of the eighteenth century, when administrative reforms cut off the city of Cuzco from major colonial trade routes, Arequipa gradually replaced that city as the region's economic center (Jacobsen 1993; Galindo 1977). Foreign and Peruvian merchant houses established businesses in Arequipa, from where they penetrated southern markets mostly through contracted retailers and peddlers. By the mid-1850s, the British Consul in Arequipa presented a positive picture of southern Peruvian market conditions: "The major share of commerce is in the hands of British merchants. Trade has increased considerably during the last two or three years and it will continue to do so as civilization advances and the needs of the masses of the population increase."[10] Particularly during the second half of the nineteenth century, sales prospects were closely linked to the region's export of sheep and alpaca wool. Such foreign goods as hardware and cheap cloth were often bartered for raw wool, while luxury items required access to cash (Jacobsen 1993).

Rapidly expanding demand for imports, like those observed in the central highlands since the late 1840s, developed in the interior of the southern sierra only by the late nineteenth century. Economic growth and the emergence of more diverse urban societies were linked to favorable conditions of the international wool trade and the construction of a railroad line. The geographical isolation of Cuzco prevented wholesale merchants from establishing branches there before the War of the Pacific (1879–83). Only when telegraph and railroads facilitated communication between Arequipa and the interior did merchants begin to open branches in the former Inca capital (Burga and Reátegui 1981). Yet the railroad advanced slowly into the Andes. The Arequipa-Puno line was finished in the early 1870s, but construction of the connecting line to Cuzco was frequently interrupted and it reached the city of Cuzco only in 1908. During the late nineteenth and early twentieth centuries, the period that Jacobsen calls the "golden age" of large wholesale merchants in southern Peru, consumption capacity increased in the southern region, mostly due to booming wool exports (Jacobsen 1988). By then even in Cuzco a well-to-do middle sector of society began to emerge.

With the arrival of the railroad the amount of imports on markets of the southern highlands expanded and diversified. In 1873 a hacendado from Azángaro (Puno) purchased, among other imported items, Norwegian beer and Spanish canned fish from a store in Puno. Inventories of Puno stores show that the selection of imported goods increased by 100 percent (from 74 to 148 different items) between 1858 and 1890 (Jacobsen 1993). When the wealthy Garmendia and Nadal families of Cuzco imported French machinery for the south's first textile factory in the early 1860s, even *Limeños* paid attention. At that time the heavy equipment had to be transported on mule backs some 500 kilometers to the family's hacienda in Lucre (Quispicanchis) at the outskirts of Cuzco.[11] But in the early twentieth century, European furniture and other bulky items, rarely seen and very prestigious in Cuzco in the mid–nineteenth century, could be brought into the city by railroad. Such progress was welcomed by many and no elite family was able to escape the social pressure to gradually replace traditional Cochabamba chairs with British furniture (Valcárcel 1981).

Construction of the Central Railway was not completed much earlier than the southern line. It reached La Oroya in 1893 before it finally arrived in Huancayo in 1908. But in the central sierra the development of the consumer society did depend far less on railroads. By the early twentieth century most inhabitants were already integrated in a cash economy, and most segments of society were well acquainted with the consumer world, due to the region's proximity to Lima. In southern towns such as Cuzco the railroad established new markets. In contrast, in the central highlands, improved infrastructures, combined with the effects of a booming mining industry, widened already existing markets and favored the development of mass consumption of manufactured goods, known until then only in the nation's capital and perhaps a few other coastal cities.

During the century following Independence, access to imports was not a major problem for those inhabitants of the central and southern highlands who desired them and could afford to pay for them. It is surprising how many pianos, desks, and other heavy items were carried into the mountains before better roads and railroads were built.[12] Peddlers brought smaller goods even to the most remote villages. However, improved transport conditions facilitated the introduction of foreign goods and caused prices to fall. In the central sierra, people consumed larger quantities of imports and consumption behavior changed faster than in the southern highlands, due to the region's extensive contact with Lima. Although southern elites were less familiar with European fashion trends, and imported goods were slightly more expensive in Puno than in Jauja, imports were appreciated for their practical (cheap cloth, hardware, etc.) as well as for their symbolic value (luxury items).

Civilization, Progress, and Modernity: The Symbolic Value of Imports

Foreign goods on provincial markets did not have the same impact on all segments of society. While peasants appreciated the cheap price of imported cloth and the practical value of scissors and shovels, they did not fully share the enthusiasm of elite families for consumer goods. Consumption patterns differed along class and ethnic lines, and such differences did not only have to do with the economic conditions of potential consumers and their access to cash. In this section I try to identify the forces that led provincial elites to change their consumption behavior and the factors that influenced the extent to which other segments of society adapted to consumption patterns practiced by local or regional elites. Once provincial upper classes began consuming foreign goods, middle sectors followed their example promptly, even if it required considerable economic sacrifices. An elite family had a bigger house than a master craftsman, but at church or at other social occasions the craftsman's suit, in order to be deemed appropriate, could not be of much lesser quality than the one the hacendado was wearing. The often rather humble economic conditions of social middle sectors did not protect them from social forces that required the expression of a modern and progressive attitude.

Consumption played a key role in Peruvian politics and society during the century following Independence, and perhaps no other aspect of economic theory has been more controversial than *consumo*. Since the 1820s some elite factions expressed their worries that unrestricted consumption of foreign luxury goods by elites and by some middle sectors drained too much capital from the productive sector, where it was so desperately needed.[13] Only for a short period of time between the mid-1840s and the 1860s, when staggering amounts of state revenues from the sale of guano (bird dung extracted from islands off the Pacific coast and used as a fertilizer in European agriculture) silenced protectionists temporarily, were some segments of the Lima society allowed to dream unhindered of Peru as a "nation of consumers."[14]

The symbolic value of imports was no less appealing to provincial elites than to the upper class of Lima. Even owners of rural textile manufactures, who fervently supported the protectionist course during the first decades of the post-Independence period by demanding high tariffs for foreign textiles, enjoyed Scottish whisky and French soap.[15] Protectionists did not hide their admiration for British industrialism and French culture and they were by no means anti-European. Spending a good deal of money on European goods was meant to underscore a family's wealth and status, to demonstrate one's links with what was considered the civilized world, and to appear modern and up-to-date. At times, relations between regional elites and the Lima upper class could be somewhat frosty, due to political rivalries or disputes. But the two groups firmly shared the basic notion of modernity that dominated the political and social discourse of the Peruvian capital.

The motives of upper-class consumers of the interior in adopting the consumption behavior of the Lima elite could vary. It is likely that merchants, mine owners, and hacendados of the central highlands assumed that dressing correctly (i.e., "modern") and placing some European furniture in the parlor of their homes were necessary to build or maintain economic and social ties to Lima business partners they depended on. In this case, people put considerable effort into being on top of fashion and consumer trends as early as in the 1830s or 1840s. During the early post-Independence period, elites of the southern sierra, on the other hand, were not so much worried that lagging behind Lima consumer trends could cause them economic disadvantages. They feared that Lima's attempts to emphasize imported ideas of progress and civilization by adopting European consumption behavior could lead to even further social and political marginalization of interior elites. For them, copying the consumption patterns of the capital's upper class served the purpose of trying to close a growing social gap between Lima and the provincial elites. But outside of Arequipa, southern elites felt less pressure to always meet Lima consumption standards than did the upper-class families of Tarma or Jauja.

The pace, intensity, and scope of changes in consumption patterns were not only dependent upon elite families' intentions and desires. The amount of cash circulating in a local or regional economy determined the consumption capacity of a market and was perhaps the single most important variable influencing consumer behavior. Demand for foreign goods was also influenced by the degree of economic exchange and social contacts between an interior province and the coast. Frequent exchange with the capital offered opportunities to become better acquainted with new fashions, styles, and the variety of goods available. Wealthy people from the central highlands had clearly better opportunities to keep up with Lima consumption trends than did most members of the upper classes of the southern highlands.

The Lima market for agricultural products, which had expanded considerably since the 1840s, and increasing sales of regionally produced *aguardiente* in the central highlands' mining camps provided the money for elite families to follow the standards of Lima consumption behavior more closely (Wilson 1982). By the mid-1840s, efforts of the more affluent segments of the Tarma society had already paid off, although the amounts of foreign goods on regional markets would still considerably increase during the following decades. Tarma enjoyed an excellent reputation among coastal upper-class circles. The town was described as "one of the most pleasant and civilized places of the whole sierra, where the superior classes . . . wish to adopt the customs of the capital as their own."[16] It was obviously the desire of members of the upper class to imitate the customs of Lima that made Tarma pleasant and civilized.

After 1850, it was no easy task for elite families of Tarma, Cerro de Pasco, and Jauja to keep up with the consumer culture of the Lima elite, who thoroughly enjoyed the blessings of the guano boom. Keeping track of quickly changing fashion trends and newly introduced consumer items was expensive and required serious attention. But by the 1860s frequent contacts with people from Lima and abroad had sharpened the minds of the Jauja and Tarma elites for international fashion trends and allegedly good taste. Regional markets had even grown enough to attract foreign tailors, dressmakers, and other artisans who began to set up shops in central Andean towns.[17] These foreigners helped to assure that European fashion trends were copied appropriately and increased the pressure on local producers to keep up with fashion trends and to perform quality work. Increasingly, women no longer accepted any fine French cloth offered for sale; they desired specific brands, colors, printing patterns, and types of embroideries, as dictated by current fashion trends.

By the 1880s, but even more so after the region had recovered from the destruction of the War of the Pacific in the 1890s, the town of Huancayo emerged as a new commercial center in the area, competing with Jauja and Tarma, and increasing the regional supply of consumer goods. As early as 1880, three Chinese restaurants were operating in the town, and consumers supported eight general stores and fifty-two shops in the town's permanent market (Long and Roberts 1984). In 1895 the city council was very much concerned about the activities of Lima merchant houses, which took advantage of increasing consumption of consumer goods in the region. Members of the council claimed that commercial agents brought large amounts of samples (of imported goods, as well as the output of such infant domestic industries as leather and textile factories) to the city and left it with considerable profits without paying local taxes (Long and Roberts 1984).

However, even in the central sierra, where elite families often had close links to Lima, where a steadily growing variety of imported goods was available and the upper class disposed of some purchasing power, people introduced new consumption behavior only cautiously. Some segments of the Andean society did not so fully embrace the idea that consumption was an integral part of progress. Among their Lima friends, adaptation to the consumer society earned members of regional elites the reputation of being civilized. But for Indian peasants, and even for more conservative members of the local elite or the parish priest, consumer goods could have different meanings. Conspicuous consumption of foreign goods could be interpreted by others as an exaggerated demonstration of wealth and power or it could be viewed as ostentatious, decadent, and immoral. New consumption behavior had to be woven into the sets of traditions, customs, and values of the regional and local societies.

This was particularly true in the central sierra. There the elite was embedded in a complicated network of social and economic ties not only to other local and regional upper-class families, but also to Lima business partners, friends, and political authorities, and to local Indian peasants (Long and Roberts 1978; Samaniego 1978; Alberti and Sánchez 1974). Controlling local economic and political affairs required cooperation with Lima authorities as well as negotiations with Indian peasants over such issues as land use, taxes, and public work projects. For these diverse systems of social relations, consumer goods could be used as social and political tools, if they were carefully chosen. A new suit made of English tweed could let the Tarma hacendado impress a business partner from Lima. It was also an appropriate garment to wear in front of the local court, where the judge decided over a dispute the landholder had with an Indian community. However, if the hacendado was interested in settling the case outside the court, he was best advised to approach the villagers wearing a traditional poncho and to bring along a jar of chicha instead of beer.[18]

Social relations between Indian peasants and members of regional elites were often tied to the Andean notion of reciprocity and *compadrazgo*. Despite their political and economic power, hacendados and mine owners had to obey to some basic rules, which characterized these social ties. Offering a village leader a box of imported nails as a gift could contribute to strengthen social bonds between *compadres,* because peasants appreciated the practical value of nails. But demonstrating wealth and power by displaying European fashion in an Indian village could have the opposite effect. It increased the social distance between the two men. Indians clearly rejected the use of luxury consumer goods in these kinds of situations and insisted on respecting tradition. In the Indian village the hacendado could impress no one with a jar of beer, as long as Indians agreed that chicha was superior to beer. Nineteenth-century travelers often emphasize that hacendados spoke Quechua fluently. Talking to Indians in their own tongue served the same purpose as wearing traditional clothing and drinking chicha in the countryside. It symbolized social bonds, mutual understanding, and respect for Indian culture, and it was designed to facilitate social and political negotiations.

Through experience, elites of the southern highlands knew that imitating Lima consumption behavior was a delicate matter. In the nineteenth century, European travelers frequently tried to ridicule the way provincial people attempted to demonstrate civilized manners by attempting to dress in European style. Upper-class families of the remote and allegedly backward southern sierra were particularly vulnerable to such mockery.

According to the Frenchman Laurent de Saint Cricq, who visited Arequipa in the 1840s, upper-class *Arequipeñas* had trouble following contemporary European fashion trends:

> Dressmakers, modistes, and hair-dressers being as yet unknown in Arequipa, it is the ladies themselves who cut out, sew, and trim their garments and fripperies; who disentangle, arrange, and curl their hair. To say that these arrangements are made in exquisite taste, and copied from the engravings of the latest fashion, would be to gloss the severe truth. To speak frankly, there is generally in the cut of the corsage and the sleeve, in the shortness or scantiness of the skirt, that mysterious something that characterized the fashion of the Restoration, and gave to the women of that epoch a certain resemblance to birds of the order of waders. Some fashionable ladies of Arequipa wear, along with the high tortoise-shell comb of the Andalusians, bunches of borrowed ringlets imported from England under the name *anglaises,* the shade of which is not always exactly the same of that of their own hair. These lionesses also generally adorn their heads with a bird of paradise, one of those aigrettes of glass-thread made in Germany, or toy butterflies mounted upon a spiral wire, which they name *tembleques,* and which vibrate at every moment.[19]

Of course, the comment that Arequipa was without modistes or dressmakers is not the only exaggeration in this arrogant statement. However, it is true that seamstresses and local tailors produced garments out of imported cloth that did mix traditional Spanish and modern French elements. Women also combined items of English, German, and French origin without hesitation. At times such mixture of styles may have been due to lack of information about the most recent fashion trends or was the result of the persuasiveness of clever shopkeepers and peddlers who were more interested in sales than in taste or styles. But gradual change in the way women dressed could be a concession to their social environment as well. In the 1830s and 1840s neither Arequipa nor other towns of the central and southern highlands were cosmopolitan urban centers. Extravagant styles may have been considered indecent, and not only the parish priest may have disapproved of them. Even the wealthiest women risked becoming the subject of local gossip if their desire to copy Parisian fashion went too far. Rarely did visitors consider such concerns.

When Saint Cricq reached the town of Cuzco in 1846, he portrayed the life-style of the city's wealthy families with pungent irony. He claimed that members "of the doubtful nobility" placed their expensive pianos from England or Chile in the entrance room of their homes and noted that "no one ever touches it, for reasons that it is easy to conceive, but the show it makes is satisfactory to the *amour propre* of the family. It is at once a certificate of civilization and an attestation of taste and genteel manners."[20] The French visitor did not realize or did not acknowledge the social, and to a certain extent also economic, strains that pressured his hosts in Cuzco and other Andean towns. Enhancing one's social status within the local or regional society through the consumption of foreign goods did not require extraordinary expenses. Using French terms to describe a specific kind of fabric or offering a glass of whisky to visiting neighbors was often enough to demonstrate civilized manners in Puno or Jauja during the 1840s. Things became more complicated and more expensive when visitors from Lima or foreign guests—people who were presumably more civilized—had to be convinced of the modern character of provincial elites. When foreigners were to be hosted, the wine had to be chosen with care and the most fashionable and expensive dress had to be worn. Wealthy people could not afford to be cheap when it came to status and prestige. Saint Cricq's comments show, however, how difficult it was for people of the hinterland to please visitors and to fight their image of being backward, poorly educated, and not really acquainted with modern lifestyles. Not even an expensive foreign piano could guarantee success.[21]

In Peru the struggle of provincial elites for social acceptance by their coastal counterparts always had an ethnic component, too. The French visitor had doubts of the noble origin of the Cuzco elite because of people's manners, limited wealth, and—perhaps most important—their skin color. For him the elite's Indian background was somewhat hidden "under the varnish of education," but it was "uncontestable."[22] Foreigners as well as *Limeños* were inexorable in questioning the ethnic background of provincial elites. While wealth, power, and lifestyle may have "whitened" a hacendado's skin within his local social setting, outsiders were more critical. They assumed that the majority of members of provincial elites were mestizos, and the further away from the coast somebody lived, the more likely it was that he or she was not white. Wearing ponchos and speaking Quechua—a hacendado's important instruments for managing local social relations—could be interpreted as an indication of the lack of civilized manners in the eyes of a foreign visitor. Thus, southern elites in particular fought not only their image as backwoods people, they also struggled against racial prejudices in a society in which ethnic boundaries determined social status to a large extent. The burden of proof that one was white rested with the person from the interior.

Before the War of the Pacific (1879–1883) the southern highlands represented an unevenly developed market for foreign goods. Large parts of the rural areas consumed only cheap textiles, limited quantities of hardware, and some inexpensive items of European origin. Outside of Arequipa, elite families were scattered over regional towns and even in remote haciendas. In the 1840s the majority of the population of Puno and Cuzco had little money left for European luxury items. Reports on the quantity of imports actually consumed in the southern sierra during the first decades after Independence are therefore somewhat contradictory. Protectionists tended to exaggerate the impact of imports on regional markets. For example, in a report from 1845 about the conditions of Peruvian agriculture, Francisco de Rivero demands the introduction of high tariffs for foreign luxury items because consumption of foreign goods contributed to "the complete rupture of the equilibrium between our products and our consumption." With respect to the southern region he complains that consumption reduced the amount of productive capital, and that twenty years after Independence even "the middle and lower classes" enjoyed luxury goods.[23] The author's argument is that demand for consumer goods had to be balanced with the output of the Peruvian productive sector.

Rivero must have had the city of Arequipa in mind when he was concerned that even the southern middle and lower classes spent their money on imported consumer goods. In towns like Puno or Cuzco, the reality of the 1840s was different. Following scattered earlier newspaper notices of the arrival of Italian wine and French liquor in the city of Cuzco, bargain sales of foreign goods, so-called *baratillos,* were frequently announced in the late 1840s.[24] Long lists of such goods as French soap and eau de cologne, German and French velvet, English leather, French ties, fine European glassware, and a large variety of fabrics of all qualities offered at bargain prices were advertised in local newspapers. These advertisements indicate that European luxury goods had lost their novelty character even in the remote southern sierra by the 1840s, and they suggest that the Cuzco market could absorb only very limited quantities of foreign goods. It is most likely that bargain sales were held not because merchants continued to ship huge quantities of imports to the interior, but because local retailers had problems finding buyers even for limited quantities of expensive imports.

Outside of Arequipa, wealthy people of the southern highlands became better acquainted with European or Lima consumption behavior only toward the end of the nineteenth century. Poor transport conditions and more limited demand delayed the expansion and increase of consumption of foreign goods. It is likely that increasing wool sales ensured that more iron tools were sold in the Puno and Cuzco areas in 1880 than in 1840. But the demand for luxury items was low in comparison to the central highlands due to the lack of cash resources and limited numbers of upper- and middle-class consumers. Markets became more dynamic only in the early 1900s, when in expectation of the completion of the Arequipa-Cuzco railroad, foreign merchants had established their stores in Cuzco. Now a sizable urban middle sector began to develop, and increasing sales of raw wool made cash available to larger parts of the population. Under these circumstance the demand for luxury items rose. Luis E. Valcárcel, perhaps the city's most famous *indigenista* of the 1910s and 1920s, states in his memoirs:

> In spite of the limits of the Cuzco environment, luxury articles were very much in demand. Pianos, perfumes, fine liquor, canned foods, cloth, crockery, jewelry, etc. were imported. They even brought European furniture that started gradually to displace the colonial furniture that predominated at the beginning of the century. The wealthy families considered it out of fashion. . . . With the arrival of the railroad this type of trade intensified. (Valcárcel 1981, 35)

However, the southern towns were still lagging behind those in the central highlands. Their economies and societies did not share the dynamics that drove other provincial urban centers. Until the late 1910s, not a single immigrant tailor had established his shop in Cuzco. By then only a few of the most affluent local master tailors announced proudly that their sons had received training in European trade schools.[25] By the early twentieth century, consumption had become a tool some urban people used to draw a clear line between urban and rural life-styles. In the central Andean towns of Tarma and Huancayo, upper-class women had become used to paying regular visits to the stores of Italian immigrants to browse through a large selection of imported goods. Less wealthy women chose Chinese and Peruvian merchants who sold foreign and Peruvian merchandise of lower price categories. The notion of going shopping had become a part of the urban consumer culture. Wilson makes the point that the most illustrative symbol of urban life-style became the acquisition of bedding. While upper-class families may have slept in French silk, Wilson shows that even relatively poor families purchased cotton and woolen blankets produced in Lima factories (Wilson 1985). Although people from central Andean towns increasingly considered sleeping on animal hides as a sign of backwardness, it was still very common in Cuzco and Puno during the 1910s.

Consumption behavior of the emerging urban middle class was determined to a large extent by standards set by regional elites. During the second half of the nineteenth century participation in the consumer society became a key characteristic of the middle class's way of life. Shopkeepers, master craftsmen, clerks, and government employees enjoyed a middle-class status because of their occupations, skills, education, or positions they held in a company. But increasingly their status had to be underscored by a life-style that reflected the middle class's close association with the modern world. However, cash income of many middle-class families was often rather limited and in economic terms they were further apart from elite families than their social status suggested.[26] Fulfilling expectations that were linked to their social position thus absorbed a significant share of a family's budgets. For a bank employee or railroad conductor, for example, it was not enough to dress correctly during working hours. The lifestyle of their entire families had to reflect their professional positions. Middle-class families not only sent their children to private schools, they also introduced European furniture into their homes, purchased European garments, and ate canned food from overseas on holidays.

Whenever economic conditions allowed upper classes a more luxurious way of life, the middle sectors were forced to adapt. As long as elite families consumed mostly foreign fabrics, food, and some other luxury goods, shopkeepers and clerks would buy similar products of lower price categories. But once elite families were socially obliged to own a foreign piano, the less wealthy storekeeper had to purchase at least an imported chest of drawers or some other furniture, even if it cost him a substantial part of his savings. In the central sierra this snowball effect became evident during the 1850s, when the elite intensified their efforts to copy Lima consumption patterns, the number of middle-class families increased, and cash became more widely available. The fact that by the 1910s the use of bedding had become an integral part of the consumer culture of the towns of the central highlands proves how certain consumption patterns penetrated various segments of society. In the southern sierra similar processes were closely linked to the gradual advance of the railroad into the mountains.

Maintaining a middle-class status could become particularly difficult in periods when costs of living rose and little money was left for the purchase of luxury items. In the late 1910s, when prices of basic goods increased tremendously on the Cuzco market, urban middle classes were facing serious economic and social difficulties (Krüggeler 1993, 213–26). In 1919 a Cuzco newspaper tried to turn attention to the hardship of the urban middle sector. The paper claimed that in contrast to peasants, workers, and capitalists, the middle class had no voice in the city, although this sector was in a particularly difficult situation. Middle-class families "have enormous needs," but "their incomes are not enough to take care of their decency." The author of the article reminds the reader that white-collar workers "must live in decent homes, dress correctly, and may not give the impression of suffering." If they failed to maintain their decent lifestyle they could easily lose their position.[27]

The author of this newspaper article views the middle class as part of the social group of *gente decente*. Decent people do not necessarily compose a unified social class, but they represent the non-Indian sector of the Andes (De la Cadena 1994). They are considered to be morally and socially advanced and link the hinterland to the modern world. During the second half of the nineteenth century, when this link to the modern world became increasingly important, consumption became an unmistakable criterion for determining somebody's decency. At times, limited economic resources could make it difficult to live up to these standards and under those circumstances consumption was not necessarily a pleasure. It served the purpose of publicly demonstrating one's social status at almost any cost. In times of crisis, the middle-class family ate less meat and the father skipped a visit to the dentist before the woman of the household would buy less expensive shoes.

Lower Classes and the Consumer World

Provincial lower classes were not strongly integrated into the consumer world until the 1920s. Even in the central highlands, where cash became more widely available during the second half of the nineteenth century, Indians and the urban poor consumed foreign and Peruvian manufactured goods in very limited quantities. But poverty was only one factor that excluded lower classes from the world of goods. Equally significant is that poor people, and particularly Indian peasants, had a different attitude toward the rising consumer culture than did the middle and upper strata of the regional societies, and that peasants were often reluctant to integrate themselves into the market economy. In the eyes of the elite, the peasantry's somewhat cautious position toward consumption confirmed old prejudices that Indians were lazy and without needs and ambitions. Although sources do not allow us to draw a clear picture of to what extent lower classes purchased consumer items, we can explore what Peruvian politicians thought of the Indian as a consumer, how Indians viewed the consumer world, and under which circumstances they participated in it.

Although most peasants produced their own cloth, urban as well as rural lower classes bought imported textiles in small quantities. For their daily clothing people appreciated British cloth, which was of higher quality, lasted longer, and was cheaper than the coarse material that came out of Andean *obrajes*. In fact, British textiles had flooded Andean markets to such an extent that the Peruvian textile sector collapsed only a few decades after independence. By the 1840s many urban lower-class inhabitants of Puno and Cuzco, who were not obliged to follow communal dress codes, were wearing shirts made of British cotton cloth, and even saddle-cloth for mules was imported. Local textile producers complained that their looms "served only our chickens to sleep on."[28] However, for many poor people occasionally purchasing British cloth was their only link to the consumer world.

In the 1860s, when it became increasingly evident that the sale of guano was not the solution to all economic and social problems Peru was facing, social conditions of the interior provinces were again blamed for the lack of national integration and for the difficulties to establish internal markets. But now the issue of consumption was approached from a different angle than in the 1840s, when protectionists were most concerned about consumption of imports as a waste of domestic capital. In the 1860s consuming manufactured goods was identified as the fuel of the economy and both a motivation for people to work and a source of employment. Mass consumption of imported and domestically produced goods became recognized as a central element of progress and development. Politicians were worried that "one single Lima upper-class family consumes more manufactured goods than many Indian villages combined."[29] Consequently, the goal was to spread consumption into the countryside:

> Simply by expanding the demand of Lima to all of Peru, could total consumption have increased a hundredfold. And because this is only

possible through commerce or industry, work would also have increased a hundredfold.[30]

The elite claimed that lack of *necesidades* (needs) prevented Indians from working harder and from appreciating the consumer goods that the industrial age provided. Peru could not join the circle of modern and progressive countries if large parts of the population worried primarily about family subsistence and had little or no nexus to the national economy. The elite was convinced that only by instilling needs in allegedly backward Indians could Peru increase demand, production, and consumption, make Indians work, and establish an economy that could rely on expanding domestic markets.

Suggestions about how to turn the Indian into a consumer and how to integrate peasants into what the elite perceived as mainstream Peru covered a broad range of possible measures. The idea of settling European immigrants with allegedly superior work ethics among lazy Indians reflected only the image most Latin American intellectuals had of industrious Europeans, but the reintroduction of the colonial *repartimiento* (forced sale of goods) or of Indian tribute were more radical proposals.[31] Some members of the elite concluded that if Indians were without material needs that went beyond their immediate subsistence and if they lacked any social and economic ambitions, only forced consumption and taxation could make them work. They claimed that even the Incas had used forced labor systems to overcome Indians' "natural tendency to limit work to the absolute indispensable effort to satisfy their limited needs."[32]

This type of suggestion demonstrates that many authors understood little about the cultures and economic dynamics of the Andean world. They simply interpreted the peasants' critical and hesitant attitude toward the consumer world as a natural or cultural deficit of backward people. Apparently, Indians did not respond to the economic rule that desiring consumer goods is an incentive for hard work and that demand fuels production and commerce, which in return creates work. If Indians were indeed so ignorant and stubborn as to ignore this simple principle, the state had the right to make them understand the civilizing effects of consumption by force. But these authors overlooked the fact that the historical experience of being forced to purchase consumer goods under the *repartimiento* system of the eighteenth century was a major reason for Indians' hesitant attitude toward the world of goods. Distrust of the non-Indian world remained a constant feature of the Andean Indian world well into the twentieth century.[33]

To be sure, Indian communities were not immune to the appeal of imported goods. Practical items, from needles and frying pans to iron shovels, could facilitate everyday work, while luxury items fulfilled important social functions. Consumer goods could easily be integrated into the system of Andean reciprocity (Alberti and Mayer 1974). Introducing relatively expensive goods into reciprocal exchange patterns (labor for goods or goods for goods) could help to strengthen ties between individuals and families and contributed to define power relations within the community. If a peasant could contribute a bottle or two of imported alcohol to a communal festivity, it was as much a demonstration of wealth and status as it was outside the community. Indians were willing to spend money even on luxury goods and would share them with the community, if it contributed to the enhancement of their social status.

Peasants could obtain consumer items through the use of cash, through barter, or as a wage substitute. All options required some sort of integration into the market economy. But participation in the market economy was often a double-edged weapon. It could mean access to cash and it could increase a household's income, but it meant also that one was exposed to economic forces (e.g., price fluctuations) Indians could not control and to deal with merchants and hacendados Indians did not trust.

Take the example of the southern highlands with its large number of Indian communities. During the second half of the nineteenth and in the early twentieth centuries, the wool trade became the single most important nexus between Indians and the market economy. Usually trade did not take place on equal terms. Indian wool producers were often not in a position to control if prices they were offered reflected actual market prices. Of course, Indian producers had some bargaining power in the market place. They could try to make themselves familiar with price developments, could take advantage of competition between merchants, and they had always the option not to sell their wool, if prices seemed unacceptably low (Jacobsen 1993). However, Indians remained skeptical of the market economy and the uncertainties it contained for them. Even at present, Indian communities hesitate to give up their system of subsistence economy based on the Andean notion of reciprocity. Economists and anthropologists explain such behavior as an attempt to avoid becoming too dependent on market forces. What looked "backward" to a nineteenth-century observer (and may still look anachronistic today) was and continues to be an effective strategy for those living in communities. The combination of subsistence economy and limited market integration is a rational adaptation to a market economy that offers uncertain conditions for peasant producers (Figueroa 1984; Lehmann 1982).

In the central sierra the situation was rather different. In the Mantaro valley, for instance, individual peasant farmers dominated the economic landscape and the contrast between the hacienda system and Indian communities was less pronounced than in the southern sierra (Long and Roberts 1978; Samaniego 1978). Cash was also more widely accessible to lower classes than in the southern region and the cash economy expanded significantly during the second half of the nineteenth century. A growing mining industry that depended partly on wage labor and changes in the region's agricultural sector turned the central sierra increasingly into a cash economy. Since the 1840s, Indian communities of the cane producing area of Tarma had come under pressure. Haciendas expanded aggressively into community territory, invading community land and turning peasants into agricultural wage laborers in the process. But peasants also switched voluntarily from a largely subsistence oriented economy to market oriented production. The increasing demand of the Lima market for agricultural goods made a closer integration into the cash economy attractive (Peloso 1985).

Although increasing cash resources did not immediately cause a consumption boom in the central sierra, it proves that growing numbers of people became involved in the cash economy. As early as in the late 1820s, the Englishman W. B. Stevenson reported enthusiastically that in the hinterland of Lima English merchants could sell considerable quantities of "large common scissors for sheep-shearing, as the natives are unacquainted with the kind of shears used in England" and that in the countryside a great demand existed for "hardware, such as pots and pans; these last ought not to be flat-bottomed, but deeper in the middle than along the sides, with two small rings instead of a handle."[34] Remarks of the American traveler William L. Herndon confirm that by the 1850s Indians of the central highlands were well integrated in regional commerce: "The Spanish Creole population is small; they are generally shopkeepers, the only dealers in foreign goods, which are retailed to the Indians at enormous profit."[35]

If shopkeepers could make "enormous profits" with the sale of imports to Indians, it was even easier for large landholders to take advantage of Indian workers. Hacendados, but even more so mine owners, tended to substitute wages with goods they distributed among their peasant-workers. This practice, which had its origin in the colonial period, allowed them to reduce their cash expenditures by manipulating the prices of items they used as wage substitutes. In the central Andean mining industry cheap rum (*aguardiente de caña*) was the most common wage substitute. In the 1850s it replaced chicha, made from maize, as the most important alcoholic beverage, because chicha production could not keep up with rapidly increasing demand (Wilson 1982). But iron tools and other hardware or cheap textiles could also be provided as a replacement for wages.

Poverty and a critical attitude toward the market economy were two factors that limited Indian peasants' full integration into the consumer world. But economic considerations alone do not explain peasants' relation to the consumer culture. Most nineteenth-century observers of the Andean world paid little attention to the fact that peasants did not construct a direct relation between consumption behavior and civilization, because they did not share the elite's notion of progress and modernity. Indians were not plagued with the fear of lagging culturally behind other parts of the world. Thus, they did not suffer from the notorious desire to express manners and demonstrate behaviors Europeans considered civilized. Instead, they concentrated mostly on the practical value of manufactured goods and demanded things that facilitated their daily work.

Furthermore, peasants often associated different meanings with consumer goods than urban people did. They reworked them according to their taste and traditions and integrated them into the Indian world. Colors, printing patterns, and embroideries of textiles, for instance, varied from community to community, and European textiles usually did not meet the taste of Indian consumers. However, a couple of yards of inexpensive plain English cloth or ribbon were appreciated. Such items could be turned into prestigious consumer goods after they were reworked so they would fit into the system of local customs. Reworking could mean to dye cloth or to attach it to traditional clothing, made of domestically produced textiles. The meaning of other European goods, from metal and horn buttons to glassware, could also be transformed. In some communities of the southern highlands, for instance, imported buttons became somehow fashionable on Indians' traditional knit caps (*chullos*) as additional decoration to the traditional ones made of horn.

To sum up, provincial lower classes and Indian peasants were not without needs and desires, although they did not share the concept of consumption and civilization the elite represented. The single most important factor that prevented lower classes from participating more intensively in the consumer world was the lack of resources. Indians were not "naturally lazy" or "without ambitions," but they often hesitated to engage in business with non-Indians and to integrate themselves into the market economy because they were the weakest link in the chain of participants in this economic system. Geographical isolation and lack of acquaintance with price fluctuations made Indians vulnerable to fraud and abuse. However, in the central highlands, with its more dynamic economy, peasants were considerably better integrated in the regional cash economy than they were in the southern sierra. They were, thus, also in a better position to participate in the consumer world. But Indians generally viewed the consumer culture from a different angle than non-Indians. They stressed more the practical value of goods than the prestige connected to them, they did not accept the idea that consumption had something to do with civilization, and they were not convinced that increasing consumption could result in better economic conditions for themselves.

Producers, Markets, and the Emerging Consumer World

The emerging consumer societies of the central and southern Peruvian highlands in the early twentieth century can be viewed from two different perspectives. Consumption clearly increased and contemporary observers described how the availability of consumer goods rose with the completion of new railroad lines. Growing amounts of imports competed with the output of the first domestic factories, and most traditional artisans continued to remain competitive against the flood of goods of mass production. How did the competition between these different groups of suppliers work out on the marketplaces of the central and southern sierra? On the other hand, provincial markets were still small. Businessmen who were looking for rapidly expanding markets on which considerable amounts of goods of mass production could be sold were disappointed. Reports from the United States on market and trading conditions in Peru, frequently published since the mid-1910s, reveal that provincial markets of that Andean country could not absorb the quantities of mass consumer goods American salesmen had expected to sell. How can we explain this discrepancy between merchants' expectations and economic reality?

Far from offering a ready market for the output of American factories, conditions of the central sierra came closer to merchants' expectations than any other region of the Peruvian hinterland. A well-developed cash economy that had penetrated most segments of society, a sizable middle class that was willing to spend money for consumer items, and an expanding mining economy represented a relatively attractive market for the sale of consumer goods. By the early 1900s several ice factories and small-scale manufacturing plants were operating in Huancayo, the region's newest commercial center, and Lima agents supplied numerous local stores with goods from foreign as well as Lima factories (Long and Roberts 1978). British consuls were somewhat astonished that the first "large and very modern" American store opened its doors in the mining town of Cerro de Pasco in 1902, selling everything from imported hardware to kitchen utensils and textiles.[36]

The output of Peruvian factories, particularly leather products and textiles, had found ready sale in the central highlands since the last quarter of the nineteenth century. Although merchants appealed to consumers' patriotic feelings by praising the products of *industrias nacionales* that they had in stock, upper-class consumers did not attach the same prestige to Peruvian consumer goods as to English and French imports (Gootenberg 1993). Affluent consumers were proud that Peru began to manufacture shoes and soaps, but the problem was that Peruvian consumer goods did not have the exclusive character that made imports so desirable. They could be purchased from any trader, not only from selected stores like "La Bella Jardiniera"—Tarma's most prestigious Italian-owned store of the early twentieth century. By the 1900s, almost all consumer groups of the central highlands purchased domestically produced goods. Peruvian textiles and shoes were of middling quality and less expensive than imported items. Wealthier consumers would perhaps use shoes from a Lima factory on weekdays, but they would wear their pair of Italian shoes on Sundays. They stockpiled dozens of blankets from Peruvian textile factories for daily use, but the woman of the house would prefer expensive imported blankets to decorate more public areas of their home.

In the central highlands, consumer goods of Peruvian mass production were particularly attractive to the growing number of less affluent people who were only in the process of entering the consumer world. Early industrialization efforts in Lima coincided with the expansion of a money economy in the central sierra. Wilson presents the case of a "relatively poor Tarma family" that was the victim of a robbery in 1910. According to the local newspaper, the family was hit hard because one family member had just spent a considerable amount of money on consumer goods in the town of Cerro de Pasco. The list of stolen goods mirrors nicely the kinds of goods poorer families consumed. Among other things it contains ponchos, a pair of shoes, two bedcovers, two straw hats and "two blankets of Santa Catalina"—a Lima textile factory (Wilson 1985).

Provincial artisans were struggling against foreign competition since the 1820s and complaints about their misery and their disappointment for not receiving much state support are not difficult to find (Bonilla, Rio, and Zevallos 1978; Gootenberg 1989). However, provincial craftsmen were rarely driven into bankruptcy by foreign competitors. First of all, not all trades were threatened by imported consumer items. Bakers, masons, painters, and like professions were not confronted with foreign competition; while tailors, hatmakers, and shoemakers were among the worst hit by imported consumer items. But even they often had the option of using foreign raw material and transforming it into finished goods. Particularly during the first half of the nineteenth century, foreign cloth was imported on a massive scale, not ready-to-wear clothing. More affluent craftsmen would also try to purchase foreign tools and machinery to improve the output of their workshops and they eagerly tried to copy foreign products. Even the poor blacksmith, whose business was reduced by the import of horseshoes, did not close down his workshop entirely. He may have dismissed his journeyman, worked perhaps part-time on a nearby hacienda, and relied more heavily on his wife's income as a market vendor, but he always considered his forge as one source of income.

The emerging consumer society put much more pressure on craftsmen of the central sierra than it did on their colleagues of the southern highlands to deal with ever-growing foreign and domestic competition of factory-produced consumer goods. Although a thorough study of the central highland's artisan sector is not yet available, it seems that developments in this part of Peru were similar to what happened in the region's retail sector. Just like French and Italian merchants, immigrant artisans penetrated the regional towns since the 1840s and shared the attractive buying power of wealthier consumer groups, while most Peruvian producers were increasingly left with the market of the middle and lower classes and with repair work.[37] Upper-class consumers took advantage of the better training of foreign artisans, trusted their judgments in matters of fashion and taste, and increased the pressure on domestic artisans to adapt to foreign consumer goods as well as to immigrant producers.

In the southern highlands, competition between different groups of producers was less pronounced. As late as during the 1890s, the southern countryside and small towns were little integrated into the consumer world. Cash was scarce, many Indian communities remained tied to a subsistence economy, and geographic isolation hampered distribution of goods. However, even in the remote town of Cuzco some industrialization projects were undertaken during the second half of the nineteenth century. The textile factory of the Garmendia family in Lucre, just outside of Cuzco, opened in the mid-1860s, and the German immigrant Gustav Mangelsdorff started the first beer brewery in 1872. Arequipa emerged as the industrial center of the region during the early twentieth century. In 1922 seventeen foundries, fifteen soap factories, and eleven tanneries, among other enterprises, operated in the city. Most of these "factories," however, were more accurately described as large artisan workshops and cannot be compared to modern industrial enterprises (Jacobsen 1988).

The urban artisan sector remained strong during the first century after independence. Before the War of the Pacific only Arequipa attracted foreign artisans in substantial numbers. Elsewhere (e.g., in Puno, Sicuani, and Cuzco) economic conditions were not promising enough before the early twentieth century. Until the 1880s, only a few Cuzco craftsmen (mostly affluent tailors, hatmakers, and shoemakers) worked with imported raw material and it was only used for specific orders. In the case of tailors and hatmakers, clients bought imported fabrics and cloth from a local merchant and handed it over to the artisan with detailed instructions. The shoemaker purchased English leather only if the customer paid for it in advance. Cash was so scarce among southern artisans that they could not afford to keep costly materials in stock. Lack of cash also prevented most craftsmen from purchasing imported tools and machinery on a larger scale, although foreign equipment could have improved a workshop's image considerably. Smiths have certainly purchased imported hammers, and tailors bought English scissors, but "Singer" sewing machines from Germany, so prestigious during the early decades of the twentieth century, were rarely found in the southern sierra before the War of the Pacific.

During the 1890s the Cuzco artisan sector began to respond more forcefully to the challenges of changing consumption behavior of customers. These changes had to do with the regional economic upswing that began during the last decade of the nineteenth century and with efforts of local craftsmen, organized in the town's *Sociedad de Artesanos* (Artisan Society), to improve the social and professional image of their economic sector.[38] As early as in the 1880s, but much more so after 1900, more affluent master artisans began to give their establishments specific names instead of identifying them simply by the owners' last names. Craftsmen certainly thought that the measure was a progressive step and hoped that it would be appealing to their modern clientele. Shop names, as they appear in newspaper advertisements, can be divided into two groups. The first refers to Peruvian nationalism and patriotism, for example, the tailor workshop "La Patria" or the shoemaker shop "Admiral Grau" (after the hero of the War of the Pacific). These names were designed to emphasize the patriotic attitude of the master artisans. Other popular workshop names referred to the presumably progressive character of local artisans as up-to-date entrepreneurs. These names reached from the fancy tailor's workshop "Parisienne" to the more moderate shoemaker's workshop "La Moderna" or "El Progreso." The function of such names was to assure clients that the enterprise was modern, reacted quickly to fashion changes, and that the owner was a dynamic businessman, who shared a vague vision of regional progress with merchants and politicians. At the same time, fancy names concealed the fact that most artisan workshops of the southern sierra lacked modern machinery and capital and that they depended on regional merchant houses.

The ever-increasing competition of foreign consumer goods on southern Andean markets and the attempts of local producers to compete with imports forced provincial artisans to increase their business relations with wholesale merchants as suppliers of both equipment and raw material. Attempts to modernize their workshops linked craftsmen to the same economic group that partly caused their economic hardship. By the 1910s, even Cuzco and Puno artisans, who had their establishments right next door to a wholesale merchant house and who served a wealthy clientele, had to pay attention to such issues as decoration of the shop, professional attendance of customers, and quality of materials and production. Business relations to merchants were so important that Cuzco artisans frequently mentioned in their advertisements the names of the merchant houses from where they bought their materials.

In Cuzco, artisans' attempts to modernize their workshops or to improve the appeal of their goods by purchasing raw materials from import-export merchants were not very successful. Their own limited capital reserves forced them into debts. Between 1897 and the mid-1910s artisans sent hundreds of petitions to the Cuzco treasurer complaining about exaggerated business taxes. Their most powerful argument (often underlined through attached receipts) was that they could not bear higher taxes because most of their income was used to pay off debts to wholesale merchants (Krüggeler 1993). The case of the tailor Francisco Hermoza demonstrates the problems artisans often faced. Since the 1880s members of the Hermoza family ran several tailor shops in Cuzco and had enjoyed a high reputation in town. However, in November 1921, Francisco Hermoza was forced to sell his workshop to another local tailor. Of the 3,000 soles he received for his shop Hermoza used 2,330 soles to pay his bills at the merchant houses Braillard, Stafford, Emmel Hermanos, and Fernando Emmel, where he had bought cloth and other merchandise.[39]

In neither the central nor the southern highlands did the dream of turning little artisan workshops into modern shops, and perhaps even into factories of mass production, come true. Craftsmen could not compete with the capital reserves of merchants and landholders and they had to leave even modest local industrialization projects to them. But mass consumption did not reach such proportions in the Andes that artisans were pushed out of business. It was perhaps the "backwardness" of the hinterland, so frequently lamented during the nineteenth century, that prevented traditional artisan products from being replaced by goods of mass production before the 1920s, and even much beyond that decade.

The British traveler Samuel Haigh warned English merchants as early as 1829 that "the South American markets have been much overrated; they are scattered over an immense surface of the globe, with a very limited population in proportion to the extent, and there is much difficulty in making favorable returns."[40] This statement is an undue generalization, but it refers to key shortcomings of Latin American markets. In Peru, poor transport conditions and large distances between marketplaces were still major obstacles for merchants during the 1910s and 1920s. When World War I offered the chance to U.S. manufacturers to increase their exports to South American markets previously controlled by the British, French, and Germans, the U.S. government supported these attempts by publishing detailed reports on market and trading conditions.[41] Markets for hardware, shoes, textiles, ceramics, and the like were analyzed by American consuls, attachés, and special agents in various South American republics and published by the U.S. Department of Commerce.[42] Specific analyses of the southern or central Andean markets are not available, but reports tend to repeat the following findings for the interior provinces of Peru. Firstly, some 50 to 60 percent of the entire population of Peru could not be considered as potential customers because they were so poor that they did not have the necessary means to purchase imported goods. Secondly, although several railroads connected some parts of the remote Andean highlands with the coast, transport conditions were still very poor in Peru and hampered commercial exchange. A network of traveling salesmen was required to cover potential markets most effectively. Finally, while Peruvian mass production of consumer goods was significant only in a few sectors (particularly in the textile and to a lesser extent in the leather sectors), local artisans were controlling considerable shares in practically all markets in which American manufacturers could try to get a foothold.

Commissioner H. E. Everley draws a rather dark picture of the future prospects of American furniture manufacturers on Peruvian markets.[43] From the producers' perspective the consumption capacity of the entire country was too small, particularly in comparison with other Latin American countries. Everley did not find enough demand for kitchen cabinets, couches, office furniture, and similar items that would justify considerable American investments into distribution and trade networks. Furthermore, the market was not uniform enough to be supplied with furniture of American mass production:

> The native Peruvians dislike very much to buy a suite of furniture that is just like another person's set. Hence, because of the many styles and kinds of furniture demanded in one market, it is necessary that the domestic factories build their product entirely to order. In no case do they endeavor to cut a quantity of any one style unless it be office furniture, chairs, flowerpot stands, or some other less important things. Such a market seems almost hopeless to any American manufacturer, since his organization, quality of work, and economy of production are based largely on a big production of current patterns.[44]

In Peru provincial consumers enjoyed foreign goods, including furniture, but they were not prepared to obey to the rules of factory production that were about to begin to dictate American consumer behavior. Furnishing a room did not mean to become the proud owner of a factory produced set of furniture. On the contrary, in the Andes consumption of luxury goods remained embedded in a network of local social relations. Decorating a room included hiring a local carpenter. He would take measurements in the client's home, engage in the ritual of price negotiations, pay attention to specific orders, and produce an individual set of furniture at a reasonable price. An imported lamp, or perhaps a foreign chest of drawers may then have rounded up the picture. Everley concluded:

The great bulk of the furniture used in the country is turned out by small, insufficiently lighted, and unsanitary carpenter shops, where from one to a dozen or even more men are employed in the most difficult, crude, and uneconomical way, as most of the furniture is made entirely by hand. Every city and small town has its share of these shops, which supply almost entirely the furniture needs of the community.[45]

Market analyses of the textile sector sound different from what Everley wrote about furniture. American observers were much more optimistic about the prospects of U.S. cloth on Peruvian markets. They thoroughly analyzed market conditions for all kinds of fabrics, recommended colors and printing patterns people preferred, and made specific comments on many different kinds of garments. Authors reached the conclusion that the market for cloth, particularly for cotton textiles, would expand over the next years and that U.S. manufacturers were in an excellent position to take advantage of growing demand in Peru.[46]

Yet, similar to the report on furniture, commercial attachés emphasized the strong position of local craftsmen in textile markets. They agreed that old-fashioned tailor shops and seamstresses produced most of the clothing for men and women and that consumers had little confidence in ready-made dresses. In the introductory paragraph of his report W. F. Montavon says frankly that "in Peru people do not buy imported ready-to-wear garments."[47] He then points out:

Anyone who has visited a Peruvian city is surprised at the large number of tailor shops. These shops are to be found in every street of Lima and even the smallest provincial village is not without one or more tailors. . . . The tailored suit is still supreme in Peru.[48]

Markets for finished products were so difficult to develop that agents advised producers to first open stores in Lima to accustom the clientele to their products, just as the French had done many years earlier. In a second step Americans would enter the interior markets through traveling salesmen and later through contracted retailers.

In towns like Tarma, Jauja, Arequipa, and Cuzco foreign furniture was available, but the quantities did not make any impression on foreign observers. The differences in descriptions of local market conditions as presented by American trade commissioners and local residents are striking. The first were looking for markets able to receive considerable amounts of goods of mass production, while the latter described the impact of novelties on often small markets. Residents of southern and central Andean towns noted carefully the newly imported items that appeared in local salons, offices, and living rooms, but rarely made reference to quantities. In fact, it was often the novelty and exclusive character of lamps, furniture, and typewriters that determined the prestige associated with them. In these cases Peruvian producers had a different notion of consumption than American factory owners had.

Conclusion

The Peruvian Andes had been supplied with imported consumer goods since the late colonial period, but the rise of regional consumer societies depended on more than the availability of goods. In this chapter I have tried to identify three main sets of factors that made people in the Peruvian hinterland change their consumption behavior. Firstly, economic conditions such as regional economic structures, links to national and international economies, and access to cash determined the quantities of goods regional markets were able to absorb. Secondly, the spreading desire of provincial elites and emerging social middle sectors to use consumption as a tool to connect themselves to the modern world was a major driving force behind the expansion of the consumer society into the Andes. Thirdly, consumer items were used by social classes, ethnic groups, and rural and urban groups to mark identities within national society. We have seen that marking identities can also mean rejecting luxury consumer items or transforming the meaning of goods.

The emerging consumer society of the central highlands was always a step ahead of the southern region. A more dynamic regional economy put the central Andes in a better position to follow consumption behavior demonstrated by coastal societies. But the region's proximity to Lima also confronted the elite more directly and more forcefully with the notion that modernity and civilization had to do with consumption. Spreading this idea was facilitated by less-pronounced regionalist sentiments and closer social ties to Lima upper-class families. The region's peasantry, which was less rooted in communities and which became integrated into the cash economy earlier and to a larger degree than peasants of the southern sierra, allowed the consumer world easier access to rural markets.

Provincial elites had special problems of adjusting to the consumer society, and consumption could be a delicate matter in the Peruvian hinterland. For upper-class families, demonstrating civilized manners meant first of all getting over their image as being uneducated and somewhat backward people. But the display of luxury consumer goods required caution. Inaccuracies in copying European fashion earned provincial elders ridicule on the part of foreign and coastal visitors and confirmed stereotypes people were eager to cast off. Provincial societies also imposed limits on upper-class families' conspicuous consumption. The parish priest could find certain dresses immoral, and the Indian village leader expected the hacendado to wear a traditional poncho, not a foreign suit, when negotiating with him.

The role of a developing urban middle sector in establishing the consumer world in provincial societies is often overlooked. Teachers, clerks, bank employees, and many other professionals and white-collar workers felt enormous pressure to underline their social status by participating in the consumer society. In the central sierra, this process began probably as early as during the 1850s, while in the south, urban middle classes developed only toward the end of the nineteenth century. This consumer group spent a far larger share of their cash resources on clothing, furniture, and other imported goods than did local elites. Active participation in the consumer world was often designed to hide the difficult economic conditions with which middle-class families had to cope.

Peasants used their limited resources to consume foreign goods, but their buying power did not allow the development of solid domestic markets. Indians were eager to obtain hardware; reworked foreign textiles according to their taste, traditions, and customs; and could even transform the meaning of certain goods. Their often critical attitude toward the consumer world had nothing to do with cultural inferiority or a lack of needs and desires, as frequently claimed by elite authors. Most Indians did not share the common notion that consumption had a civilizing effect or proved one's civilized manners. On the contrary, the historical experience of forced sales of consumer goods (from gewgaw to imported textiles) had increased their suspicion toward non-Indians and their ideas of consumption. This skepticism had not vanished during the first century of post-Independence Peru.

Had provincial markets for consumer goods considerably grown between the 1820s and the early twentieth century? Around 1910, the presence of thirty or forty pieces of foreign furniture on their market was most alarming to the association of carpenters of any Andean town. Yet, the

American merchant could make a reasonable profit only after he would sell a hundred units. Market analysts were disappointed to see that provincial markets were still poorly prepared to absorb large quantities of goods of foreign mass production. Merchants had clearly underestimated the economic flexibility of the provincial artisan sector and its low labor costs. But more importantly, the emerging notion that industrial mass production lowered prices of consumer goods and allowed all segments of society to enjoy the blessings of industrial capitalism was not fully shared in the Andes. Cloth from Lima and foreign textile factories was appreciated, but dresses and suits were tailored by local artisans. Consumption was somehow still integrated in a network of local social relations and it was not a simple act of purchasing a mass product. Furthermore, the social value of many consumer goods still depended on their exclusive character and high price, and on restricted access to them. The idea of mass consumption did not fit into the economic and social setting of early-twentieth-century Andean society.

NOTES

1. For the Central Andes, see Magdalena Chocano, "Circuitos comerciales y auge minero en la Sierra Central a fines de la época colonial," *Allpanchis* 19, no. 21 (1983), 3–26. For the southern region, see Nils Jacobsen, *Mirages of Transition: The Peruvian Altiplano, 1780–1930* (Berkeley: University of California Press, 1993), chap. 2.

2. Samuel Haigh, *Sketches of Buenos Aires, Chile, and Peru* (London: J. Carpenter and Son, 1829), 380–81.

3. Temple, Edmond, *Travels in Various Parts of Peru, Including a Year's Residence in Potosí* (Philadelphia: E. L. Carey and A. Hart, 1833), 2 vols., vol. 2, 84–85. Jacobsen also confirms that markets of southern Peru were oversupplied in the 1820s. See *Mirages,* 51.

4. William B. Stevenson, *A Historical and Descriptive Narrative of Twenty Years' Residence in South America* (London: Hurst, Robinson and Co., 1829), 2 vols., vol. 2, 77–79; Haigh, *Sketches,* 380–83; Temple, *Travels,* vol. 2, 85–89.

5. Heraclio Bonilla (comp.), *Gran Bretaña y el Perú: Informes de los cónsules británicos,* 5 vols. (Lima: IEP, 1977), vol. 5, "Los mecanismos de un control económico," 84–91.

6. "De Charles Milner Ricketts a George Canning," December 27, 1826, in: Bonilla (comp.), *Gran Bretaña,* vol. 1, 17–83, 69.

7. William Herndon and Lardner Gibbon, *Exploration of the Valley of the Amazon Made Under the Direction of the Navy Department* (Washington, DC: House of Representatives, 32d Congress, 2nd Session, Exec. Nr. 36, 1853), 2 vols., vol. 1, 123.

8. Nelson Manrique discusses in detail how the trade between the central highlands and the coast was organized. "Los arrieros de la Sierra Central durante el siglo XIX," *Allpanchis* 19, no. 21 (1983), 27–46. See also his book, *Mercado interno y region. La sierra central, 1820–1930,* (Lima: DESCO, 1987), chaps. 2 and 5. One of the most exciting contemporary studies of the Jauja region, its conditions and its potentials for future development, is Manuel Pardo, "Estudios sobre la Provincia de Jauja (1862)" in: Jacinto López (comp.), *Manuel Pardo* (Lima: Imp. Gil, 1947).

9. See, for example, Herndon and Gibbon, *Exploration,* vol. 1, 117.

10. "Puerto de Islay. Informe del Sr. Withew, Consul británico en Islay, sobre el comercio de ese puerto. Año 1856," in Bonilla (comp.), *Gran Bretaña,* vol. 4, 97–114, 99.

11. Carlos F. Oliart Garmendia, *Como y quienes fundaron la primera fábrica de tejidos de lana en el Perú* (Cuzco: n.p., n.d.).

12. Johann J. von Tschudi, *Travels in Peru during the Years 1838–42 on the Coast, in the Sierra, across the Cordilleras and the Andes, into the Premival Forests* (London: David Bogue, 1847), 364.

13. See Francisco de Rivero, *Memorias o sean apuntamientos sobre industria agrícola del Perú y sobre algunos medios que pudieran adoptarse para remediar su decadencia* (Lima: Imprenta del Comercio por J. M. Monterola, 1845), 12 and 24.

14. Paul Gootenberg, *Imagining Development: Economic Ideas in Peru's "Fictitious Prosperity" of Guano, 1840–1880* (Berkeley and Los Angeles: University of California Press, 1993), 63. On the guano era, see by the same author, *Between Silver and Guano: Commercial Policy and the State in Postindependence Peru* (Princeton: Princeton University Press, 1989a).

15. On the southern textile manufacturing sector after Independence, see Heraclio Bonilla, Lía del Río, and Pilar Ortiz de Zevallos, "Comercio libre y crisis de la economía andina: El caso del Cuzco," *Historica,* 2:1 (1978), 1–25.

16. "Bosquejo general del Perú: 1877. por George McGregor," in: Bonilla (comp.), *Gran Bretaña,* vol. 1, 111–72, 117.

17. On German immigrants in the region, see Friedrich Gerstäcker, *Viaje por el Perú* (Lima: Biblioteca Nacional, 1973), 67–69.

18. On consumption of chicha and beer in the Peruvian Andes, see Benjamin S. Orlove and Ella Schmidt, "Swallowing Their Pride: Indigenous and Industrial Beer in Six Andean Regions," *Theory and Society,* 24:2 (1995), 271–98.

19. Paul Marcoy [Laurent de Saint Cricq], *Travels in South America. From the Pacific Ocean to the Atlantic Ocean* (London: Blackie and Son, 1875), 3 vols., vol. 1, 41.

20. Ibid., 240–41.

21. Haigh, *Sketches,* 381–82.

22. Marcoy, *Travels,* vol. 1, 243.

23. Rivero, *Memorias,* 12 and 27.

24. *El Demócrata Americano* (Cuzco) January 29, 1847 and June 4, 1847.

25. References to foreign training of Cuzco craftsmen can be found in *Guía General del Cuzco 1937* (Cuzco: Barscht and Florez, 1937).

26. David S. Parker discusses similar tendencies for white-collar workers of

early-twentieth-century Lima in his important article "White Collar Lima, 1910–1929: Commercial Employees and the Rise of the Peruvian Middle Class," *Hispanic American Historical Review* 72, no. 1 (1992): 47–72.

27. "Al Margen de la campaña obrera" *El Sol* (Cuzco), June 23, 1919.

28. The economic hardship of many Cuzco artisans and of the urban poor is well presented in Narciso Arestegui's novel, *El Padre Horan* (Lima: Editorial Universo, n.d.), 2 vols. The quote is taken from vol. 2, 107. This novel, originally published in 1848, is considered an early example of Andean *indigenista* literature.

29. Claudio Orambela, *Investigación de los medios más oportunos y eficaces de estimular a los habitantes del Perú según la situación social al trabajo más ordenado y provechoso* (Lima: Imprenta del Estado por J. E. del Campo), 12.

30. Ibid.

31. *Algunas questiones sociales con motivo de los disturbios de Huancané* (Lima: Imprenta dirigida por J. M. Monterola, 1867), 8–11.

32. Ibid., 8.

33. On the effects of the colonial *repartimiento* system on Indian society, see John R. Fisher, *Government and Society in Colonial Peru. The Intendent System, 1784–1814* (London: University of London, Athlone Press, 1970), and Jürgen Golte, *Reparto y rebeliones, Túpac Amaru y las contradicciones de la economía colonial* (Lima: IEP, 1974).

34. Stevenson, vol. 2, 78.

35. Herndon and Gibbon, *Exploration,* vol. 2, 5.

36. Bonilla, "Informe sobre el intercambio comercial y la situación general del Perú para el año 1902, por Alfred St. John," in: Bonilla (comp.), *Gran Bretaña,* vol. 2, 39–68, 55.

37. Gerstäcker, *Viaje,* 67–69.

38. On economic cycles in the southern region in the late nineteenth and early twentieth centuries, see Nils Jacobsen, "Free Trade, Regional Elites, and the Internal Market in Southern Peru, 1895–1932," in: *Guiding the Invisible Hand. Economic Liberalism and the State in Latin American History,* ed. by Joseph L. Love and Nils Jacobsen (New York: Praeger, 1988), 145–75. On the importance of the artisan society of Cuzco see Thomas Krüggeler, "Unreliable Drunkards or Honorable Citizens? Artisans in Search of Their Place in the Cusco Society, 1820–1930," (Ph.D. thesis, University of Illinois at Urbana-Champaign, 1993), chap. 5.

39. "Transferencia de establecimineto de sastrería," book 3, f. 17, (1921–22), Archivo Departamental del Cuzco, Notario Emilio Muñíz, 1920–1930.

40. Haigh, *Sketches,* 381.

41. The share of American goods among all imports to Peru increased from 29.8 percent in 1913 to 65.1 percent in 1917. See "Informe sobre las finanzas, la industria y el comercio del Perú al finalizar el año 1919, por F. W. Manners," in Bonilla (comp.), *Gran Bretaña,* vol. 2, 349–76, 375.

42. U.S. Department of Commerce, Bureau of Foreign and Domestic Commerce, Miscellaneous Series, No. 39, *Peruvian Markets for American Hardware,* prepared under the Supervison of the U.S. Commercial Attaché at Lima, Peru (Washington: Government Printing Office, 1916); ibid., No. 74, *Wearing Apparel in Peru,* prepared by William F. Montavon (1918); ibid., Special Agents Series, No.

152, *Market for Boots and Shoes in Peru,* by Herman G. Brock (1917); ibid., No. 158, *Textile Markets of Bolivia, Ecuador, and Peru,* by W. A. Tucker (1918), 49–95; ibid., No. 176, *Furniture Markets of Chile, Peru, Bolivia, and Ecuador,* by Harold E. Everley (1919), 54–102; ibid., Trade Promotion Series, No. 25, *Peru. A Commercial and Industrial Handbok,* by W. E. Dunn (1925).

43. See U.S. Department of Commerce, *Furniture Markets.*

44. Ibid., 74.

45. Ibid., 74–75.

46. U.S. Department of Commerce, *Wearing Apparel in Peru,* and ibid., *Textile Markets of Bolivia, Ecuador, and Peru.*

47. U.S. Department of Commerce, *Wearing Apparel in Peru,* 5. The reason why even upper-class Peruvians rejected factory clothing was, according to the author, that people had traveled to Europe and knew only the allegedly terrible quality of European ready-to-wear products. It was the task of American manufacturers to convince customers of their high quality production. Ibid., 23.

48. Ibid.

Chapter 3

From Benches to Sofas: Diversification of Patterns of Consumption in San José (1857–1861)

Patricia Vega Jiménez

After 1850, with the production and sale of coffee, the inhabitants of the Central Valley of Costa Rica, particularly those living in the capital, experienced a decided increase in income. This allowed them to increase consumption of imported articles, especially those from Europe. But in what measure, and in what way, did patterns of consumption become diversified? This essay will try to answer that question, which has not so far been taken up by any researcher because only a handful of references exist in the writings of a few travelers who left a record of what they observed in their visits to Costa Rica during the first half of the nineteenth century.

Several different sources have been used to answer our query, but the most important is one that has been little used previously: the commercial advertisements published in newspapers of the period. Three of these publications were examined: *Crónica de Costa Rica, Nueva Era,* and *Album Semanal.* Five years, from 1857 to 1861, were selected, during which a total of 1,025 advertisements were published. From these advertisements those offering food, liquor, furniture, household goods, clothing, accessories, and medicines were chosen. Advertisements having to do with offers of services related to these categories were also analyzed. The total number of these advertisements studied amounted to 213.

This is certainly a limited study, insofar as it is concentrated on San José; this choice is justified by the city's commercial development after 1840, with the successful cultivation of coffee. The five years studied, from 1857 to 1861, include the last two years of the crisis brought on by the National Campaign, the cholera epidemic, the scarcity of credit, and the decline in coffee exports (1857–58), along with their subsequent recovery beginning in 1859. The study is based on a sample of more than 1,500 advertisements taken from newspapers that circulated in Costa Rica between 1833 and 1861.[1] The advertisements that have been selected allow us to analyze how the market for goods and services grew and became diversified within the urban space of San José.

I.   Food, Drink, and Medicines

The large number of advertisements concerning food, especially imported foodstuffs, is attested to by the statement of the Chilean diplomat Francisco Solano Astaburuaga, who wrote in 1857:

> . . . trade in Costa Rica will surely develop on a not insignificant scale. England, France, the United States, Chile herself, and the other sister republics maintain considerable exchanges with Costa Rica. Her trade movement is represented by more than 20,000 tons, importing and exporting to the value of $2,600,000. Imports consist of European merchandise, machinery, flour and other agricultural products from those countries, and exports are made in coffee, timber, cocoa, pearls and the shell that produces them, raw sugar, hides, sarsaparilla, etc. . . . (Fernández 1982, 310)

At that time, Costa Rica's commercial trade with the outside world was carried on chiefly with Great Britain, though some commercial relations were maintained with other European countries and with the United States. Ever since the eighteenth century, the British had maintained active trade with the Spanish colonies, and Costa Rica was not excluded from this mercantile traffic (Naylor 1988, 177); but after 1821 the British definitely replaced the Spaniards in this area. Great Britain became the chief market for Central American products and a direct source of manufactured goods for the region (Naylor 1988, 187). There is no doubt that by the middle of the nineteenth century foreign trade increased quantitatively in the Central American isthmus: between 1849 and 1851 the value of merchandise from the United Kingdom rose from 949,513 to 2,523,200 pounds sterling (Naylor 1988, 192).

Among British articles imported, textiles occupied a preferential place: 85 percent of the total value of British products imported into Central America between 1857 and 1860 (Quesada 1985, 85). However, in the Costa Rican newspapers of the period, the promotion of food products was stressed. Shopkeepers, both Costa Rican and foreign, offered Westphalia ham, Swiss cheese, Scotch codfish, asparagus, fruit both canned and in syrup, dried fish, "petit pois," salmon, and other foodstuffs from the Iberian Peninsula and Western Europe. If imports of textiles and clothing were quantitatively greater at that particular time, why did the shopkeepers advertise foodstuffs so insistently?

This emphasis may have been due to the fact that textiles had circulated very widely ever since the eighteenth century, and hence did not require much advertising; foreign foods, on the other hand, were just beginning to come into the market, and this obliged merchants to advertise them so that the well-off segment of society would purchase them. Furthermore, foodstuffs, because they were in large part perishable, could not be carried from town to town by peddlers, as were textiles (Molina 1991, 71–178). Moreover, as can be deduced from the advertisements, in which the consumption of foreign foods was associated with social distinction, owners of stores undertook to distribute food at both wholesale and retail. The origin of imported foodstuffs was varied. Olives, olive oil, raisins, and herring came from Spain. Cheeses and hams came from Sweden, Holland, and Flanders. Flour originated in Chile, California, Colombia, or New York, and was the most widely advertised nonmanufactured product at the time, with this peculiarity: unlike most articles, it was advertised as a single product. That is, all the advertisements for the sale of flour offered it exclusively. This, plus the fact that it was advertised so frequently, suggests that there was a good market for flour in a country where wheat was virtually no longer produced.[2] In any case, local products were not excluded from the advertising of the period; in addition to foreign cheeses, English ham, and Peruvian salt, cheese from Turrialba was also offered; Francisco Gil, in May 1859, sold

> Sardines in oil, half and quarter-sized cans—Very fine cheese from Sweden—Ditto from Flanders, known as "ball cheese"—Ditto from this country (from Turrialba). Peruvian salt in blocks. Spermaceti—English and Genoese soap—Cooking oil in bottles and half-bottles . . .[3]

At that time the basic diet of Costa Ricans began to be linked to rice and beans. According to Gil's advertisement, rice was already being imported from Sonsonate in 1859.[4] Also, European seasonings had become indispensable in the preparation of meals. The result of this, according to the German scientist Moritz Wagner, who visited the country in 1853, was that "dishes were loaded with pepper and English-style condiments . . ." (Wagner and Sherzer 1974, 185). Even salt was imported; thus, in May of 1857, an advertisement that did not give the merchant's name announced the sale of "English salt of higher quality than that produced in this country, at the price of five pesos for a load of eight and a half arrobas."[5] Foreign products were already competing with local ones in price and quality. Competition, however, did not prevent the establishment of food-processing factories in Costa Rica. Juan Lang, a merchant and craftsman of European origin, decided to compete with imported articles by producing a good variety of products himself. In June 1858, he advertised that he

> . . . has again established, on a larger scale, his gelatin factory, composed of the animal substances so often recommended by medicine for convalescents as the strongest and most appropriate tonic. The factory will also always have on hand a selection of jellies made from the juice of various kinds of fruits, prepared with exquisite care in sealed earthenware jars, a procedure that will permanently preserve them against the acetic fermentation produced in such jellies by the entrance of air; and in addition a number of excellent and delicious preserves in which, most unlike the foreign product, there is no coloring substance that could be injurious to health. To further serve his clientele, he has added to the delicious sweets already mentioned a variety of ice creams that he will prepare to order whenever a quantity with a value exceeding four pesos is required. He further offers to provide this article for sale every Monday and Thursday of the week, from 10 in the morning to 3 in the afternoon, in addition to furnishing it occasionally from 7 to 10 at night, which will be announced by hanging a lantern or colored lamp over the pastry-shop door . . .[6]

What seems obvious, in view of the prices of the articles being advertised, is that they were not always cheap products, as can be seen in table 3.1, especially in the case of ham. In this regard, Wagner said that ". . . almost all European merchandise costs 50% more here than in the markets of the Old World" (Wagner and Sherzer 1974, 188); but not only foreign products were high in price. This same visitor noted that Costa Rican products were expensive: "the box of potatoes costs two reals and a half, corn four and beans five reals. The inferior butter of the country costs from three to four, and cheese a real and a half the pound; a chicken is worth a real and a half, and a dozen eggs one real" (Wagner and Sherzer 1974, 183).

Prices of foodstuffs were not invariable, a statement that can be proved by following for four months the advertisements of Breucker, an importer of Chilean flour. He began by offering the quintal of flour at seven pesos and half a real in October 1860, and in February of the following year he had reduced the quintal to six pesos. Corn flour, on the other hand, a Costa Rican product, maintained a stable price during this whole period (see table 3.1). The high price of foodstuffs is related to a certain degree of displacement of subsistence agriculture and stockbreeding by coffee, within a context of population growth and increased movement toward the cities (Samper n.d., 1–49; Samper 1978, 123–217; Alvarenga 1986, 115–32; Hall 1976; Molina 1991). It is important to emphasize this, for the more sophisticated foodstuffs offered by merchants were aimed at the wealthier groups, especially prominent citizens within the city of San José.

Besides imported foods, liquors were very important and occupied a privileged place in the advertisements. The customer could choose between Burgundy and "Haut Sauterne" champagne, but the range of wines offered to the public was much more varied: "Haut Brion," "St. Emilion," "Benicarlo," "Tenerife," "Madeira," "Barsac," "Margaux," "Medoc," "Gran Vin," "Priorato," "San Julián," and so on. Obviously French and Spanish wines occupied a preferential place in nineteenth-century commercial

TABLE 3.1. **Price in Pesos and Reals of Some Foodstuffs and Wines, San José (1858–61)**

Article	Year	Measure	Price
Sweets	58	Quintal	4
Ham	58–59	Pound	2.4–3.4
Noodles	59	Pound	0.2
Corn flour	60	Quintal	5
Salt	60	Quintal	2.1
Wheat flour	60–61	Quintal	6–7.5

Wines[a]	Price per Bottle	Price per Case
Bordeaux	0.4	4.2
High-grade champagne	2	17
Port and Madeira	0.6	7
Sherry and Pajarete	0.6	7
Barsac	0.6	6.4
Tenerife and Benicarlò	0.6	6
Málaga	0.6	6
Guignolet	1	10

Sources: Album semanal, Crónica de Costa Rica, and *Nueva Era* (1867–61).
[a]Figures taken from an advertisement published by Juan Lang in May, 1860.

establishments of the Costa Rican capital. It was enough to advertise them as beverages originating in those countries without giving further details. However, not all advertisers followed this pattern. They preferred to offer a long list of names of wines to allow the customer to choose those he liked best.

Apparently, to judge from the frequency of advertisements, the wines most often consumed were port and sherry. Some alcoholic beverages were never advertised by merchants, among them whisky; however, cognac and gin, the latter imported from Holland, were permanently stocked in commercial establishments. Indeed, though there were no shops exclusively dedicated to the sale of alcoholic beverages, liquor almost always formed part of the lists of articles offered to the public. Permission to sell such products was allowed after payment of a warrant costing 200 pesos a month (Fernandez 1982, 310). According to the Irish traveler Thomas Francis Meagher, who visited the country in 1858, "with the exception of cognac and other distilled liquors, tobacco, and gunpowder, all commercial products are free of any restriction. Because the excepted articles are government monopolies, they are deposited in public storehouses and cannot be shipped either inside the country or abroad without a special license."[7] Merchants listed the names of the different brands of liquors that they had in stock, together with clothing, furniture, and medicines. A good example of this is Juan Lang's advertisement in May 1860. This merchant, after offering a long list of liquors, also advertised "at reasonable prices, prunes, raisins, refined sugar, noodles, gum arabic, spermaceti, flour, and other articles."[8] Even craftsmen who offered their services, such as tailors, tinsmiths, carriers, and dyers, sold liquor in their homes or shops. Undoubtedly this indicated a product in great demand, and hence a good piece of business for both permanent and occasional merchants.

There were establishments that advertised themselves as wine shops. Victor Gólcher, in June 1859, announced that "a wine shop is being established in the Hotel de Paz where all kinds of exquisite wines are to be found . . ."[9] And he advertised stocks of both foreign and domestic beer in his shop. Gólcher, however, was not the only merchant pushing the sale of domestic beer; other merchants also advertised this beverage, manufactured in the country, alongside the more prestigious foreign liquors. The presence of this product in commercial advertisements (the only domestic liquor, in fact, that did appear in them) shows that it began to be produced in Costa Rica at least as early as the 1850s.

Beverages could be obtained in cases, bottles, or half bottles, at prices ranging from 2 to 7 pesos the case, and from .4 reals to 2 pesos the bottle. A Bordeaux wine, "genuine, best quality, from the barrel," could be had for "two pesos the half-bottle,"[10] and a case of champagne for 17 pesos. According to the advertisements that stated the price of alcoholic beverages, in May 1860 there was hardly any difference in price between one wine and another (see table 3.1). The establishments that offered beverages also usually sold medicines, which were advertised in the newspapers. In April 1858, in an advertisement with no advertiser's name, it is stated that "the apothecary and wine shop on the main square offers, at both wholesale and retail, and at comparatively very cheap prices, a selection of drugs from Germany and France," in addition to "good wines of every kind, and pure wines especially selected for the use of invalids."[11]

The reason why articles so apparently different were sold in the same store is that it was thought that some liquors had curative properties; hence they were advertised along with medicines. In any case, the range of medicines offered was not very broad. Instead, much emphasis was placed on one or two products that were thought of as "magic" for curing invalids of any conceivable illness: balm of anacardium and Holloway's pills. These last were widely recommended by the country's doctors and pharmacists, among them the physician Bruno Carranza, a salesman in Costa Rica for the English firm that distributed such pills.

In an advertisement published in January 1858, Carranza described the properties of this medicine, "composed entirely of medicinal herbs," which he recommended for all ages because it was "harmless to the tiniest infant and the most delicate complection, and equally rapid and effective for rooting out illness in the most robust constitution; it is wholly innocuous in its operations and effects, at the same time seeking out and removing illnesses of all kinds, in whatever degree they occur and no matter how long-standing and deeply rooted they may be." Despite being effective in the cure of asthma, intestinal worms, jaundice, tuberculosis, and many other illnesses, they were not expensive medicines, for their cost was "boxes of 4 dozen at four reals, 12 dozen for a half-escudo, and 24 dozen at 2 pesos."[12]

Unlike the omnipotent qualities of Holloway's Pills, balm of anacardium merely had the advantage of curing "toothache and pain in the ears and face in ten minutes."[13] But its price was much higher than that of the other medicine, for its cost rose to ten pesos the dozen, despite the fact that the pills were imported from England and the balm was manufactured by Dr. J. S. Riera in Costa Rica. Holloway's pills (or ointment) were cer-

tainly a very popular medicament. Making fun of the all-powerful qualities attributed to it, the merchant Gustavo Meinecke, in an advertisement
published in April 1858, announced that he had stocks of "the best wines
and liquors, as well as Westphalia hams, meats, patés, vegetables, fresh
Holland and Limburger cheeses . . . [and other] DELICACIES even superior to Holloway's famous Pills." The products that he offered, unlike the
pills, "please the palate more, and strengthen and fortify the human constitution . . ." The pills' omnipotent qualities were reduced to almost nothing in comparison with the articles he was promoting, because hams and
cheeses "help in the most effective way to cancel IOUs, increase the coffee
harvest, and promote the process of beginning to pave the streets of our
capital."[14]

Barber shops also sold a medicinal product that had many different
uses. The soap balm offered by Alejandro Cardona, in April 1860, was
offered for shaving as well as for washing the hands, and according to Cardona served "equally well for brushing the teeth," and was also advertised
as "useful for many remedies." The balm was offered at a reduced price;
each vial cost six reals, and the barber even offered his customers the
opportunity "to try it out before buying it."[15]

Importation of medicines must not have been very widespread, to
judge from the studies carried out by the historian Rodrigo Quesada.
According to his investigations, listings of imports of drugs and medicine
from Great Britain do not appear until 1881 (Quesada 1985, 88). Advertisements indicate that fresh medicinal products were preferred, prepared
from plants considered by apothecaries to have curative properties. José
Ventura Espinach assured the public, in an advertisement published in
October 1858, that he had "a selection of medicines in the best possible
condition, because all are fresh."[16] Dr. Nazario Toledo went further: in
October 1858, he offered not only prepared products but also spices; and,
to assure their "freshness," he bought medicinal plants from dealers when
his patients asked for them. He therefore pointed out in his advertisement
that, in his shop in San José as well as his establishment in Puntarenas,
"Central American products and spices will be found in small portions, in
order to serve as samples, and to ascertain how much will be used according to the orders that are received."[17] It was also expected that the prepared
product be backed by the pharmacist who sold it. In this sense Miguel
Lara, a Guatemalan apothecary who lived in Costa Rica for a time, guaranteed in September 1858 that he would not only personally observe "the
greatest accuracy and care" in preparing his medicines, but also promised

efficient service, for his shop "will be open at any hour of the night that is necessary."[18] The sale of pesticides as well as medical instruments was common in apothecary's shops. Juan Braun offers a good example of this statement when in May of 1861 he announced to the public that he had just received from Europe "a complete selection of new drugs and medicines, in addition to syringes, trusses, nursing bottles, mortars, pillboxes, a genuine remedy to kill rats and flies, and corrosive sublimate for anthills. New pills for intestinal worms, a new powder guaranteed to combat colic in infants."[19]

II. Clothing and Toiletries

To judge from what was offered in advertisements, prominent citizens enjoyed dressing in the latest fashions being worn in the great capitals of the world, and to do so was not cheap. A pair of high-quality cashmere trousers cost twelve pesos in 1858[20] and patent-leather boots eight pesos.[21] If we consider that a fine hat cost seven pesos, three reals[22] and a linen shirt two pesos,[23] not counting undershirts, stockings, or underpants, the cost of an outfit of clothes was nearly thirty pesos. When we realize that the average monthly salary of a day laborer came to between fifteen and eighteen pesos (Cardoso 1976, 21), we may be sure that the clothing described was not bought by ordinary people.

People with lesser resources had other choices. Shoes made of second-class calfskin were offered at two pesos, and low-quality trousers at six pesos (see table 3.2). Shoes were not a particularly necessary item. According to Wagner's description, "more than 90% of the population . . . does not use shoes on weekdays, either for comfort's sake or for economy; even the children of wealthy merchants usually go about barefoot until the age of ten" (Wagner and Sherzer 1974, 178).

Despite this, the number of advertisements for shoes was highest on the list of personal clothing. Shoes were an advantage enjoyed, to judge from what we infer from the advertisements, by the wealthiest citizens. However, undershirts, underpants, and shirts were articles of masculine clothing whose frequent appearance in the advertisements suggests that these were articles often acquired by different social groups, partly because their price did not place them out of reach of less well-off persons. In a sale to liquidate the stocks of "Tinoco and Co.," advertised on 15 April 1859, "30 doz. cotton and woollen shirts at 18 reals per doz." were offered, and moreover "9 doz. shirts with linen collar, front, and cuffs at $24. per doz."[24] Certainly these were wholesale prices, but the difference between them and retail prices must not have been very great.

Clothing, more than other articles, became a symbol of social distinction. The most important citizens, says Moritz Wagner, wore patent-leather boots and top hats, the peasants went barefoot and wore "straw or palm-leaf hats with a narrow brim." Ordinary men wore, "on cold and rainy days, a striped blanket over their shirt, and wool mixture or all-cotton trousers"; on the other hand, "the rich coffee growers and merchants dress in the French style; they like well-cut suits and give much importance to elegant silk hats from Paris and narrow-brimmed Panama straw hats" (Wagner and Sherzer 1974, 178).

TABLE 3.2.   **Price of Clothing in Pesos and Reals, by Quantity, San José (1857–61)**

Article of Clothing	Price (per article)	
Military frock coat	18–24	
Military trousers	9–12	
Epaulet	17	
Trousers	0.4–12	
Three-piece suits	18–25	
Frock coats	20–24	
Dress coats	12–15	
Vests	6	
Jackets	8–10	
Capes	18–38	
Shirts	1.4–2.4	
Neckties	1.4	
Shoes and Hats	**Quantity**	**Price**
Hat	One	1.4–7
Cap	One	6
Shoes	Pair	2–8
Children's shoes	Pair	1–2.4
Women's shoes	Pair	1.2–6
Fabrics and Other Items	**Quantity**	**Price**
Grosgrain	Length	5
Printed cottons	2.8 ft.	1
Chiffon	2.8 ft.	1
Alpaca	2.8 ft.	3.4
Drill	Length	3.4–6
Cotton cloth	Yard	0.4
Damask	Yard	0.6

Sources: Album Semanal, Crónica de Costa Rica, and *Nueva Era* (1857–61).

Meanwhile women, to whom the merchants addressed a goodly proportion of their advertisements (see table 3.3), could choose among ribbons, beadwork, earrings, gloves, and stockings as accessories for their dresses in addition to perfumes, colognes, and rice powder. To make their dresses, the stores offered the most varied materials: cotton and linen, silk from Paris, London, and China. It is not surprising that advertisements should emphasize the existence of these kinds of materials in the commercial establishments of San José. According to Quesada's studies, 85 percent of the British products imported by Central America between 1856 and 1860 were textiles and manufactured goods. Of the textiles, 91 percent were cottons and the rest woolens, linens, and jutes, materials used for popular consumption, in addition to silk.[25]

Clothing and notions occupied a much smaller place in Great Britain's total imports to Central America than did dress materials, for, as the advertisements show, it was the custom not to buy dresses ready-made but to acquire the materials and have them made to measure. Both rich and poor followed this practice. The importation of English materials favored development of a body of craft workers engaged in tailoring. Some of these workers managed to earn enough money to open their own shops, where they not only made clothing to measure for their customers but also

TABLE 3.3. **Distribution of Sixty-one References to Different Articles, Addressed to Specific Groups (1857–61)**

Articles	Men	Women	Boys	Girls	Military	Clergy
Hats	8	9	1	3		1
Shoes	5	5	2			
Dresses		1		1		
Crinolines		1		1		
Boy's caps		1				
Hair ornaments		1				
Collars and sleeves		1				
Riding habits	2	2				
Toys			1			
Trousers					6	
Ornaments					1	
Frock coats					4	
Jackets					1	1
Caps					1	
Epaulets					1	
Total	15	21	4	5	14	2

Sources: Album Semanal, Crónica de Costa Rica, and *Nueva Era* (1857–61).

offered other articles. Iturraran Lara, for example, in August 1858, stated that, "desirous of selling good quality at a low price, he announces that he has a fine selection of materials of all kinds to make the garments for which he receives orders, in shawls, cashmeres, merinos, velvets, etc., etc. as well as in linen cloth." In other words, he made articles of clothing for both rich and poor; but not only did he offer these services, he also "guaranteed that if the garment does not fit, it will be altered within a few hours until it is entirely to the buyer's taste."[26]

In any case, importation of clothing from Europe or other parts of the world was not an entirely unknown activity for Costa Rican merchants. When this happened, they made sure that they were exclusive garments and that they were brought in small amounts. Wilhelm Marr, for instance, announced in May of 1857 that he "has just received from Europe a small selection of ready-made clothing"; these consisted of tailcoats, overcoats, frock coats, jackets, and trousers, "all of the latest style."[27] As with the men, dress was what distinguished society ladies from ordinary women. When Wagner described the dress of the latter group on market day, he referred to the use of "beaded necklaces or metal ornaments with crosses or pictures of saints, often two or three mingled together; they do not use earrings, but wear rings on their fingers" (Wagner and Sherzer 1974, 178). Printed cottons were the cloth that distinguished "the barefoot wife of the poor day laborer" from "the rich woman dressed in silk, and with a black mantilla on her head" (Wagner and Sherzer 1974, 199).

Printed cottons were sold in large quantities and were available in many colors and patterns. Federico Roger and T. Lacoste, in January of 1860, had in stock for purchasers in Puntarenas "505 lengths of printed cottons . . . 11 of blue cotton . . ."[28] Six months later, David Arguello was promoting, in a bargain sale, "wide printed cottons, very fine."[29] It is not surprising that this material was preferred by poorer women, for a 2.8-foot length of "fine printed cottons, very good quality and patterns"[30] cost only one real. To judge from the comments of the English traveler John Hale, lower-class women dressed badly, unlike ladies of the wealthier classes who liked to dress expensively. As early as 1824, Hale noted that "when I reached the city of Cartago I was invited to a party, and when I entered the room I was surprised to be presented to so many richly dressed ladies. The pearls and gold ornaments some of them wore were worth at least a thousand dollars" (Fernández 1982, 31). Later, in 1859, when coffee had broadened the buying power of the different social groups, lower-class women changed their attire. The English traveler Anthony Trollope observed that they were no longer badly dressed or out of style, and described them as follows: "They are addicted to crinoline, as all the female species is nowadays; but everything seems to come down to having billowing skirts . . ." (Fernández 1982, 474). Indeed, crinoline, like the printed cottons, was one of the materials most frequently offered by merchants of the period, of various qualities and in considerable quantities. Dujardin, for example, advertised in November 1859, that he had stocks in his store of "150 crinolines of all kinds for ladies and girls."[31] In any case, there is no doubt that France furnished the best example of the styles to be followed by well-to-do settlers. This interest afforded Boulanger an opportunity to specialize in one line of goods: French shoes;[32] and Castanet did the same with hats. This latter merchant advertised in October 1859 that he "has received a new selection of straw hats for women and girls, in the latest Paris style. Also of felt and beaver, very fine."[33] Invoking the fashions of Paris seemed to be an advertising ploy that gave good results. Perhaps for this reason Saturnino Tinoco, in March of 1858, announced that his store "has recently received a complete selection of French footwear, for ladies and gentlemen. Also silk vests, trousers, frock coats, and overcoats of fine cloth."[34] On the other hand, persons with a certain amount of buying power had the chance to send their clothing to a dry cleaner's, where in addition to having it cleaned and pressed, it could be given the color desired by the customers. Miguel G. Molina had installed an establishment of this type, where he offered a number of services: "dyeing in all the colors of this art, in silk, wool, or cotton, and he has brought from Europe all the equipment necessary for the purpose . . . He also cleans and removes stains from all kinds of woollen clothing, removing the grease and enhancing the colors if necessary."[35] The economic growth of Costa Rica permitted importation of the technology of the industrialized countries, which gave artisans the necessary machinery for plying their trade as efficiently as possible, as Molina did.

In their advertisements, neither craftsmen nor merchants customarily gave the price of the articles they sold; and the ones who did were apt to give the buyer a wide choice of options. This was probably due to the fact that haggling was the usual form of doing business. A short account written by Wilhelm Marr, in which he describes his travels in Costa Rica in 1854, before he settled there as a merchant, shows that when he tried to buy matches in a shop in San José, the clerk told him that their price was four for a real. Marr says, "I put my real on the counter and got my matches. He looked at me in surprise because I didn't haggle" (Fernández 1982, 164).

Lastly, it is important to stress that the products described could be acquired not solely with money. Barter was still a common form of commercial exchange. Emilio Loper, a successful shopkeeper of the period, left this option open in an advertisement that the published in May 1858, in which he offered to barter "foreign liquors for coffee from the next crop."[36]

III.   Furniture and Household Goods

When the German Wilhelm Marr visited Costa Rica in 1854, he observed that glassware, gilded tables, and oil paintings, along with table clocks and lamps, were changing the interior decoration of the homes of prominent people both new and old in San José:

> though they do not offer comfort in the sense we give to this word, the tendency to imitate things European has, however, become more noticeable. Here it may be a magnificent piano, which forms a strange contrast with the two dozen modest caned chairs lined up along the walls and the rest of the furniture lacking; there it may be two elegant sofas placed very near each other, which make what is lacking all the more obvious. Sometimes you can even see two beautiful mirrors hanging on a white wall, amid roughly carved wooden benches and ordinary wicker chairs . . . (Naylor 1988, 198)

Marr's description is evidence of the change that had begun to take place in the country. The kind of furniture that had been common in houses ever since the last days of the colony was gradually being replaced by imported articles. A great deal of porcelain from Great Britain was coming into Central America. However, to judge from commercial advertisements, the kinds of household goods brought from abroad were very diverse. Among other items, chairs, pianos, guitars, sofas, glassware, marble tables, mirrors, mattresses, decorations, and chests of drawers were advertised. These were not articles of basic need but of luxury, which adorned the homes of the wealthiest citizens. Indeed, it was not only the facades, size, and layout of these buildings that distinguished them from those of the peasants, but also their furnishings.

The large number of lamps offered in commercial advertisements leads us to believe that the use of such appliances, imported from Europe, must have become commonplace in the homes of well-to-do families. Clocks also occupy a prominent place in newspaper advertisements, a circumstance surely related to the capitalization of agriculture, very slowly changing the concept of time, which in its turn very slowly began to become money (Thompson 1977, 239–93). In any case clocks (especially French ones) became utilitarian and decorative objects, and indispensable in the homes of the most prominent citizens of San José.

Other kinds of furniture, not such useful kinds, were often advertised. In fact, in April 1858 Pedro Ganini advertised the sale of marble drawing-room tables and a number of marble pieces suitable for a mausoleum, which were at the public's disposal in the Hotel Costa Rica, where he was lodging.[37] In the same month Wilhelm Marr offered customers who did not have the means to acquire genuine marble furniture "elegant gilded tables, with an imitation-marble top . . ." Moreover, in the largest shops in the capital there were abundant supplies of porcelain in different patterns,[38] and imitation-marble paper was sold in the bookshop of the printery known as "El Album."[39]

As offerings of products increased, customers became more demanding. Not only did they yearn for things European, but they were struck by whatever was new and peculiar. Obviously the merchants took advantage of this curiosity. To promote the sale of merchandise, they stressed what their customers were looking for: originality. Wilhelm Marr referred to this in May 1858, when he advertised a product that at the moment was very common in Costa Rica: "wax figures, both sacred and profane," but with a difference; these were articles "such as have never been seen here before!"[40] Consumption of furniture and household goods increased greatly, and as a result of this rise in demand the merchants had to adjust to the rules of the marketplace in order to make a profit. Reducing the prices of things, for instance, allowed them to sell products that had been part of the stock of their shops for a long time. In 1858 Wilhelm Marr's company offered, in addition to two upright pianos built for tropical climates, sturdy chairs at thirty-six pesos the dozen;[41] a year later these chairs had not been sold. Consequently the company decided to lower the price to thirty-two pesos the dozen,[42] and by May of 1857 only three were left. The sale was a great success.

Other merchandise was not so easy to place in the market. Alfonso Meinecke imported two pianos in 1858 and it took him more than two years to sell one of them; in 1860 he was still advertising the remaining piano. Probably this was not a typical case, for pianos were an article frequently acquired among wealthy urban dwellers. These instruments could even be an investment, for they could be disposed of at a later date, as was done by Don Rafael Escalante, who in May 1857 offered for sale "in exchange for coffee or money, a piano of the finest quality . . ."[43] In the opinion of the German Moritz Wagner, these musical instruments were a fad among wealthy citizens, serving "to exercise young ladies' fingers"; and in fact many of them, in the scientist's opinion, "learned to play Strauss waltzes and polkas charmingly" (Wagner and Sherzer 1974, 226).

Parallel to the increase in consumption of foreign goods, new urban services developed in San José that led in their turn to changes in furnishings and domestic architecture. For example, in April 1858, Messrs. Francisco Kurtz and Guillermo Nanne, after signing a contract with the government, announced the building of a water main in the capital, capable of "providing water to private houses for a period of five years" (Carballo 1982, 21; *Album Semanal* 1858, 4). The new service being advertised opened possibilities for selling "statues, monuments, elegant fountains for patios and gardens, spigots, drains, sprinkling systems, pumps, etc., etc., and other objects necessary for supplying the rooms . . ."[44] Kurtz and Nanne gave customers the option of choosing the design of the things they required. In an advertisement published several days later, the German contractors offered, in addition to the other articles mentioned, "water closets" that gave to outstanding citizens of San Jose an opportunity to defecate with distinction.[45] These changes in habits of consumption led, as was to be expected, to competition and cooperation with craftsmen, either native or foreign, who were established in the country. On the one hand, skilled workers undertook to manufacture articles that could compete with those brought in by European merchants. This was the objective of Bradway and Manson, who in December 1857, advertised that "we are certain that we can not only satisfy the persons who deign to hire us, but are also completely convinced that they cannot procure foreign articles . . . as cheaply as we can manufacture them."[46] Using newspaper space, harness makers, upholsterers, and carpenters began to advertise their services. Enrique Browdorff, whose trade was specialized and directed chiefly at urban consumption, offered in May 1858, "to the worthy public of this capital, my services in my profession of painter and upholsterer. Any person who wishes to hire me may call at the house of the late Jesús Cordero, Calle de los Almacenes."[47] Despite this preoccupation on the part of artisans, ready-made foreign products continued to inundate the market. Silver objects, bronze candlesticks, mirrors, and statues, as well as sofas and carpets, became "necessary" household products in the homes of well-to-do citizens. Poor peasants probably could not afford to spend more than half of their monthly income to exchange their rustic bench, made of cedar wood, for a comfortable, elegant German sofa. When Wagner describes the house of an apparently prosperous peasant, he says that it was "extremely simple; a table and an occasional wardrobe, a long wooden bench, or a dozen chairs ranged around the walls . . . Mirrors are rare; the crucifix and a few pictures of saints, sometimes engraved on copper, or family pictures on the whitewashed walls, fill in the extremely scant decoration of the wretched living room" (Wagner and Sherzer 1974, 171).

On the other hand, craft workmanship became a complementary type of work in this process of change in patterns of consumption. Some craftsmen found an additional source of income in repairing the articles, both domestic and foreign, that were acquired on the market. Bradway and Mason advertised, in December 1857, that "any desired repairs in machines of the type we have indicated, or in any other objects included within the scope of our business, will be carried out promptly and satisfactorily."[48] Promptness was a quality proclaimed by craftsmen as part of their virtues, in a world that was becoming more and more competitive as the market increased and society became more complex.

This firm of foundrymen furnishes a typical example of the links that existed between urban consumption and the productive structure of craft and agrarian work. Unlike Browdoff's, Bradway and Mason's work was not aimed exclusively at the urban public, for some of their products were addressed to farmers. They offered to manufacture "iron presses, mills for cleaning coffee, horns for carts, grillwork for balustraded windows, bells for churches and chapels, plows of all descriptions, machines for sawing, mills for grains, gratings, etc. . . . , [offering in addition] not to charge for consultations held with us in our establishment."[49]

IV.   Commercial Infrastructure and the Merchants

In 1854 Wilhelm Marr noted a phenomenon that is evident in commercial advertisements during the years 1857 to 1861: "Commercial imports are almost exclusively in the hands of foreigners. Costa Ricans who engage in commerce have their businesses in the interior of the country" (Fernández 1982, 134). In fact merchants from Europe, especially from Germany, were prominent in the importation of articles of any sort, and became some of the largest merchants in the capital, sometimes as representatives of British commercial houses (Obregón 1982, 59–69).

Business was successful. The foreign importers succeeded not only in enlarging their shops, but some even opened branches to satisfy their customers. A good number of merchants, both Costa Rican and foreign, had stores both in Puntarenas and in San José, the two largest centers for commercial trade at the time. For example, in October 1860, Juan Knohr advertised the sale of fresh flour from New York both in the capital and in Puntarenas;[50] and in April of the following year Doña Ana Benita Escalante was advertising the sale of sugar "in Alajuela at the house of Don Cirilo Martín: in Heredia at the house of Doña Ana Zamora."[51]

On the other hand, Dujardin Roumien and Dubreuil announced, in October 1860, that they had opened "a new and large shop in the Calle de la Puebla, house of Sra. Doña María Esquivel," although "the old shop will continue to be open also."[52] Obviously the sale of imported articles was a lucrative activity for Dujardin. In June of the same year he had installed a commercial house in Paris, under the company name of "Dujardin Roumien Dubreuil,"[53] from which commercial transactions for his establishments in Costa Rica were carried out.

Shops, however, were still appendages of private houses. Usually one room of the building was used for commercial purposes. The owner of the house could be the merchant, or he could rent one or several parts of his dwelling to a merchant, as Doña María Esquivel de Quesada did in October 1858. For a monthly rent she leased several rooms in her house to Juan Lang, so that he could carry on the activities connected with his pastry shop.[54] The broadening of commercial activity, however, rendered these spaces inadequate, especially for those merchants like Meinecke or Dujardin who carried on large-scale commercial transactions. The former of these had a store-cum-wine shop, so large that it had ". . . sufficient capacity to store merchandise" and hence "was offered [in February 1861] to commerce, for the execution of any type of commission . . ."[55]

In view of how prosperous business was becoming, several people decided to build shops and rent them to merchants. José María Mora and Félix Madrigal advertised, in November 1858, that they had finished construction of a building that "contains twenty shops with all the necessary conveniences."[56] In her turn Doña Rosario de Fernández, in June 1859, announced that opposite the house of Gordiano Fernández "two good-sized shops, which can even serve as warehouses, are for rent . . ."[57] The rapid increase of shops and independent workshops strengthened the commercial and craft identities of such establishments. Despite the fact that people continued to speak of Dujardin's or Marr's shops, or those of Manuel Sánchez or Julián Carmiol, to mention only a few, their establishments were advertised by their commercial names: "French hat shop," "Shop of the volcanoes," "German bakery," "German tailor shop," "French shoe store," "Puntarenas druggist," "Steamboat grocery store." These commercial and craft centers became basic points of reference within the capital city.

Shops needed space because the selection of products was very large, to judge from the variety of articles advertised in public announcements. The detailed description of a store made by Wilhelm Marr in 1854 corroborates this: "I entered a mean little shop located in the Calle del Carmen. Behind the counter, and surrounded by a real chaos of all possible and impossible objects, was a small and rather lean man . . . beside him a simply dressed lady . . . Both moved with difficulty through the confusion of goods that surrounded them. Cups, glasses, axes, toys, strings of glass beads, bolts of calico, stearine candles, silks, shotguns, swords, candlesticks, olive oil, merino woolens, yellow soap, bottles of ink and cologne, umbrellas, walking sticks, whips, hats, boots, iron pots, machetes, guitars, accordions, cruet stands: all these things lying, hanging, or standing, in heaps or one on top of another and crammed together. It seemed there was no space left to breathe and much less to move about. And yet the couple moved in that cage of merchandise, wielded the measuring stick, weighed, and counted, and as the woman talked with remarkable speed, she sold silk ribbons to several ladies, and he demonstrated to a youth in a jacket, with a resounding 'Jesús!', how small a profit he was making on a pair of spurs he was selling to him" (Fernández 1982, 181).

The preceding description is consistent with the mercantile activity that can be inferred from the advertisements. There were very few who specialized in only one branch of commerce: shoes, hats, clothing, or food. Most sold every kind of merchandise in their establishments, like Gustavo Meinecke, who advertised indiscriminately meals, liquor, clothing and accessories, furniture, household goods, etc. In addition he had space for storing merchandise in his warehouse, and he also transported merchandise from Puntarenas to the capital.

The magnitude and variety of the activities carried out by these merchants is confirmed by the inventory of assets made for the "Tinoco y Compañía" store in April 1859, for the purpose of auctioning off its stocks in order to pay its creditor, Crisanto Medina (Villalobos 1981, 35–38, 62–65). The value of the articles to be sold off, according to the legal announcement, was quite high: 43,170 pesos (see table 3.4). The amount of capital represented by the stock in Tinoco's store shows the large scale of the business. To judge from the volume of merchandise, its strong point was clothing and accessories: shoes, buttons, thread, lace, ribbons, hats, silk and wool umbrellas, shawls, fringes, hatbands, woolens, mufflers, and dusters; however, in terms of their worth, it was construction materials and manufactured goods that had the highest value, owing to the fact that the price of these articles (steel, nails, hinges, window glass, windows, and iron balconies) was much greater than that of other products.

The stocks of food and drink of "Tinoco y Compañía" were very small, but in any case the announcement of the liquidation makes clear that the store sold everything to everyone. Its customers were society ladies as well as countrywomen, farmers and craftsmen, rich or poor, members of the professional class and businessmen. The store offered, indiscriminately, tires for carts and playing cards, French shoes and hinges, swords for military men, iron pickaxes and ladies' silk caps.

Trade was not an exclusive activity of professional merchants. Doctors and pharmacists also engaged in it, and some created commercial companies for importing and exporting products. Others, in addition to offering services such as tailoring or sheet-metal work, sold many different kinds of articles in their shops. Women were not excluded from this phenomenon. Many of them worked with their husbands in the business, either in selling or services. Alejandro Escalante advertised the use of a cocoa mill for his customers and stated that anyone wishing to use it could speak with him "or with his wife."[58] His wife not only operated the machine, but also served the perfumes and sugar that were sold in his store.

TABLE 3.4.   Value, in Pesos and Reals, of the Assets of the "Tinoco y Compañía" Store (1859)

Type of Assets	Value	%
Construction materials	14,809.4	34.3
Clothing and accessories	11,987.4	27.8
Farm implements	4,949.6	11.5
Furniture and household goods	4,089.4	9.5
Textiles	3,650.2	8.5
Paper and books	1,820.4	4.2
Toiletries	1,254.0	2.9
Beverages and foodstuffs	609.4	1.4
Total	43,170.4	100

Source: Crónica de Costa Rica. April 16, 1859, p. 4.

As early as 1858, some advertisements were addressed to specific social groups. Ramón Ortiz, for example, announced to carpenters and contractors, in August 1860, that he was selling sawn wood of good quality and at favorable prices:

> . . . as he is certain that it is his desire to favor small contractors or the general public, he is sure that they will employ his services, and he promises that all will be efficiently delivered according to the orders with which he is favored, and that everything will be placed in their workshops and homes with the greatest punctuality; his clients may send whatever they like to his home [located in Poas] . . .[59]

Despite the appeal to particular sectors of society, some groups were not considered to be important buyers. The absence of toys for children in commercial advertisements of the period is very noticeable. They appear on only one occasion, in June 1859, when David Argüello announced to his customers the existence of such items—among many others—in his shop.[60] However, advertising of adult games such as dominoes, chess, and billiards was more frequent.

On the other hand, advertising began to specialize: in the advertisements special devices were used to capture the attention of the public. Articles being advertised were emphasized by showy letters within the text, either in bold type, italics, or capital letters. Sometimes reiteration of the key word was used to attract the reader; for instance, Victor Gólcher, in February 1861, headed his advertisement in the following way: "FLOUR, FLOUR, FLOUR."[61] A few used headlines praising the properties of the product being advertised, as Antonio Pupo did in May 1860, when he announced the sale of "Batchelor," a liquid for dyeing the hair; his advertisement was headed: "THE END OF GRAY HAIR."[62]

By this time some advertisers had created a type of advertisement that they published periodically in the newspapers for a certain length of time—from two to three months—without changing a word. Most merchants employed a careful description of what they were offering, whether it was an article or a service. In August 1858, Winter specified that his "mill produces excellent flour, exactly to the taste of owners, at the price of one real the small box." And he added that "as the mill is capable of grinding five boxes an hour, it is delivered sooner than in any other." And in addition, "the wheat is weighed and the same weight is returned in flour, less three ounces per box";[63] and the advertisement continued giving details of the service being offered.

In a similar but rhetorically more sophisticated example, Herbert Parry announced the sale of "Grover and Barker" sewing machines, and to establish the qualities of the machine, he made use of comments that had been published in different newspapers and magazines in the United States.[64] Another expedient used by merchants to increase their sales was to hold bargain sales in their stores. This activity was not sporadic but cyclical, and a number of different articles were sold at reduced prices. In April 1859, Lucas Fernández advertised "a sale of printed cottons, of very good quality and patterns, at one real per length of 2.8 feet, in his shop on the plaza."[65] Meanwhile David Argüello, in June 1859, had "arranged to sell at very low prices a selection of merchandise in stock in his shops." These were chiffons, alpacas, drill, and mixed woolen and cotton fabrics, in addition to silk dresses and ball gowns for ladies, silk ribbons and fringe, embroidered gloves, table clocks, artificial flowers, and children's toys.[66]

Epilogue

The diversification of patterns of consumption, obvious in the first half of the nineteenth century, became much more marked by its closing years. Commercial establishments, some of them already transformed into large department stores, advertised articles that had not been announced in the 1850s; for example, ladies' underclothing. In July 1891, Uribe and Batalla offered, among other garments, "corsets . . . [and] silk underclothing [for ladies]."[67] Madame Tessier had even specialized in this type of garments, referred to at that time as "lingerie"; in an advertisement published on July 3, 1891, she announced that she "has just received a magnificent selection of lingerie for ladies, girls, and newborns, all in exquisite taste and capable of satisfying all demands . . . in this line, nothing can be desired that she does not have in stock, in her shop on the main street."[68]

In a more macabre vein, A. K. Harrison, also in July 1891, announced to the public that he had available "a splendid hearse, just received from the United States"; moreover, he sold coffins.[69] Jenaro Castro, in his turn, looking forward to the Feast of All Souls, announced in October of the same year the sale of "tombstones in low and high relief. Can be made in all price ranges. Come early, before too much work has piled up."[70] Funerary technology kept pace with other kinds of progress produced by the Second Industrial Revolution, led by Germany and the United States. In the store of Macaya and Rodríguez, in July 1891, the following products were offered: "American doors, sheet lead, lead pipes, washboards, galvanized iron. Machines for making ice cream, slicing potatoes, making cookies, grinding meat, pressing meat, shelling corn . . ."[71]

At the end of the nineteenth century, after half a century of diversification and change in patterns of consumption, San José was already showing a well-defined urban and secular culture. This culture was led by a bourgeoisie of tradesmen and farmers, enriched by coffee exports, whose intellectual group had just undertaken a number of liberal reforms (Salazar 1990) that were indispensable for the ongoing process of inventing the nation of Costa Rica (Palmer 1990). In the commercial advertisements of the 1890s, just as in the streets of San José, it was obvious that the Costa Rica that had preceded the period of Juan Rafael Mora (1849–1850) was being relegated more and more to feature articles, old news stories, and nostalgic descriptions of outdated customs.

NOTES

1. The period 1850–60 is analyzed in Rodríguez Saenz, Eugenia, "Estructura rediticia, coyuntura económica y transición al capitalismo agrario en el Valle Central de Costa Rica (1850–1860)" (postgraduate thesis in history, University of Costa Rica, 1988). For the period before 1850, see Molina Jiménez, Iván, *Costa Rica (1800–1850), El legado colonial y la génesis del capitalismo* (San José, Editorial de la Universidad de Costa Rica: 1991), 183–336. This author also emphasizes the documentary importance of advertisements: "Aviso sobre los 'avisos'. Los anuncios periodísticos como fuente histórica (1857–1861)," *Revista de Historia* No. 23 (January–June 1991). The first version of the present chapter was published in this number. The research upon which the article was based was aided by a grant from the University of Costa Rica. The author wishes to thank Anthony Goebel for his help in collecting the data.

2. Meléndez, Carlos, *Costa Rica: tierra y poblamiento* (San José, Editorial Costa Rica: 1977), 114. The author states that owing to the cultivation and exportation of coffee, gold coinage began to circulate, and imports of merchandise from England and other European countries proliferated in Costa Rica. All this contributed to a rapid decrease in wheat farming. Low prices of Chilean wheat made importing this crop cheaper than growing it. By 1890 production of this grain had disappeared almost entirely.

3. Crónica de Costa Rica, May 18, 1856, 4.

4. Ibid.

5. Crónica de Costa Rica, May 6, 1857, 4.

6. Crónica de Costa Rica, June 12, 1858, 4.

7. Fernández, Costa Rica en el siglo XIX, 345. On the monopoly of alcoholic

beverages by the Costa Rican government, see Kierszenson Rochwerger, Frida, *Historia del monopolio de licores (1821–1859)* (graduate thesis, University of Costa Rica, 1986).

8. *Nueva Era*, May 20, 1860, 4.
9. *Crónica de Costa Rica*, June 4, 1859, 4.
10. *Nueva Era*, May 20, 1860, 4.
11. *Crónica de Costa Rica*, April 28, 1858, 4.
12. *Album Semanal*, January 22, 1858, 4.
13. *Nueva Era*, November 17, 1860, 4.
14. *Album Semanal*, April 24, 1858, 4.
15. *Nueva Era*, April, 1860, 4.
16. *Crónica de Costa Rica*, October 9, 1858, 4.
17. Ibid.
18. *Nueva Era*, September 6, 1858, 4.
19. *Nueva Era*, May 16, 1861, 4.
20. *Crónica de Costa Rica*, November 27, 1858, 4.
21. *Crónica de Costa Rica*, June 3, 1858, 4.
22. *Crónica de Costa Rica*, April 9, 1858, 4.
23. *Crónica de Costa Rica*, April 14, 1859, 2–3.
24. *Crónica de Costa Rica*, May 16, 1859, 2–3.
25. Quesada, "El comercio entre Gran Bretaña y América Central," 88.
26. *Crónica de Costa Rica*, August 18, 1858, 4.
27. *Crónica de Costa Rica*, May 23, 1857, 4.
28. *Nueva Era*, January 14, 1860, 4.
29. *Crónica de Costa Rica*, June 4, 1859, 4.
30. *Crónica de Costa Rica*, April 16, 1859, 4.
31. *Album Semanal*, November 27, 1859, 4.
32. *Crónica de Costa Rica*, June 3, 1857, 4.
33. *Nueva Era*, October 18, 1859, 4.
34. *Crónica de Costa Rica*, March 27, 1858, 4.
35. *Crónica de Costa Rica*, November 10, 1858, 4.
36. *Crónica de Costa Rica*, May 26, 1858, 4.
37. *Crónica de Costa Rica*, October 10, 1858, 4.
38. *Nueva Era*, February 11, 1858, 4.
39. *Album Semanal*, January 22, 1858, 4.
40. *Crónica de Costa Rica*, June 20, 1858, 4.
41. *Crónica de Costa Rica*, April 10, 1858, 4.
42. *Crónica de Costa Rica*, March 10, 1859, 4.
43. *Crónica de Costa Rica*, May 25, 1857, 4.
44. *Album Semanal*, May 1, 1858, 4.
45. *Crónica de Costa Rica*, April 28, 1858, 4.
46. *Crónica de Costa Rica*, December 23, 1857, 4.
47. *Crónica de Costa Rica*, May 20, 1857, 4.
48. *Crónica de Costa Rica*, December 23, 1857, 4.
49. Ibid.
50. *Nueva Era*, October 24, 1860, 4.

51. Nueva Era, April 18, 1861, 4.
52. Nueva Era, October 18, 1860, 4.
53. Nueva Era, June 2, 1860, 4.
54. Crónica de Costa Rica, October 13, 1858, 4.
55. Nueva Era, February 21, 1861, 4.
56. Crónica de Costa Rica, November 20, 1858, 4.
57. Crónica de Costa Rica, June 15, 1869, 4.
58. Crónica de Costa Rica, May 18, 1859, 4.
59. Nueva Era, October 18, 1860, 4.
60. Crónica de Costa Rica, June 4, 1859, 4.
61. Nueva Era, February 21, 1861, 4.
62. Nueva Era, May 20, 1860, 4.
63. Crónica de Costa Rica, August 28, 1858, 4.
64. Nueva Era, December 10, 1859, 4.
65. Crónica de Costa Rica, April 16, 1859, 4.
66. Crónica de Costa Rica, June 4, 1859, 4.
67. El Heraldo, July 1, 1891, 1.
68. El Heraldo, July 3, 1891, 3.
69. El Heraldo, July 1, 1891, 1.
70. El Heraldo, October 20, 1891, 3.
71. El Heraldo, July 1, 1891, 3.

Chapter 4

Foreign Cloth in the Lowland Frontier: Commerce and Consumption of Textiles in Bolivia, 1830–1930

Erick D. Langer

El chiriguano por ser soberbio no se rebaja a usar los adornos de las tribus limítrofes que le son inferiores, pero se amolda fácilmente a usar los vestido y adornos de razas que le son superiores. No se rebaja a usar las plumas de aves, a grabarse el rostro y los brazos, a usar zarcillos de palo, como los Tobas y otros, pero imita y pretende superar a sus superiores los blancos, vistiéndose como ellos, usando el sombrero fino los hombres, la manta de lana y seda las mujeres, el calzado y la bota los jóvenes, el zarcillo extranjero las doncellas.
—Bernardino de Nino, *Etnografía chiriguana* (La Paz 1912, 198)

Introduction

The import/export complex of Latin America has been studied in great detail for the nineteenth and twentieth centuries. Scholars often have presumed that the region fell under the neocolonial control of the industrialized countries of the North Atlantic because of trade dependence, in an unequal exchange of raw materials for manufactured goods. Many have assumed that this type of unequal exchange reproduced itself on a local level in Latin America, where indigenous groups became increasingly dependent on manufactured goods supplied through urban centers. Certainly, we have studies that appear to document trade between Europeans (or their creole successors) and Indians, which gradually forced the latter into dependence on the former. This has been documented for Amazonian groups among others, as well as for the Araucanians of the pampas region.[1]

This increasing dependence on creoles through trade relations, how-

93

ever, varied according to the relative power of the indigenous groups and the creoles and the varying ability of each group to adjust to new circumstances. The ability to adapt and to change, to not assume that indigenous peoples either change very slowly or that they follow a linear, evolutionary pattern imposed by Western ideas of how natives are supposed to act, is essential to understanding the case of the Chiriguanos, who lived in what is now the southeastern section of Bolivia, in the foothills of the Andean mountains.[2] As we shall see, assumptions about the evolution of market participation and consumption of Western goods (in which we assume that people in the present consume more than people in the past), or assumptions about power relations between indigenous peoples and those of European descent, do not hold true in conventional ways for the Chiriguanos. I will try to show this through a study of the consumption of imported cloth among the Chiriguanos during the post-Independence period, concentrating on the nineteenth century. While these peoples might be in many ways exceptional (but then, which people are not in some way exceptional?), I suspect that some of the patterns in consumption and relative power found here might apply to other ethnic groups as well.

It is difficult to find information on the consumption of foreign-made textiles among indigenous groups in the historical past. Descriptions of such consumption by travelers and anthropologists, potentially prime sources for such a study, are hard to come by. In the case of the Chiriguano Indians, anthropologists in the early twentieth century focused on what they considered "traditional" material culture, trying to reconstruct images of unadulterated, precontact indigenous cultures in which the only material culture admitted was that which did not contain European-made materials. This is certainly true of the pioneer anthropologist Erland Nordenskiöld's classic treatise on this subject, *The Changes in the Material Culture of Two Indian Tribes Under the Influence of New Surroundings,* published first in 1920. Even Fr. Bernardino de Nino's sensitive 1912 ethnography on the Chiriguanos, the most complete source on this ethnic group for the early twentieth century, in the chapter on clothing and adornments assumes that the "ancient Chiriguano dress was very simple and too immoral," as among the "Chacobos in the north of Santa Cruz and others in the Bolivian Chaco," although the economic basis of the latter ethnic groups was very different (Nordenskiöld 1979; De Nino 1912, 189). In other words, De Nino, as was common in early-twentieth-century discourse influenced by Social Darwinism, assumed that there was a neat evolutionary progression in history that could be seen in part through clothing patterns. The "nomadic" (thus "primitive") peoples of the Chaco, who relied primarily on hunting and gathering, were seen as a type of mirror into the past for other groups, such as the Chiriguanos, whose economy was based on swidden agriculture, a "superior" type of organization.

The Guaraní-speaking Chiriguanos, residing in the lush subtropical valleys of southeastern Bolivia, relied primarily on the bountiful maize harvests that the mild climate and superb soils provided. A political culture that emphasized individual and village independence permitted only relatively loose alliances between villages and the development of regional chieftainships that successfully attacked Inca-held Andean highlands and later resisted Spanish and creole conquest (Pifarré 1989; Saignes 1990; Susnik 1968; Calzavarini 1980). Indeed, the main reason for the successful assertion of independence from Spanish dominance over many centuries (the Chiriguanos were fully conquered only in the late nineteenth century) was this ethnic group's ability to continually adapt to new circumstances and to change if necessary (Saignes 1990, 21–82).

The Importance of Imported Cloth on the Frontier

My need to understand the Chiriguanos outside of a conventional framework within which Latin Americanists generally put indigenous peoples began a few years ago, when I realized that what scholars assumed to be the usual relationship between Europeans and Indians was rather different in the case of these particular peoples. I found that frontier ranchers and even the Bolivian government, in reverse of the procedure in the highlands, were paying tribute to the Indians! Although the landowners, for example, tried to assuage their honor by calling these payments rental fees for utilizing frontier grazing lands, it was in fact a tributary relationship. For one thing, landowners were paying "grazing fees" for land that they, at least on paper, owned. This included even one of the great warriors and heroes of the Independence movement, General Francisco Burdett O'Connor, who in the early Republican period became the largest landowner in the department of Tarija. O'Connor, as well as other ranchers in the region, "provide[d] gifts to the Indians every year so as not to receive damages" to their cattle herds and other possessions along the frontier.[3]

In addition to the reversal of ordinary tributary relations between Indians and Europeans, an analysis of merchant records from the city of Tarija showed another unexpected characteristic of the Chiriguano frontier. Records from prominent merchants in the second half of the nineteenth century show that every important trader was heavily involved in trade with the Chiriguanos along the eastern frontier. For example, Juan de Dios Trigo's probate records from 1854 reveal that at least one-quarter of this merchant's resources, representing approximately 3,000 pesos, were related to trade with the frontier. His son, Bernardo, in the late 1840s and early 1850s accumulated 6,000 pesos of capital in the eastern frontier region before venturing to Valparaíso and Buenos Aires. The Trigos, as well as all the other traders from Tarija and elsewhere, sold mostly imported cloth from Britain, France, Belgium, and Germany (Langer and Hames 1994, 285–316).

A significant amount of cloth had been manufactured within Bolivia itself during the colonial period, but during the nineteenth century this industry was dying. While no exhaustive study has been made of the Bolivian textile industry, a number of studies have shown that even high tariff policies were ineffective in preventing the triumph of foreign-made cloth. Bolivian *obrajes,* or textile mills, many located in the Cochabamba and La Paz areas, could not compete in terms of quality or price against the onslaught of European textiles. It is also likely that Tarija merchants, located near the poorly controlled border with Argentina, simply ignored official pronouncements and avoided paying customs duties on most of their imports. In any case, the Chiriguanos in this sense followed the trend noted throughout Latin America when their consumption changed from domestically produced to imported cloth.[4]

Who were the merchants' consumers along the frontier? We know that few mestizos or whites lived in the vast frontier fringe where cattle by far outnumbered Bolivian citizens. Unfortunately, demographic data on the eastern frontier is sparse for the nineteenth century, although what information there is confirms the impression of a lack of members of a national society. Cordillera province, the largest and southern-most province of Santa Cruz department, in the 1830s contained only around 2,000 inhabitants.[5] Salinas province in Tarija had a similar pattern. Unfortunately we do not have a census of Salinas before 1871, when the economic boom of the eastern frontier had already begun and presumably a significant number of migrants had entered the region. Even then, the province, with 11,053 inhabitants, but half the department's surface area, had the smallest population (20 percent) in Tarija, except when one counts "the savage population which is encountered between the Pilcomayo and Bermejo rivers" that the census taker calculated topped 50,000.[6]

Moreover, as far as we know, the settlers along the frontier were a poverty-stricken lot. Cattle ranching, the predominant economic activity of the region, was not yet lucrative as it would be in the following decades, when the renascent silver mining industry brought about increasing demand for livestock. If the diaries of Francis Burdett O'Connor, the largest landowner of Salinas province and a man obsessed with the efficient administration of his properties, are any indication, cattle ranching did not bring in great earnings in the 1850s.[7] In turn, the other potentially lucrative market for merchants like the Trigos along the frontier, the military, was in even worse shape. Soldiers in the forts were paid infrequently and often wore rags because they could not afford to purchase new clothing.[8]

Thus, much of the trade was not with the poor and sparse mestizo population along the frontier, but with the Indians on the other side of the frontier. Other evidence also suggests that this was the case. One of the five clauses in the 1843 peace treaty between the Chiriguanos and the Bolivian military specified that "all Christians [i.e., whites or mestizos] who want to enter the Cordillera with any type of trade may do so with complete security," suggesting that commerce with the Chiriguanos was an important activity for the Bolivians.[9]

Another piece of evidence, though somewhat late for our purposes, are the many photographs taken in the late nineteenth and early twentieth centuries of the Chiriguanos. The use of European textiles among men is universal. Indeed the few pictures of Chiriguano men in their "traditional" costume, such as the one exhibited in the 1892 exposition of Catholic missions in Turin, Italy, look deliberately contrived and artificial.[10] The photos of Chiriguano chiefs in particular are noteworthy for their use of European dress, including pants, belts, shirts and, in some cases, portions of Bolivian military uniforms (De Nino 1912, 157; Pifarré 1989, 299). It is more difficult to determine the origins of women's clothes, but it is most likely that the wide swaths of cloth even of "traditional" dress that the women used also were of foreign manufacture.

Why did the Chiriguanos want imported cloth? It is easy to speculate about aesthetics; imported cloth had brighter colors than natural dyes and came in different textures and patterns. Most of all, foreign textiles provided prestige that the Indians associated with the white man. Since colonial times, the Chiriguanos had called the Spaniards *karai,* the term used prior to the European invasion to describe powerful but malignant spiritual beings.[11] By the nineteenth century, this term had come to represent all creoles. As far as I can determine, the Chiriguanos made no distinction between Europeans and native-born creoles, nor regarding the origins of the cloth. Be that as it may, European cloth by the nineteenth century was a prestige item among the Indians, especially for male attire.

Given the use of imported cloth by the Indians, how important was it? Estimating the actual volume of trade along the frontier is unfortunately impossible because the government had no interest in keeping this information. Until we find the records of the most important merchant houses that traded along the frontier, we will not know the exact numbers. However, we have some data for the turn of the century on the most important fair, held in Sauces every August, that shows the significance of this trade. In 1900, two of the largest merchant firms of Tarija (Mateo Araóz é Hijos and Trigo Hermanos) turned over at least 40,000 Bolivianos (Bs) worth of merchandise from the fair; in 1902 the representative of one merchant firm, Jofré é Hijos, returned with 50,000 Bs from Sauces to purchase letters of exchange with which to buy more cloth.[12] These figures are even more surprising because at this point the Sauces fair was already on the decline: the conquest of the frontier by cattle ranchers, the growing predominance of German and Argentine merchant firms, and Chiriguano migration to Argentina had greatly diminished living standards and eroded the consumer base of the frontier region (Langer and Hames 1994, 302–3).

Gaining Access to Cloth Imports

Although in many cases the evidence is only suggestive, a strong case can be made that the Chiriguano Indians participated in the consumption of imported cloth to a much greater degree than previously realized. Through what mechanisms did this ethnic group gain access to this consumption good? The trip from the factory floor in Liverpool or Brussels to, say, a Chiriguano village in the Huacaya valley was a tortuous one, involving many different intermediaries and different types of exchange. After all, we know that money was scarce, if not completely absent from the frontier. In addition, what resources did the Chiriguanos have that made possible the acquisition of these goods?

Both of these issues, mechanisms of access to imports and Chiriguano resources, are closely related. Indeed, it is possible to periodize how Chiriguanos gained access to these goods based on an understanding of shifting political and military power, access to lands, labor relations, and migration patterns. Three overlapping periods are discernable, characterized by slowly shifting means of acquiring imported cloth. The first period, covering the first four decades from Independence to the 1860s, is characterized by tributary relations and Argentine trade. In the second period, from about 1850 to the early twentieth century, Indians acquired imports through fairs. By the 1880s, a new mode of acquisition began to take hold, characterized by advances in goods and money from cattle ranchers as part of a debt peonage system, and acquisition of goods through purchase directly in Argentina, in return for wage labor. This last phase lasted for about a century, though in the past decade these types of relationships have waned somewhat. Let us now examine each of these phases in somewhat greater detail.

Tribute and Trade

We have already briefly alluded to the tributary arrangements between Chiriguano peoples and cattle ranchers in the early republican period. This was, however, only one means in which the Chiriguanos received tribute. Local authorities, from the subprefect to lower officials, also provided Chiriguano village headman, called *tubichas,* with goods and money. Thierry Saignes has published a partial list of the disbursements by the Tarija departmental treasury. While treasury officials listed monetary amounts, it is clear that a significant portion of this money was actually spent on clothing, such as in 1842 "24 pesos 4 reales to pay for the clothing and other items which have been bought to give to Captain Aracua" (Saignes 1990, 178–80). According to Saignes, between 1840 and 1865 the Tarija treasury paid an average of 85 pesos per year to the "Indian allies," but this was only one level of government for which we have precise figures. I have evidence that this list is at best incomplete and that in fact much higher sums were paid to tubichas during this period (Langer and Ruíz 1988, 208). I suspect that earlier in the century, especially in the 1830s, cattle ranchers paid more than government officials. Tribute possibly went from a "private" function to a "public" (i.e., governmental) duty as the nineteenth century wore on.

Regional chiefs, or *mburubichas,* traveled to the city of Tarija to negotiate the terms that would make these chiefs into Bolivian "allies." We have the description of such a voyage in the diary of Francis Burdett O'Connor, who in 1850 helped Guayupa, the powerful chief of the Ingre valley, get to the city of Tarija with some of his men and helped pressure the new prefect to pay the 100 pesos that the mburubicha demanded. When the prefect refused, O'Connor himself borrowed money to pay a portion of the fee.[13]

When exactly this money was used to purchase cloth is not clear; I suspect that in many cases the Chiriguano chiefs purchased cloth while in the city of Tarija, undoubtedly a less expensive proposition than buying textiles from frontier merchants.

In other words, the Chiriguanos parlayed their political and military power into access to goods not available within the indigenous economy. Tribute payments, whether in coin or cloth, were just one means. Another important way in which Chiriguanos achieved access to cloth was through the "theft" of cattle. As in the case of the Araucanian Indians of the Argentine pampas, the taking of cattle can be interpreted in many ways. Along the southeastern Bolivian frontier, as in the pampas, most of the land (despite the paper assigning the land to creole ranchers) in fact was controlled by the Indians. What ranchers might have interpreted as thefts, in the Indians' eyes was only the rightful taking of animals on their own land. In the nineteenth-century pampas, the Araucanians built their own commercial empire by selling the livestock across the border to Chilean customers (Jones 1987, 311–36; Goñi 1986–87, 37–66; Palermo 1988, 43–90). The Chiriguanos and Chanés did likewise, selling cattle on their lands to entrepreneurs in thriving Orán, on the Argentine side of the eastern frontier.[14] While this commerce was probably on a lesser scale than the massive trade on the pampas, it was nevertheless significant. Many of the wars between Chiriguanos and creole forces can be seen as struggles over these livestock sources. As I have explained elsewhere, the Chiriguanos' strategy in conflicts with the settlers up until the 1860s was not to kill cowhands or soldiers, but to kill or take as many cattle so that the creoles had little reason to remain in Indian lands. In fact, government authorities ascertained that conflict was imminent when the warriors began killing or "stealing" cattle (Langer 1989). Was this one way in which the Chiriguanos showed their superiority over the creoles—by asserting control over frontier resources?

Unfortunately, the exact mechanisms for gaining access to textiles are not very clear. We do know that the Indians bartered cattle for other goods, though the product for which they bartered is not specified. Given the fact that the Salta merchants, who also controlled trade to Orán, were mainly cloth merchants and, up to the 1860s, the wholesalers for Tarija merchants, it is highly likely that the major good for which the Chiriguanos bartered was cloth. In addition, a major trade route between northern Argentina, Tarija, and Santa Cruz skirted the Andean foothills, right through Chiriguano territory. Surely merchants sold (or gave as payment for transport services or simply for permitting transit) textiles to the Indians on their way to Santa Cruz. They might have exchanged cloth for cattle along the way as well. This was the case with Joaquín Ligeron, who in the 1860s bought young bulls "in exchange for the *efectos* [foreign goods] I have brought from this city [Tarija]." Although much of his commerce was with the Franciscan missions, he also listed credits among Indians living in independent villages such as Tacuaremboti and Iguembe. Indeed, the Indians of Cabezas, a mission of Chiriguanos in colonial times, owed him 40 out of the 48 pesos of debts in that town.[15]

As far as we know, the Chiriguanos did not sell maize, their staple crop that grew abundantly in their territory. Apparently, the Indians distinguished between their subsistence crop (maize) and goods that could be commercialized (cattle). In fact, the selling of cattle complemented very nicely the Chiriguanos' subsistence strategy. As one scholar has put it, the struggle between creoles and Chiriguanos can be characterized as a struggle between cattle and maize. Cowhands deliberately herded cattle onto the maize fields as a way of getting rid of the indigenous settlements (Susnik 1968, 60; Langer 1989). What better way of counteracting the ranchers' strategy than using the fissures in creole society between merchants and ranchers by selling the noxious cattle to the former? We know that Macharetí, one of the most important centers of Chiriguano resistance to creole encroachment until 1869, was one of the centers of this cattle trade. Here the Indians (which included members of the neighboring Toba ethnic group as well) traded the cattle they had captured around the important Bolivian settlement of Caiza to either other Chiriguanos or, as one author delicately put it, to "those who were neither Chiriguanos nor Indians" (Corrado 1990, 444). In this way the Chiriguanos were able to gain resources from the ranchers and use them to purchase goods produced outside the indigenous economy, such as imported textiles.

Frontier Fairs

It is likely that the region's fairs began to develop in the second half of the nineteenth century. The combination of greater penetration by cattle ranchers (by this time the balance of power was shifting in favor of creole society), a significant independent Chiriguano population, and a commercial revitalization of southern Bolivia and northern Argentina provided a vibrant market along the frontier. Fairs developed in Iguembe, Muyupampa, and Sauces to take care of increased supply and demand. The fair in Sauces (present-day Monteagudo) was by far the most important fair, located between the large independent Chiriguano communities of the Caipipendi valley to the north, and the cattle estates and the populous Franciscan missions to the south. Sauces also was the most important node of commerce between the frontier regions and the highlands. The fair, held in the month of August, attracted the most important cloth merchants from Tarija, coca and cloth traders from Cochabamba, mule and donkey breeders from Argentina, and merchants from Santa Cruz who hawked sugar, coffee, and rum (Mendieta 1928, 61). As we have seen, even in the early twentieth century the volume of trade in Monteagudo was quite high. It is significant that all three fairs were located next to regions with the highest number of independent Chiriguano communities. While we have no description of the fairs' consumers, Chiriguanos undoubtedly helped maintain the vitality of the fairs through their barter or purchase of cloth and coca, a favorite item of consumption among members of this ethnic group.

The importance of fairs along the frontier represents a transitional stage in the development of markets in the region. One development, the predominance of Franciscan missions, probably restricted the growth of fairs, though in the long term it probably stimulated consumption. The Franciscans encouraged the Indians' dressing in European clothes. The friars gave schoolchildren European clothes to wear, as a means to attract the children to school, and as a visible means of "civilizing" them (Langer 1995). Many missionaries equated the wearing of European-style clothes as a step from the Indians' innate "barbarism," to show that the Indians had indeed become citizens of the nation. The missionaries' conceptions are somewhat ironic, for, as Thierry Saignes has asserted for the eighteenth century, the Indians saw the friars' distribution of clothes as one clear sign of their own superiority. In the Chiriguanos' eyes, the Franciscans' frequent presents were payments to keep the Indians there, perhaps not unlike the tribute payments by ranchers and government officials (Saignes 1990, 119–22). It is not certain that this relationship was quite as clear in the nineteenth century as it was in the eighteenth. However, Fr. Bernardino de Nino, one of the most sensitive Franciscan observers of the early twentieth century, noted that the Indians demanded clothes for their children if the friars wanted them to go to the mission schools (De Nino 1912, 117). In any case, the distribution of textiles in the long term undoubtedly made the Indians more dependent on purchased textiles and expanded the market for these goods.

The wearing of European-style clothes eventually became a mark of distinction between the mission Indians and those living in independent villages. Even among the converted girls and women, the friars insisted that they wear skirts and blouses on the model of the mestiza women [called *cholas* in Bolivia) rather than the *tipoy,* a long cloth wrapped around the body with two slits for the arms. The change of clothes put these women on the missions into the category of precisely the type of people that they were becoming—culturally neither Indian nor fully creole (Seligmann 1989, 694–712). This was in addition to two other characteristics that differentiated men born on the mission from those born elsewhere. Boys in independent villages received a chin plug (called *tembeta*) early in life, whereas the Franciscans forbade this custom on the missions. Also, independent Chiriguanos wore long hair, wound under their handkerchiefs. Mission Chiriguanos wore their hair relatively short. As time went on, these distinctions provided a marked differentiation between the two groups and a feeling of superiority on both sides that further divided Chiriguano society through visible physical distinctions.

Debt Peonage and Migration

By the late nineteenth century, two developments, the expansion of cattle ranches, and Chiriguano migration to Argentina, had begun to counteract the pattern of high consumption of textiles among Indians in the region. Both ranchers and migration to Argentina had existed before the late nineteenth century. Beginning in the middle of the 1860s an invigorated highland mining economy made lucrative an expansion of cattle ranching throughout the region. As a result, haciendas expanded dramatically and many Indians fled to Argentina.

The conquest of Chiriguano territory in the late nineteenth century was a complex process. The silver boom in the highlands not only made possible the expansion of the cattle market, but it also provided the Bolivian state and local settlers with resources they did not possess before. The settlers were able to establish forts at Ingre and Iguembe in 1866 and, for the first time, had the resources to maintain these stockades. Likewise, settlers from the Santa Cruz region built two forts near Cuevo. Chiriguano guerrilla tactics were unable to eliminate fortifications, providing the settlers with points far in Chiriguano territory from which to strike Indian villages. This, combined with the introduction of the repeating rifle that vastly outperformed the bows and arrows or old flintlock muskets of the

Indians, finally put the Chiriguanos on the defensive. In addition, Chiriguano groups pressured by the ranchers permitted the establishment of Franciscan missions in their midst. While serving to protect Indian land claims to a certain extent, the missions also divided Chiriguano society. Mission Indians became the permanent military allies of the creoles and upset the system of ever-changing village alliances that had made Chiriguano autonomy possible to that point. After establishing the small missions of Itau, Chimeo, and Aguairenda on the fringes of Chiriguano territory, in 1845, 1849, and 1851, respectively, the Franciscans were able to found missions in the core area with the foundation of Tararí (1854), Macharetí (1869), and Tiguipa (1872).

The Huacaya War of 1874–78, when the independent Chiriguano villages in conjunction with Toba allies attempted to eliminate the missions and the forts, brought about massacres and a stream of Chiriguano refugees into the Chaco regions controlled by the Tobas. When the Indians returned to their homelands, they found them divided up among the victorious settlers. Ranchers forced the remaining Indians into debt peonage to control the labor force and prevent escapes (Langer 1989, 123–42; Pifarré 1989, 269–391). As a result, living standards among the captive Chiriguano population plunged. Each year, landowners gave their workers a set of clothes, often of very poor quality, the value of which they were then required to work off. In addition, administrators discounted food and coca rations. Although I have not been able to gain access to actual hacienda account books in the region, it is likely that prices of clothes and food were highly inflated, for it is clear from other records that hacienda peons were never able to work their way out of debt (Langer 1989, 148–50; Nordenskiöld 1979, 300).

The only way for the Indians to improve their condition was to escape the oppressive hacienda regime, and escape they did in increasing numbers in the late nineteenth century. The sugar plantations of northern Argentina, located in eastern Andean valleys of Jujuy and Salta, were the Chiriguanos' most common destination. We do not have statistics on the transnational migration, since the Chaco frontier was poorly guarded on both sides and nobody bothered to keep this type of information on indigenous peoples. Not only did hacienda peons escape, however; Indians from the Franciscan missions (which held about 40 percent of the total Chiriguano population by 1900) also left to work in the sugar cane fields of northern Argentina (Langer 1987). On the missions and in the surviving independent communities, much of this migration (at least initially) was seasonal. After the sugar cane harvest, most men (and the few women migrants) returned to their villages.

The Chiriguanos did not only leave because of oppression at home; they also had positive reasons to go. The Indians knew Argentina as *mbaporenda,* "the place where there is work" (Hirsch 1989). Not only did they find work, but also access to the goods that they desired, including clothes. In fact, descriptions of Chiriguanos returning from Argentina almost uniformly mentioned not only the bad habits they presumably picked up in the plantation labor camps, but also the new clothes and the mule or donkey they had acquired (De Nino 1912, 79n; Nordenskiöld 1979, 6). Migration thus depressed trade in cloth in two ways. First, the Chiriguanos received clothes in return for their labor in Argentina or purchased them there rather than in Bolivia. Secondly, many Indians (especially those who escaped the haciendas) left Bolivia permanently, diminishing significantly the number of consumers in the region. From 1875, when one estimate pegged the Chiriguano population at 46,000, the number of Indians diminished largely because of emigration, leaving probably less than 20,000 by the 1920s.[16]

This pattern of hacienda control and emigration has persisted until very recently. Only in the 1980s have conditions loosened somewhat on the haciendas for the Chiriguanos; beginning in 1989 poor economic conditions in Argentina have finally led to a decrease in migration to the sugar plantations of Jujuy (Healy 1982). Thus, the domination of the hacienda in the region continued for about a century, while in turn migration patterns and the drain of the frontier population of Indians (at least in part as a reaction to the oppression of the haciendas) persisted for about the same period.

Effects on Chiriguano Society

We have thus far discussed the scope of the textile trade along the frontier and the changing means by which Chiriguanos achieved access to imported textiles. While the study of consumption patterns is a valuable goal in itself (since very little work has been done on this, particularly on historical indigenous societies), the most important issue must be what effect consumption patterns had on indigenous societies themselves. How did the demand for textiles not made within indigenous society shape social and political roles? How, if at all, did the Chiriguano economy change as a result of this demand?

The changing means of access to imported cloth give us important clues as to the role of imported textiles in Chiriguano society. While, as I have suggested, the consumption of cloth is an important factor to keep in mind when discussing changes in Chiriguano society, it is by no means the only causal factor. Changing patterns in textile consumption also serve as indications of larger transformations of indigenous society. Alterations in consumption patterns formed part of a complex web of interactions that transformed indigenous society in conjunction with changing political, economic, and social conditions in Chiriguano territory, as well as within Bolivia, and, to a certain extent, Argentina.

As discussed above, during the first four decades after Bolivian independence, the political power that the Chiriguanos wielded along the frontier to a large degree provided them with access to imported textiles. Tributary relations, both with the various levels of the Bolivian government and with the landlords, favored the *capitán* (or tubichas), the leaders of Chiriguano society. While Chiriguano political culture emphasized individual freedom of action, once the chiefs had been selected by the community and convinced the village of a certain course of action, the village's adult males (tellingly called *soldados* by the creoles) were expected to follow their capitán's orders to the letter. The tubichas in turn kept their position through the redistribution of goods that they obtained. In this way, they presumably kept the village content with their rule and created obligations among its inhabitants to follow their suggestions. Lengthy community meetings, where the adult males talked and talked until they came to a consensus, highlighted this process. As Pierre Clastres has shown, for most "face-to-face" societies such as the Chiriguano, requirements for chiefdomship included good oratorical skills. Those who spoke powerfully were able to create a consensus that translated into what the Europeans interpreted as unquestioning loyalty once an action was decided upon (Clastres 1977, Bloch 1975; Brenneis and Myers 1984). Heredity was important for leadership as well, for the Chiriguanos invariably selected a member of the traditional chief's family (though not necessarily his son) to succeed him in the position.

Bolivian ranchers paid their tribute to the tubichas; high government officials paid the regional chiefs, the mburubichas, for their "services." This provided another resource for the chiefs with which they consolidated their power in their communities. Unwittingly, the creoles thus strengthened the hand of the militarily powerful chiefs, often to their own detriment. For the policy of paying tribute was in many ways an abject failure. As Francisco Pifarré asserts, the period between 1840 and 1875 was one of almost constant warfare in which Chiriguano groups frequently changed sides and used the creole troops for gaining advantage in the Machiavellian world of Chiriguano power politics. Moreover, the various departmental governments (and probably the ranchers as well) supported different village alliances, confusing the political situation along the frontier and providing goods for a large number of different chiefs (Pifarré 1989, 285; Langer 1989). Since the chiefs served as nexus for the redistribution of textiles, the main form of tribute payment, they were able to accumulate greater power than they had had in the eighteenth century. Using Karl Polanyi's paradigm, the chiefs' ability to rely more on redistribution than reciprocity (which is an exchange among equals) created a greater sense of hierarchy than existed previously (Polanyi, Arensberg, and Pearson 1957; Sahlins 1972). The payment of textiles promoted a more hierarchical indigenous society at odds with the emphasis on individual liberty in Chiriguano society.

Most textiles and other goods paid as tribute could be distributed among the "soldiers" and also among the women. Thus, in 1839 a tubicha received "one and a half *varas* of cloth and a dozen knives," or in 1843 the Tarija prefect provided his Indian "allies" with "ponchos made of Castilian cloth, blankets, knives, tobacco, and some trinkets for their women" (Saignes 1990, 178; Ruíz 1988, 208). These goods, in all likelihood, were meant for redistribution by the chiefs among the mass of the Chiriguano population. The redistribution consolidated the tubichas' hold on power because of their ability to deliver highly valued goods not produced within Chiriguano society.

Of course, the distribution of textiles was by no means egalitarian in Chiriguano society. The chiefs received clothes made especially for them, for example, the 24 pesos 4 reales spent on "clothing for capitán Aracua" in 1842 (Saignes 1990, 179–80). The creoles, like the Spaniards before them, were very conscious of status differentiation. Chiefs were to wear better clothes, even militia uniforms in some cases, to distinguish themselves from the mass of the Indians. The differential dress codes probably played into the chiefs' hands, since here was a visual sign of their superiority. Dressing better was only part of this status differentiation; chiefs also often had more than one wife, as well as other marks of high status.[17]

The adoption of ready-made textiles changed the role of Chiriguano women, one of whose main occupations had been weaving the cloth for the *tiru* and the *cutuma,* respectively the main male and female clothing pieces.

The introduction of voracious cattle into Chiriguano territory destroyed cotton production, forcing the Indians to rely on imported textiles. The expansion of the cattle ranches coincides with the flourishing of the frontier fairs, suggesting a causal relationship between the decline of Chiriguano territorial integrity (and thus cotton production) and the need for imported cloth. The woman's long cotton or wool dress made of European textiles and worn by those in independent villages even changed its name (though apparently not its shape) to *tipoy* (De Nino 1912, 185). The decline of weaving diminished the status of Chiriguano women. As far as it is possible to tell, production of cloth was only for the domestic sphere; women did not commercialize the cloth they made nor did they become market women. That was left to mestizo traders who came to the settlements and fairs.

The decline of Chiriguano power on the frontier was extremely rapid after the Huacaya War (1874–78). Much of this can be explained by causes external to Chiriguano society, such as the introduction of the repeating rifle, the increasing resources of the state due to income from the silver mining boom, and the like. However, it is likely that differential access to textiles also played a role, for it is in this period that the tubichas lost some of their control over the distribution of textiles in their villages. Not only did ranchers and the government refuse to continue to pay tribute, but the mass of Chiriguanos began to gain access to cloth by migrating to work on the Argentine sugar plantations. In many cases, the sugar plantations paid their workers directly in cloth, such as in 1855 in the Zenta valley, where plantation owners paid the Indians a piece of tobacco each week, a daily food ration, and eight varas of rough cloth per month.[18]

The items acquired in Argentina by returning migrants diffused throughout their villages very quickly. Good Chiriguano manners included the sharing of scarce goods among relatives and friends; individual accumulation, so common in Western culture, was not acceptable behavior (De Nino 1912, 125). The textiles and other goods thus began to be distributed through horizontal networks, competing with the vertical networks the tubichas had fostered for much of the nineteenth century. This "democratization" of access to textiles in Chiriguano society probably also helps explain the rapid demise of the independent villages once migration to Argentina became prevalent. The combination of external pressures through the aggressive expansion of the ranches with the decreasing authority of the tubichas made Chiriguano society much more vulnerable. Although this point should not be overdone—external causes were in all probability more important than the more egalitarian distribution of textiles—the lack of armed resistance after 1878 by Chiriguanos is notable. Significantly, the last major attempt to throw out the creoles occurred under the aegis of a messianic leader in 1892 who had no claim to tubicha heritage. Indeed, when a year later some of the major Chiriguano chiefs attempted to revive the rebellion, they were unsuccessful (Fernández 1972; Saignes 1990, 187–98, 210–11).

The way in which the Chiriguanos had gained access to textiles also affected relations between landowners and their peons. Debt peonage was the rule on haciendas along the frontier, but the Indians helped make possible the accumulation of debt by insisting on advances when they went to work for an hacendado. Apparently, many insisted on an advance and then left the ranch; in 1927 two important ranchers petitioned the government for "guarantees for the landowners in the contracts with the peons they employ; because the flight of peons to Argentina and other distant places is frequent, defrauding (the landowners with) the advances received (clothes and money). It must be said that it is *impossible* to get any peon without an advance."[19] In addition to being a tactic for cheating the landowner out of his goods, the provision of textiles at the beginning of the contract also fulfilled a need to create a redistributive relationship between landlord and peon, as had earlier occurred between tubicha and soldier. I have argued elsewhere that landlords in many ways took over the functions of the tubicha (though clearly for their own ends) (Langer 1989, 154). However, hacendados could never muster the same kind of legitimacy—nor was it necessarily in their interest to do so—making it easier for Chiriguanos to renege on these exploitative labor contracts. Ranchers also used other means to hold their Chiriguano workers. To bolster their hold over their peons, landlords provided their workers with alcohol and coca. Moreover, a severe competition developed between landlords to attract Chiriguano women to their estates, for they calculated that the emotional bonds created between their workers and the women made the men less likely to leave (149–50).

These supplementary means to keep workers on the estates shows the ineffectiveness of simply distributing textiles. As observers noted, the quality of these clothes was often inferior, certainly of poorer quality than what the Chiriguanos could get in the sugar plantations of Argentina (Nordenskiöld 1979, 300). Beyond the issue of quality, it is clear that the Indians' standard of living decreased significantly under the hacienda regime. The yearly distribution of clothes among the men (which were then discounted heavily from wages) was much less than what the Indians had been able to afford previously. Thus, consumption dropped along the former frontier, also spelling the eventual doom of the fairs by the late 1920s (Mendieta 1928, 61).

Conclusion

We can see how the consumption of imported textiles was an important part of the history of the Chiriguano frontier. Consumption patterns, the ways in which the Indians gained access to these goods, and the transformations in Chiriguano (and frontier) society intermesh very nicely. These patterns help us understand another dimension of the Latin American frontier that is rarely discussed. It also shows that the evolutionary models common for understanding indigenous peoples, a holdover from racialist assumptions of the early twentieth century, are still implicitly imbedded in these paradigms and should be reexamined. The consumption of imported textiles remained relatively high while the Chiriguanos remained independent of creole society. In the first forty-odd years after independence the Indians parlayed their military and political strength (relative to the weak Bolivian state and ranchers) into access to imported cloth, often by selling to frontier merchants the cattle the ranchers paid the Indians not to take from the Chiriguanos' own territory. Almost continuous warfare and the payment of tribute mainly in cloth by both government officials and ranchers to Chiriguanos chiefs kept vertical ties within the communities strong.

Only with the growing strength of the cattle economy and the conquest of the Indian villages beginning in the late 1860s did this pattern rapidly change. As Chiriguanos migrated in increasing numbers to the sugar plantations in northern Argentina, they gained independent access to quality textiles in return for their labor. This eventually weakened the position of the tubichas (who also were receiving little or no tribute from creoles), leading to a rapid breakdown of village society and the ability of the Chiriguanos to resist encroachment. While the landowners also distributed cloth among their workers, the debt peonage arrangements in general depressed Indian living standards and also diminished the demand for imported textiles. This, as well as seasonal and permanent migration of the Indians to Argentina, led to the decline of the frontier fairs by the 1920s. Thus, through looking at patterns of textile consumption we can question the notion of frontier "development" and the relative advantages—even in terms of classical economic concepts of supply and demand—of frontier conquest in Latin America.

NOTES

1. See, for example, Robert F. Murphy and Julian H. Steward, "Tappers and Trappers: Parallel Process of Acculturation," *Economic Development and Cultural Change* 4 (July 1956), 335–53, and Kristine L. Jones, "Conflict and Adaptation in the Argentine Pampas" (Ph.D. dissertation, University of Chicago, 1984). Jones in particular makes extensive reference to the North American experience, which in many ways serves as her model for understanding relations in the pampas. It is for North America, of course, that the model of indigenous dependence on trade is most highly developed.

2. The word *Chiriguano* has become controversial because of its presumed negative connotations. Some have assumed that the word comes from two Quechua words signifying "cold" and "feces." See, for example, Guillermo Pinckert Justiniano, *La guerra chiriguana* (Santa Cruz, 1978), 33–36. However, more recent scholarship has tried to show its Guaraní origin and the term's more positive meaning. See Isabelle Combès and Thierry Saignes, *Alter Ego: Naissance de l'Identité Chiriguano* (Paris, 1991). The Chiriguanos themselves by the nineteenth century called themselves *ava* ("men" or "people"), but in contemporary scholarship this name refers to only one of three groups of Chiriguanos. Thus I have chosen to keep the label "Chiriguano."

3. For a more in-depth discussion of tributary relations, see Erick D. Langer, "Las 'guerras chiriguanas': Resistencia y adaptación en la frontera surboliviana (siglo XIX)," Paper presented at the Primer Congreso Internacional de Etnohistoria, Buenos Aires, 1989. The quote is from Tomás Ruiz to Governor of Tarija, Tarija, Nov. 24, 1836, 3–4, Correspondencia Oficial, Ministerio de Guerra (hereinafter MG), vol. 90, no. 55, Archivo Nacional de Bolivia (hereinafter ANB).

4. For the decline of the nineteenth-century Bolivian textile industry, see Brooke Larson, *Colonialism and Agrarian Transformation in Bolivia: Cochabamba, 1550–1900* (Princeton, 1988), 258–69; José María Dalence, *Bosquejo estadístico de Bolivia* (La Paz, 1975 [1851]), 253–57. For a somewhat similar case in Peru, see Alberto Flores Galindo, *Arequipa y el sur andino: Ensayo de historia regional, siglos XVIII–XX* (Lima, 1977) and Paul Gootenberg, *Tejidos, harinas, corazones y mentes: El imperialismo norteamericano de libre comercio en el Perú, 1825–1840* (Lima, 1989).

5. In 1834, the government counted 1,817 inhabitants. In 1839, the province only contained 2,127 individuals. This was out of a total of 54,457 and 62,727 inhabitants respectively in Santa Cruz department. See "República Boliviana, Departamento de Santa Cruz, Censo jeneral de almas que tiene el expresado, correspondiente al prócsimo pasado año de 1834," Correspondencia Oficial, Ministerio del Interior (hereinafter MI), vol. 55, no. 33; and "República Boliviana, Departamento de Santa Cruz, Censo jeneral que manifiesta el número de almas que tiene

el espresado correspondiente al año prócsimo pasado de 1839," MI, vol. 82, no. 28, ANB.

6. "Tarija: Cuadro sinóptico jeneral del censo Urbano i Rural del Departamento," MI, vol. 195, no. 93.

7. O'Connor for example appeared to lose more cattle to disease and theft than he was able to sell. See for example, "Diario de Francisco Burdett O'Connor," Nov. 26, 1854, Private Archive of Eduardo Trigo O'Connor D'Arlach (hereinafter AETOD).

8. See, for example, E. Borda to minister of interior, Tarija, Feb. 14, 1884, MI, vol. 221, no. 55, ANB.

9. J. Vicente Soza to minister of war, San Luís, Dec. 1, 1843, MG, vol. 169, no. 73, ANB.

10. See the copy available in the Archivo Franciscano de Tarija. Many photos of Chiriguanos are available in De Nino, *Etnografía;* by the same author, *Misiones franciscanas del Colegio de Propaganda Fide de Potosí* (La Paz, 1918); Arthur Chervin, *Anthropologie Bolivienne,* vol. 1 (Paris, 1908); and Erland Nordenskiöld, *Indianerleben: El Gran Chaco (Südamerika)* (Leipzig, 1913).

11. The definition comes from Antonio Ruiz de Montoya, *Tesoro de la lengua Guaraní* (Madrid, 1639), as cited in Pifarré, 541.

12. Juan de Dios Trigo to Eduardo Knaudt, Tarija, Oct. 8, 1900; José Araóz to Aramayo, Francke y Cia, Tarija, Oct. 22, 1900, "1900–1901 Tarija: Agosto 1900 to Noviembre 1901"; Jofré é Hijos to Aramayo, Francke, Tarija, August 4, 1902, "1902–1903 Tarija: From Octubre 15/901 to Febrero 2/902," Archivo COMIBOL, Tupiza.

13. "Diario, Junio 1849–Septiembre 1850," June 12–13, 1850, 57–59, AETOD.

14. See, for example, José Manl. Sánchez to Francisco B. O'Connor, Caraparí, Feb. 14, 1833, MG, vol. 12, no. 32, ANB.

15. "Juicio ejecutibo instaurado por D. Ignacio Justiniano contra Joaquín Ligeron por cantidad de 652 pesos," 1869: 334, f. 7, Fondo Prefectural, Archivo de la Casa de Cultura de Tarija. Given what we know about Tarija merchants in the nineteenth century, it is almost certain that the "efectos" Ligeron referred to were textiles or clothes. See Langer and Hames. It is unlikely that Ligeron actually charged the Indians money; the peso amount in the court case only represented the value of the goods sold on credit, to be noted in the Bolivian court.

16. Angélico Martarelli, *El Colegio Franciscano de Potosí y sus misiones: Noticias históricas,* 2d ed. (La Paz, 1918), 326; the estimate for the 1920s is my own. Also see Chervin, *Anthropologie,* 82.

17. De Nino, *Etnografía,* 204. Maintaining various wives was a necessity for the chief, because he needed the women to produce corn beer, called *cangüi,* for the many festivals he sponsored.

18. Benjamín Villafañe, *Orán y Bolivia a la márjen del Bermejo* (Salta, 1857), 37.

19. Ramón E. Cortés and José Manuel Padilla, "Estadística de la Provincia del Azero año 1927," in Eulogio Ostria Reyes, *Informe Prefectural: Departamento de Chuquisaca* (Sucre, 1927), 103, ANB.

Chapter 5

Chile in the Belle Epoque: Primitive Producers, Civilized Consumers

Benjamin Orlove and Arnold J. Bauer

We are primitive producers but civilized consumers.
—Enrique Molina, Rector of the
Universidad de Concepción (1874–95)

I. Introduction

Like many Latin American countries, Chile became closely integrated into the world economy after the 1870s with the rise of export economies. Chilean copper and nitrates had their counterparts in Colombian coffee, Venezuelan petroleum, Argentine beef and wheat, and other exports of food, fibers, and minerals. And, as in the other Latin American countries, this Chilean development toward the outside—*"desarrollo hacia afuera"*— proved less long-lasting than was hoped, collapsing in the world depression of the 1930s. In Chile, as in other countries, this cycle, running roughly from 1870 to 1930, has attracted scholarly attention not only from historians and social scientists interested in developmental economics and neocolonial relations, but also from novelists and essayists drawn to the extravagant excesses and tragic social consequences of this heady period—the "belle epoque" of Latin American history.

In this chapter, we turn to Chile in order to establish a new balance in the treatment of this period. Many writers have focused on the "export economies," often within frameworks of modernization and dependency analysis, while others have ignored the economic dimensions of historical change in this period altogether. We seek to explore the virtually unexamined reciprocal process of "import economies." Our inquiry required a greater emphasis on social and cultural circumstance and so in one sense our approach reflects the turn in academic fashions from political economy to questions of culture and identity. At the same time, we wanted to underpin our social and cultural discussion as best we could with systematic evidence. Chile appealed to us because its statistical service, unique in Latin America, provides complete runs of import data beginning when we wanted to begin, from the last third of the nineteenth century onward. And, unlike figures on, say, agricultural production or population, the information gathered in the customs houses for tax purposes are relatively reliable. So we have fairly good runs on several hundred imported items from aeroplanos and ajo (airplanes and garlic) through champagne, jewels, and lace to zapatos (shoes). At times we have been driven quite mad trying to reconcile measures—for a few years, for example, "pianos" are taxed by the kilo—and to cope with changing forms. Coffee, for example, was imported in beans, ground, and in powder. Economic measures were a problem as well; it was difficult to incorporate data on shifting exchange rates, and virtually impossible to address issues of inflation. In this chapter, we have focused on three sets of goods (wine; hot drinks like coffee and tea; houses and furnishings) for which there are long runs of fairly complete and unproblematic import statistics, and for which other qualitative sources, such as consular reports, memoirs, and travelers' accounts, are available.

The Chilean case also offers extensive local writing on this period. We were particularly fascinated with the accounts of the acerbic criticism leveled at the spending habits of the belle epoque elites. Many writers point to the extravagant journeys to Europe, the immodest mansions or lavish banquets, of the *clase derrochadora,* "the spendthrift class," the squandering arrogant group of uninhibited consumers (Vial 1981, 2: 629, 642 ff.), who also appear in varying guises in the academic and anglophone literature as well. We felt that this was a firm beginning for our analysis: views from without and within that could complement each other.

During those decades after the 1870s, when favorable conditions in the world economy led to an unprecedented surge in export earnings, did a "clase derrochadora" and the state it dominated waste the opportunity to invest the earnings in local industry, squandering its wealth instead on excessive foreign travel and expensive imports? Did it matter that reference groups were foreign—and consequently that the goods consumed by Chileans furthered European industrial growth but not their own? Did the Latin American elite's unquenchable thirst for foreign goods inhibit capital formation at home? These questions, raised before by contemporary writers, must remain quantitatively inconclusive in this essay, but we believe that we add new understanding to the cultural debate. We can at least address the question of the existence and dynamic of the *clase derrochadora* in the sense of a distinct group of high-living wealthy.

To anticipate our findings, we give, as anthropologists and historians so often do, an answer that is not quite a yes or a no. The term *clase derrochadora* suggests that the great fascination for imports was confined to a single class and a single period. We show a greater range within Chile, since other groups were also attracted to imports, and the demand for foreign goods preceded rather than followed the export bonanza. In addition, we open the relation between European fashions and European goods; some goods produced in Chile seemed European to the Chileans, while other goods imported from other countries seemed Chilean rather than foreign.

In our endeavor to explain this great expansion of imports, we have focused on three forces at work in Chile during the nineteenth and twentieth centuries. The first of these, to which we have already alluded, can be termed the macroeconomic forces: the shifts in the international economy that made foreign goods far cheaper in Chile than they had previously been. This trade, controlled by Spain throughout most of colonial rule, grew slowly when Spain loosened restrictions on foreign trade in the eighteenth century and when republican governments established the freer trade policies after Independence in the 1820s. The conjuncture for the rapid growth came in the last third of the nineteenth century as a revolution in steam and rail drove global transportation costs downward, permitting the shipment of products whose bulk or weight relative to value had previously excluded them from world trade. The discovery and export of sodium nitrate and copper from the 1870s on contributed to private fortunes and also yielded unanticipated state revenue, which allowed urban improvements, the extension of railroads, and the expansion of state bureaucracies and public education. Export earnings were not felt primarily in the mining sector itself, which was dominated by foreign owners, but in the rising flood of pesos that ultimately came to rest on the high reef of new merchants, bankers, *"agricultores progresistas,"* and bureaucrats thrusting upward through the older crust of traditional landowners. In lands just recently wrested from the Mapuche Indians in the south, one José Bunster managed in two decades to amass a huge fortune and capped his social ascent in 1900 by paying 60,000 pesos (then equivalent to some 12,000 pounds sterling) at the annual auction of box seats in the prestigious municipal theater, nudging aside its owner, a member of the traditional elite (Vial Correa 1981, 1: 2, 629). From the mid-1880s on, constant erosion of the Chilean peso against the pound sterling and the dollar enabled landowners and miners to pay their workers in diminished wages. At the same time, substantial earnings, concentrated in a fairly small segment of society, permitted a volume of imports that, both to the older elite and the increasingly militant layer of critics and working class intellectuals—themselves a result of the new prosperity—seemed excessive and gaudy.

In our view, though, the macroeconomic forces alone do not account for the growth of imports. Our second set of forces consist of the use of status markers in a postcolonial context. We do not merely wish to include Chile as yet another instance of the well-established principle within anthropological studies of consumption, the near-universal tendency of humans to represent status differences by the ownership, use, and display of goods—a tendency illustrated both by the smallest, simplest, and most autarkic populations, in which dress and often diet vary for men and women, for the young and the old, and by larger, more complex, and more interdependent societies, in which goods can also mark class position, caste membership, political status, and religious affiliation. We suggest instead that there are certain dilemmas in the use of goods to mark status in postcolonial nations such as nineteenth- and twentieth-century Chile.

When Spain's colonies achieved independence, they did not merely become autonomous republics; they entered a world of nations, still fairly new at the time. Their inhabitants used goods to mark two sets of statuses: goods could indicate the firmness of their identity as citizens of the new and still somewhat ill-defined nations, but goods could also mark the firmness of their identity as participants in the world order of nations. This postcolonial context created the contradictory pressures to use goods to demonstrate national distinctiveness and global commonality—a contradiction that expressed itself in a tension between national and cosmopolitan styles. These pressures fell with particular severity on the politically dominant groups within these nations. In systems of rule whose parameters remained partly unresolved—granted the laborious and circumstance-filled paths that had led to Independence—the leaders felt an additional set of contradictory pressures. To support their authority, they used goods to mark their distinctiveness as a governing elite and to show their commonalities with the masses, the members of the nation that they ruled. Their claims to legitimacy thus rested on a simultaneous separation from and identification with the mass of their fellow citizens, both of which could seek an expression through the use of goods—a tension between sophisticated refinement and populist ordinariness.

These tensions appear clearly in the Republic of Chile, which has its own historically specific variants on common Latin American patterns. Finding a native population less rooted to sedentary agriculture than in Mexico or the central Andean zone, the sixteenth-century European invaders in Chile either absorbed the surviving native people into a seigneurial agrarian regime or pressed those who resisted into the temperate rain forests of the south. Over the following four centuries, there emerged a Euro-mestizo society joined by small but consequential numbers of French and Spanish Basques, and mainly entrepreneurial English, German, French, or North American immigrants. A factor unique to Chile undercut the Indianness of rural populations and thus heightened the mestizo aspect of this society. Unlike most other displaced native peoples in Latin America, the Mapuche never abandoned their military raids on the Spanish colonial settlements. The ongoing wars strengthened the identification between these settlements and the distant imperial center. It also reduced the sense of ethnic and racial diversity within colonial society, since the Indians in Chile—unlike those in many other portions of South America—were seen as distant, beyond *la frontera,* the line that separated the areas of firm colonial control from the unconquered Indians.

By the last third of the nineteenth century, the people who dominated the economic, social, and political life of Chile made up a provincially sophisticated, preindustrial urban elite. In a population of just less than 2,000,000 in 1870, about a quarter of the total lived in a handful of larger towns and cities. Santiago, the largest, still had less than 150,000, and of those, a few blocks of houses near the colonial Plaza de Armas held the dominant social and political families. The country they inhabited was still anchored in the rural world of the central valley that has been such a distinctive feature and enduring burden of Chilean history. Within little more than a decade, war against Bolivia and Peru extended Chilean boundaries a thousand miles north to enclose the nitrate and copper deposits of the Atacama desert. With that done, the victorious army was directed south finally to dispossess the Mapuche who had tenaciously resisted in turn the Inca advance, the Spanish Empire, and the Chilean Republic and thus brought under official, if not yet real, dominion the long southward curving tail of the country as far as the Straits of Magellan. This territorial expansion meant that at the same time that a burgeoning economy was rapidly drawing rural mestizo migrants into the cities, the national boundaries were extended to enclose other ethnic groups previously marginal to mainstream Chilean society. Employing the discourse of nationalism, the Chilean elite endeavored, on the one hand, to speak for and lead its less-fortunate compatriots while, on the other, it became attracted to irresistible models of foreign culture and consumption.

In their deeply engrained cultural ambivalence, the dominant groups in Chile reflected the unusual nature of their historical formation. From the sixteenth-century beginnings, the first generations of "creoles" had looked back from their urban outposts in America to Spain, and then in the nineteenth century toward England and France, for ideas, culture, and manufactures all the while maintaining a mixture of affection, bemused paternalism, and outright contempt for the people they ruled. If, however, the leaders of republican Chile saw themselves as separate from "*el pueblo*" ("the people") in ethnicity and culture, they were also bound to them by the same features. For if the former were somewhat whiter than the latter, they were both of the same faith and spoke the same language. Precisely because they could be confused with the common people, at a certain conjuncture of their history, the Chilean elites strained to stand out from their less cultured, less modern, compatriots by fervently embracing everything European and especially French and English. Imported items of consumption consequently served as markers of cultural identity for a partially segmented and socially insecure elite.[1]

This appeal of Europe created the third and final of the forces that we note: the great attraction of modernity. The exposure of Chileans to the world of nations demonstrated to them the backwardness of their country—a backwardness that seemed all the more acute because the key sign of the nineteenth and twentieth century world of nations was progress. In this world, a world of rapidly changing fashions, the one fixed element was newness, understood to be improvement.

Chilean elites in particular were swept up into this world of modernity. The same innovations in steam and rail that permitted nitrate and copper to reach foreign markets also enabled more and more members of the Chilean elite to follow their exports to western Europe and, to a lesser degree, to the United States. Still immersed in a rustic culture and even accompanied by its sounds and smells, Chileans carried up the gangplank to waiting steamships in the port of Valparaíso not only their children in arms but also, in the case of one don Francisco Undurraga, the children's tutor, a cook, the wet nurse, a recently delivered burro (in case the wetnurse failed), and fifty bales of hay for the burro's feed. Agog in London, Paris, and New York, they were understandably impressed with the rapid modernization: Haussmann's broad new avenues, gas and electric lights, the sartorial glitter at the Paris Opera, a fascination with goods and fashion; a thousand unimagined things to buy. More than one traveler, returned to Santiago, found the capital unbearably dull, the citizens drab and provincial. This, however, could be partly overcome by an attempt to recreate small models of Paris or England in Chile. European architects such as Guerineau, Brunet des Baines, Theodor Burchard, or the Italian Provazoli built with imported materials; English and French landscape designers laid out formal parks and gardens surrounding both city houses and country estates nearby the capital (Vial Correa I: 2, 644 ff.). Consequently, European furniture makers, textile and leather workers, and French vintners of champagne became the beneficiaries of pounds sterling and francs earned through export.

All this was part of a much larger process, the formation of a world bourgeoisie, or at least a western bourgeoisie. As Sergio Villalobos, one of Chile's distinguished historians, remarks, the avid consumption of European goods, the journeys to Europe and contact with its intellectuals, artists, and engineers, was something more than "vain posturing or following the latest fashions. It was to place one's self at the peak of the historical moment or perhaps—it might be imagined—at the center of history." It was to be *modern.* The Opera, for example could be enjoyed "with all its truculence and tenderness" by members of the "conquering bourgeoisie" in similar and familiar circumstances across the board, "in La Scala, Covent Garden, the Met, in Manaos or in the Municipal Theatre" of Santiago (Villalobos 1987, 78–79). This last, rebuilt in 1873 to the design of one French architect, Lucien Hénault, was repaired after the 1906 earthquake with the aid of another, Emil Doyere (Vial Correa 1981, 1: 236). By entering the larger world of fashion, the new elites everywhere, from Budapest to Saint Petersburg, to Lima and Santiago, could "feel European."

These three forces overlap and even coincide in many occasions. In particular cases we cannot always detect their operation as separate entities. How much of the increased appeal of French champagne is to be attributed to the macroeconomic forces that made it cheaper, to the postcolonial dilemmas of national identity that rendered it newly attractive to those who could afford it, and how much to the sense of modernity that added to the urgency with which elites felt the need to catch up with

Europe? Whatever the particular combination of these forces that operated in each specific instance, the overall consequences were similar, because these forces supported rather than undermined each other.

We have emphasized the forces that created the belle epoque in Chile, and led to a strong impulse to consume foreign goods, especially for the elites, but for other classes as well. These forces, we wish to add, placed limits on this demand as well. Once again, the macroeconomic forces of the market deserve mention. When Chilean export revenue began to decline in the 1920s, due to the collapse of nitrate earnings, the immediate decline in the exchange rate between the peso and major European currencies reduced imports; the Depression of the 1930s cut into them much more deeply. But here, as in the rise of imports decades earlier, other factors were at work.

The postcolonial dilemmas had not ended. For all the appeal of Europe, it remained only one pole of the axis that linked cosmopolitan and nationalist styles. There were many groups who would reject what they saw as excessive Europeanization. Among these were the growing urban middle sectors of employees, lower professionals, storekeepers, and artisans, eager to consume imports though often unable to do so, resentful of the wasteful displays of the wealthy. Among these, as well, were some segments of the truly rich themselves. Where the older, essentially Hispanic landowning elite saw itself as comfortably distinct from ordinary people, the new groups—some provincial elites, ascendant mestizos, immigrant entrepreneurs—thrust to prominence by economic boom, strained both to outdo the established elite and to distance themselves from their own social origins. Some turned to French or English fashions and were seen as *estranjerizado,* or self-estranged, from their own country; others, presumably more secure in their status, looked down their noses at these pretensions, for which a new term, *siútico,* developed. A new cohort of self-consciously nationalistic writers and critics condemned from below the antipatriotic practices of an entire wasteful and "squandering class."

Our third theme, modernity, created countertrends as well. In its embrace of newness and experimentation, modernity itself created the possibility of multiple avant-gardes, making room for alternative modernities. It was during the 1920s, before rather than after the collapse of the economic prosperity of the belle epoque, that writers and painters sought uniquely Latin American forms of modernity, at times turning to popular and indigenous forms: the literary experimentations of Miguel Angel Asturias, Jorge Luís Borges, and Pablo Neruda and the Mexican muralists are only among the best-known examples of such movements (Ades 1989; Unruh 1994). At a broader level of popular culture, it was at this time that Latin American soccer, with its distinctive style of rapid passing and dramatic team work, achieved prominence in what had previously been a predominantly European, and somewhat more stolid, game: the Uruguayan championships in the 1924 Olympics in Paris and the 1928 Olympics in Amsterdam may be taken as turning points (Lever 1983, 41). At this time, new music and dances such as the tango spread in popularity, suggesting not only a populist, antielitist move, but the promise of a Latin American modernity as well (Savigliano 1995), a promise that received some international affirmation with the spread of Latin American dances during the Jazz Age (Rowe and Schelling 1991). Though less strongly marked than in some other countries, such as Mexico, this search for Latin American modernities contributed in Chile as well to a return to domestic, rather than foreign, goods.

It is to this setting that we now turn, to the Chilean belle epoque, where unprecedented opportunities for wealth and movement coincided with jumbled and ambiguous identities. More concretely, it is to the actual goods consumed in this setting, the wines, the tea and coffee, the houses and furnishings—that we now direct our attention.

II. Wine

The case of wine consumption in nineteenth- and early-twentieth-century Chile shows the Chileans' concern to make distinctions between local and European products. The antecedents of this pattern, though, reflect some unusual features of the country's colonial history within the general context of Latin America. From the beginning of the Spanish occupation in America, alcoholic drink marked clear divisions between native and European populations. In Mexico and the Andean highlands, ordinary people continued, and continue still, to consume fermented drink made from maguey or maize. Beer, introduced by the Spaniards in the sixteenth century, had little appeal to Indians. European wine was generally too expensive for daily consumption, although there is evidence that some of the cheapest European wines did filter into the native and mestizo masses. Differences between native and European alcoholic consumption were reinforced by ritual and religion. As Taylor has shown in his study of alcohol consumption in colonial Latin America, pulque, "heaven's water," was offered to the gods in pre-Hispanic feasts, and after the conquest both pulque and maize remained closely associated with "planting and harvest ceremonies, marriage, birth, death and healing." Native people before and after the conquest apparently often drank to unconsciousness; indeed, "devotion was measured by the degree of intoxication." The Spaniards, on the other hand, were inclined to see grape wine a "symbol of civilization and Catholic heritage" as well as "an essential part of the diet." After all, wine was honored by Christ Himself as a noble drink and He "chose to transform it into His most precious blood" (Taylor 1973, 38–42).

Despite this Spanish predilection, however, there were few places in Latin America where the wine grape flourished. Both the tropics and the high plateaus were inappropriate. Central Chile (and, to a lesser extent, some portions of western Argentina) were the only ideal zones for this plant, and the European settlers there were producing drinkable wine as early as 1578 when Drake's coarse-palated crew managed to liberate a few casks in Valparaíso. The early friars were intent on wine making to reduce the need and bother of imports for the Mass as well as for their own consumption. They introduced a common black *Vitis vinifera* grape. Although this grape produced wine in a few niches on the Peruvian coast, in Mexico near Querétaro and Aguascalientes and in Baja California, only in Chile and present-day Argentina did ordinary people become wine drinkers, no doubt because of the greater availability and higher quality of the local product—and also because of their identification with Hispanic culture and opposition to the indigenous culture.

Chile was unusual not only for the quantity of wine that was consumed and for the wide range of social status of people who drank it, but also for the way that wine, an essentially European beverage, came to be seen as a local and American product. Elsewhere in Latin America, the word *chicha,* which the Spaniards adopted from an indigenous language of the Caribbean to denote local fermented drinks, was restricted to fermented grains and roots; only in Chile did its primary referent become fermented fruit juice. Though in the sixteenth century the word *chicha* in Chile indicated a kind of maize beer, it soon acquired the meaning of hard apple cider and, by the mid– or late eighteenth century, included lightly fermented grape juice (Graham 1824, 126–27). *Chicha* no longer stood in opposition to wine, but instead became a kind of wine—at the first stage of fermentation, just after the skins, seeds, and stems are removed. The very grapes from which it was made also came to be seen as American. Here as well, the contrast with the other grape-growing areas of Latin America is clear. In Mexico, the Spanish varieties of grapes were known as *mission grapes* (*uvas de misión*) through their association with the missionary orders that introduced and cultivated them. In Peru and Argentina, the term *creole grapes* (*uvas criollas*) was used, suggesting the American-born descendants of European ancestors, much as the term *creole sheep* (*ovejas criollas*) was used to refer to the offspring of animals brought over in the sixteenth century. Only in Chile were they called *country grapes* (*uvas del país*) with the Spanish term having the same double meaning as the English word, referring both to a nation and to its rural areas.

Travelers' accounts from the 1820s describe wine-making techniques in the first years after Independence that resembled those of previous centuries. Barefoot men trod the grapes to express the juice, which was drained off and fermented in large clay vessels half-buried in the ground. The wine itself was transported in goatskin containers (Graham 1824, 126–27). The overall production was small. Except for an occasional drink of wine at major festivals, the bulk of the population drank *chicha* and another lightly fermented wine known as *chacolí*. The wines that had undergone a more complete process of fermentation were consumed primarily by the better off.

Other accounts from the 1850s and 1860s describe the production and consumption of wine in very similar terms (Gilliss 1855, 353–56; Subercaseaux 1936, 54–56). At this time, though, the first stirrings of change had begun to take place. Some imported wines were already available for sale, and a few landowners had introduced new techniques of production, especially the use of French rootstock first introduced in 1851 and planted heavily during the following three decades. These shifts led to rapid growth. To anticipate the quantitative figures that we will discuss in detail, wine imports, which had been quite low through the early 1870s, boomed dramatically, peaking at over 500,000 liters in 1878, and remaining over 100,000 liters per year through 1920. Domestic production increased roughly fourfold in the same period, from 50,000,000 to over 200,000,000 liters per year.

This case might seem to demonstrate the straightforward working of market forces. It could be argued that the rising incomes during this period of prosperity led to an increase in demand for luxury items such as wine, further encouraged by a downward trend in the transportation costs for the importation of foreign wines and foreign wine-making equipment. The increasing availability of capital within the country encouraged some local entrepreneurs to invest in wine production.

This economic view can be complemented by an examination of the social and cultural underpinnings of the features by which different types of wine were distinguished. This period was marked not only by an increase in the amount of wine that was consumed, but also by the development of new features by which wine was described. The earlier separation into *chichas, chacolíes,* and proper wines declined in significance, as the first two categories of unaged wines dropped sharply in popularity. A new distinction—between wines made of "French" and "country" grapes—became important. Our goal in this section is to explore the origins of this distinction and to trace the shifting terms in which this distinction was understood.

The post-Independence opening to British and French markets not only brought a new range of imports into the country but also encouraged travel and often lengthy stays in London and Paris. Wealthy Chileans acquired a taste for French wines and a particular enthusiasm for the elegant and aristocratic Bordelaise chateaux that produced them. This taste was evident among a broad sector of Chilean society. Horace Rumbold, the British consul in Valparaíso, who carefully studied the market for European goods in Chile, wrote in 1876:

> No drinkable foreign wine is obtainable under 2 to 3 dollars (8*s.* to 12*s.*) a bottle, and much of the wine figuring at that price in hotel and restaurant wine cards is of native growth, and bottled on the spot; a flaming label, possibly stating that it had formed part of an Imperial or Royal cellar dispersed in times of political trouble, sufficing to make the produce of some vineyard with an uncouth Indian name pass current for the delicate "grands crus" of the Gironde. (Rumbold 1876, 407)

The clientele in these hotels and restaurants must have included many individuals who had not left Chile, as well as those who had traveled to Europe.

As Rumbold suggested, French wines were popular, and, indeed, France remained the principal source of wine imports into Chile through the 1920s. Innumerable memoirs of this period celebrate the elaborate parties and the volume of the fine reds of Burgundy and Bordeaux, the champagnes of Moet Chandon and Veuve Cliquot and only the occasional Rhine. The volume of imports, though, began to decline soon after Rumbold wrote his description, 1878 having been the peak year, at 630,000 liters. The decline in imports is due partly to the nosedive in European production following the spread of phylloxera, a tiny louse that attacks the roots of grape plants, in the 1870s, and partly to the imposition of import duties after 1897 (Hurtado Ruíz-Tagle 1966, 162). In the 1870s, there was also an increase in Chilean production of French-style wines, made of French grapes and sold in 750 ml bottles, unlike the ordinary wines made from "country" grape varieties and sold in jugs.

The composition of imported wines also shifted as shown in figures 5.1 and 5.2, in which the curves showing the volumes and values of three kinds of wine are superimposed on each other. By the end of the nineteenth century, white wines came to form a higher proportion of the shrinking overall imports, exceeding the importation of red wines for several years during the 1890s. The very expensive champagnes formed the bulk of the imports after 1910. Several factors are at work in this sequence of types of wine. The Chilean production of French-style white wines lagged behind the reds because of the greater technical difficulty of making the whites. To preserve the natural fruity aroma of the white grape in wine, fermentation temperatures are normally held below those common in red-wine fermentation, techniques most likely not available in the early stages of fine wine making in Chile. Moreover, imperfections, such as oxidization or browning, are more visible and objectionable in the whites, all of which must have given imports an advantage to those who sought European-style wines. Finally, this sequencing suggests the possibility that elites sought to keep themselves separate from other social sectors; once Chilean red wines such as cabernets and merlots were widely available, they no longer served as well as a status marker, so the elites shifted first to importing French white wines, and then later to French champagnes.

Our quantitative information on domestic wine production is less certain, because it was easier for the Chilean government to trace the importation of foreign wines entering the country through a few ports than to keep records on the production of a large series of estates. Three different sources partly contradict each other, one suggesting increases from 28 million liters in 1862 to 36 million in 1873 to 209 million in 1914; a second, from 81 million liters in 1875 to 275 million liters in 1903; a third, from some 51 million liters in 1873 to 110 million twenty years later, reaching 275 million by 1903 (Hurtado Ruíz-Tagle 1966, 176; Chile 1915, 192; Lloyd 1915, 225). Conservatively taking the larger figures for the 1870s and the smaller ones for years after 1900, there is still an increase from about 25 liters per capita per year to about 70. The actual increase was probably larger, bringing consumption to about 85 liters per capita per year, but in either case, these levels are close to the 100 liters drunk annually by

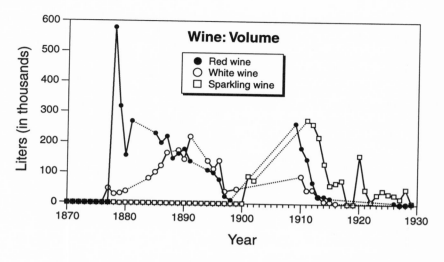

Fig. 5.1. Volume of wine imports into Chile, 1870–1929

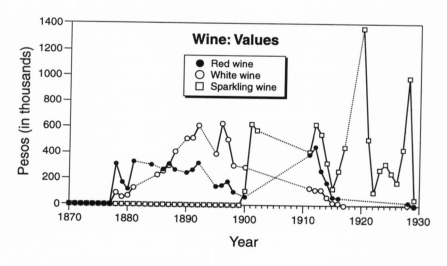

Fig. 5.2. Value of wine imports into Chile, 1870–1929

Parisians on the eve of the Revolution (Braudel 1973, 166). Much of this expansion in production was due to an increase in area planted in grapes, though an expansion of irrigation and improved management were also important.

In 1851, one Silvestre Ochagavía brought to Chile not only rooted cuttings of the noble cabernet, merlot, and white sauvignon, but also the French technicians who laid out French-style vineyards (cordon rather than Chilean head-pruned) and introduced state-of-the-art crushers, presses, and fermenters. The long-standing importance of this event in the minds of Chilean winemakers is shown by the illustration on the cover of a book entitled *Grapes and Wines of Chile* (León 1947) nearly one hundred years later: it shows an elaborate wrought-iron gate that is open to reveal a balcony from which is visible a broad plain, covered with grape vines and stretching to the Andes on the horizon. A large oval above the gate contains no words, but simply the numbers "1851." We may infer that many, if not most, of the readers of the volume would have known at once that this referred to the year that opened the period of excellent wine making in Chile.

Within thirty years after this introduction, some fifteen to twenty elegant new *viñas*—the Spanish term includes both vineyards and the winery—sprang into existence, mostly in the fertile plain within easy reach of Santiago. We may notice in passing that *Vitis vinifera* plantings throughout Europe, California, and even Argentina in the late nineteenth century were utterly devastated by phylloxera, a plague that could only be combated by grafting *Vitis vinifera* onto a resistant root stock, such as the American *Vitis labrusca.*[2] The lice, however, never crossed the Andes so there was no need for grafting. Consequently, Chile, whose plantings date from the prephylloxera era, remains today the only viticultural region in the world where grapes are produced on their original French roots, making Chilean wines, as some recent advertisements suggest, more French than the wines produced in France.

The Chilean vineyards that produced French-style wines literally created a new social space within the country. New mining and commercial families such as the Cousiño, Subercaseaux or Urmeneta as well as more enterprising members of the older landowning elite sunk their fortunes into new plantings, irrigation works, imported equipment, and also into the construction of impressive estate houses and surrounding gardens that quickly became sites for the entertainment of the local elite and visiting dignitaries as well as the odd European count or marquis. At Pirque, now in the smog belt of Santiago but once a sylvan glade, the Subercaseaux installed new cabernet vineyards and built in the center, an imposing castle in the François I style (Vial Correa 1981, 1:2, 643). The French landscapist Guillaume Renner laid out the vineyard gardens at Macul and Santa Rita. At Viña Undurraga, in the Maipo valley, the exuberant owner set out

French vines, imported barrels from Bosnia, erected over the grave of his favorite horse an oversized sculpture of the beast in white marble and designed gardens that delighted foreign presidents. Unlike the pattern of vineyards across the Andes in Mendoza, Argentina, where a smallholder Italian peasant tradition prevailed, the nineteenth-century Chilean elite imported equipment, technicians, and vines to create, in the midst of a rustic and backward countryside, the elements of a French wine industry. Through the construction of charming and often ostentatious mansions and gardens they also managed not only to confirm their status in the Chilean elite but also to further the process of Europeanizing themselves.

From the mid–nineteenth century onward, the development of Chilean viticulture was impressive not only in the new French sector but in the wines made of "country" grapes as well, produced often on more rustic estates, lacking both elaborate houses and irrigation facilities. We see, then, that in 1912 French grapes represented about one-fifth of the area planted in grapes and, since they were more likely to be irrigated than the country grapes, almost certainly a higher proportion of the total wine production of the country. Moreover, these French-style wines were substantially more expensive than ordinary wines. In 1920, the cost in Chilean pesos of a liter of wine from country varieties ranged from \$0.15–0.20, while those of French stock began at \$0.20–0.40, with the finest varieties

TABLE 5.1.   Wine Production Data in Chile

	1876		1902		1912	
	Production in Decaliters					
Wines	2,940,096	36.7%	10,619,720	77.4%	14,382,935	72.6%
Chichas	2,696,317	33.6%	560,560	4.1%	2,670,140	13.5%
Chacolíes	1,966,821	24.5%	2,309,710	16.8%	2,590,724	13.1%
Aguardientes	413,543	5.2%	231,160	1.7%	176,334	0.9%
Total	8,016,777	100.0%	13,721,150	100.0%	19,820,133	100.0%
	Area in Hectares					
French grapes	n.a.		n.a.		12,171	21.4%
Country grapes	n.a.		n.a.		44,611	78.6%
Total	n.a.		29,764		56,782	100.0%
Yield in decaliters per hectare	n.a.		461.0		349.1	

Sources: For 1876, Rumbold (1876, 496); for 1902, 1912, Lloyd (1915, 225), Chile (1915, 292).

from the best-known vineyards going for $2.75–$10.00 (Commercial Encyclopedia 1922, 988). How are we to account for the fact that French-style wines formed so large a proportion of the production, in a country with a small proportion of wealthy individuals? No doubt the models of wine drinking provided by the elite, together with a widely promoted national pride in fancier, prize-winning wine, is part of the explanation of this spread (Chile 1915, 192).

At international fairs in the late nineteenth and early twentieth centuries, the Chileans who organized their country's exhibitions placed particular emphasis on wines. These efforts, entailing the cooperation of a large number of wine makers, paid off. Chilean wines won their first major medals in France itself, at the Bordeaux exhibition of 1882, and continued to earn more: in Liverpool in 1885; a Grand Prix at the centenary fair in Paris in 1889; and a great triumph, numerous gold medals at the Pan American Exposition in 1901 in Buffalo. Chileans seemed to have been eager to show well at this last fair, where their country won more medals than any other except the United States and Mexico. The wine section of the Chilean exhibit accounted for many more medals than the much larger mining and minerals section—the base obviously behind the prosperity so evident in the entire exhibit. What distinguished Chilean wines from those of other American nations was precisely their indistinguishableness from French wines, the sole yardstick of quality in wines.

This view was stated with particular clarity in the section on wines in a book on Chile published in 1915 in English by the Chilean government with the purpose of attracting investments. "The Medoc and Borgoña of this zone [of lands close to Santiago] are not in the least inferior to the original products of these famous [French] regions" (Chile 1915, 192).

An earlier account showed the same sort of nationalist pride in which the fine quality of Chilean wines is revealed in the inability to detect them as being Chilean:

> The introduction of these wines into the United States has met with exceptional success. At a dinner party given in Philadelphia recently by a distinguished American, only the Urmeneta were served; and when the guests were told that they had been drinking a Chilean production, their surprise was unbounded. The general verdict was that Chilean wines compared favorably with the best French brands. (Wright 1904, 248)

In addition to information on these international contexts, we have a view of domestic consumption of French and French-style wines based on the collection in the Museo Histórico in Santiago of several hundred menus from banquets. This source offers evidence to the great preponderance of imported wines before 1920 at the large banquets held to honor navy officers, bishops, senior government officials, and some wealthy private individuals. Despite the evident decline in overall imports of wine after the 1870s, and the tariffs after 1897, Chilean wines appear on fancy menus only infrequently before the end of World War I. National pride seems to have surfaced in 1899, for example, at the meeting of the Chilean and Argentine presidents in Punta Arenas, in a contested border region in the far south on the Strait of Magellan. Normally an occasion for French wines, Chilean wines were served instead. The Chilean hosts no doubt intended this gesture to demonstrate the superiority of Chilean wines: both Foreign Ministries obviously could afford to purchase French wines for state dinners, but the Argentines were unable to display national wines that had won medals at international expositions. Political party leaders also made a point of serving Chilean wines at banquets where presidential candidates were announced. At other banquets, though, the guests drank wines from the Clos de Vougeot or Pommard, the "grands crus" of Bordeaux, the heavenly sauternes of Chateau d'Yquem, and other French wines. Indeed, through the years just before World War I, the predominant language of the menus themselves was French. Thereafter, the Spanish language returned, accompanied by local wines—in every instance wines made of French grapes in the French manner.

By 1920, then, Chilean wine drinking seemed to be more Europeanized precisely at time when imports declined. Wine-making techniques had shifted. Less of the immature *chichas* and *chacolíes* were produced, with *chicha* retaining its popularity only at the celebrations of national independence on September 18 and among the poor in popular districts of towns and in the countryside. Nonetheless, distinctions within these Chilean-made wines continued. The wines made from French grapes, and sold in the European-style 750 ml bottle, cost much more than the wines made from country grapes and sold in jugs. The Europeanness of these "French" wines was validated in a variety of ways—by the continued importation of small amounts of French wines that served as a kind of yardstick, by bringing foreign visitors to the vineyards, by the continued efforts to bring these wines to international expositions where European judge could evaluate their merits. Indeed, the word *vino,* "wine," has come to mark the families that established themselves during this belle epoque period. By the 1930s, *apellidos vinosos,* or "winy surnames," became a common term for the elite families that invested in these French-style vineyards: Errázuriz, Ochagavía, Cousiño, Undurraga, Subercaseaux (Edwards Bello 1994, 19). Generations removed from their nouveaux-riches forebears, these families by the end of the nineteenth century had joined the Chilean elite. The distinctions created in the nineteenth century between the country and French grapes, and between the wines made from them, still serve to mark off segments of the country.

III. Hot Drinks

The British consul Rumbold, writing in 1875, commented on the shift in the hot beverages that Chileans drank:

the increased consumption of such articles of food as rice, sugar, coffee, and tea . . . points to greater well-being among the lower orders, while the steady falling off in the imports of Paraguayan tea (*yerba mate*) would seem to show that the Chilean *peon* is being gradually weaned from the ruder tastes of his forefathers. (1876, 377)

Our review of the national import statistics shows that his account was accurate and, at least in the narrowest quantitative terms, offered a prediction of future trends that would prove to be true. However, writing in a later and more self-conscious era, we will explore the question of the definition of the "well-being" of which he wrote, and discuss the features that make certain tastes "ruder" than others. In this matter, our efforts are aided by the fact that the three hot drinks (coffee, tea, and yerba mate) offer their consumers very similar sets of substances—caffeine or closely related stimulants, bitter flavorings, and hot water.

The import figures for the period from 1870 to 1930 demonstrate that the per capita consumption of coffee and tea increased, while that of yerba mate—the major hot beverage of the late colonial period—fell off. This is shown in figures 5.3 and 5.4 (the curves showing the volumes and values of the hot drinks are stacked on each other). The rates of increase for coffee and tea are remarkable, granted the length of the period under consideration: an average annual rate of 2.8 percent for coffee, and 3.9 percent for tea. By contrast, per capita consumption of yerba mate declined, changing at a much less dramatic average annual rate of –0.3 percent.[3] Dividing this

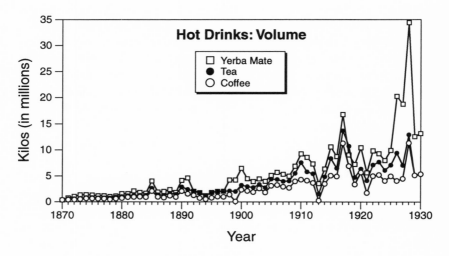

Fig. 5.3.   Volume of imports of hot drinks into Chile, 1870–1930

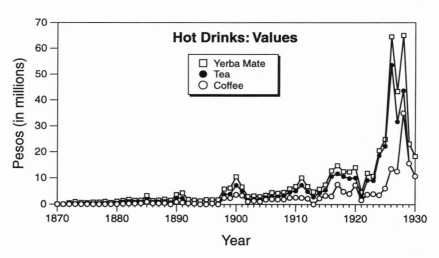

Fig. 5.4.   Value of imports of hot drinks into Chile, 1870–1930

period in half, the per capita consumption of tea grew at the dramatic pace of 5.8 percent per year in the last three decades of the nineteenth century and then slowed to the still impressive annual rate of increase of 2.2 percent in the first three decades of the twentieth century. By contrast, coffee consumption accelerated from a 2.0 percent annual rate in the former period to 3.4 percent in the latter. The decline of yerba mate slowed, going from –0.5 percent in the first period to –0.1 percent in the latter.

Rumbold wrote not only of aggregate consumption, but of the consumption of particular classes. It is much easier to demonstrate that coffee and tea were consumed almost exclusively by elites in the early decades of the nineteenth century than it is to document the spread of these beverages downward through the social hierarchy to "the lower orders" of whom Rumbold wrote. Coffee was occasionally drunk in Chile at the end of the eighteenth century—it was served to the British explorer Vancouver in 1798—and by the 1820s had become the beverage wealthy families served after dinner. Unlike mate, it was served in the European manner, brought to the table in a pot, from which it was poured into individual cups. The expansion of coffee was linked to the eponymous institution, the café or coffee shop. The first of these appeared in Santiago around 1808 (Silva Vargas 1992, 315), and others followed there and in Valparaíso, and, later on in the century, in the mining camps in the north. Silva Vargas suggests that the cafés began to increase in number in the 1820s and 1830s, and to become fully established by the 1840s. They were places where men gathered to drink coffee and, on occasion, alcoholic beverages. Billiard tables, another recent introduction to Chile, were also common there. They drew almost exclusively from the wealthy and the small middle groups of artisans, sales clerks, and office workers, since poorer men went to other establishments (*chinganas, picanterías,* and *bodegones*) to drink *chicha* and other alcoholic drinks (324). Many of the foreign males in Chile, which included many single British and French citizens who were employed by trading firms, spent a good deal of their free time in the cafés. By 1872, there were twenty-nine cafés in Santiago (Tornero 1872, 93), where foreigners were still a large proportion of the clientele. These associations with dinner and with public places seem to have lasted well into the nineteenth century and into the twentieth: the collection of menus of banquets describing meals served in public places include seventeen that mention the hot drinks served after the meals. Of these, coffee alone was served at thirteen, both tea and coffee at four. It does not matter greatly whether this difference indicates that tea was actually served less frequently, or that the word "café" on a menu sometimes meant "hot drinks like coffee and tea will be served"; in either case, coffee seems to have been the normative drink at banquets.

By contrast, tea—also apparently an upper-class drink at the time— appears to have been consumed almost exclusively at home. A number of sources report that it was served not at the end of dinner, but later in the evening, to guests who would gather for conversation, card-playing, and singing. As with coffee, a pot of the beverage was brought to the guests and then poured into individual cups. On the occasions when women would visit each other (the men of the family were presumably out at cafés, clubs, or *chinganas*), tea was almost always served, rather than coffee. Like coffee, tea seemed associated with newness and Europeans. Eduard Poeppig, a German scientific traveler in 1827 described an evening visit to a well-off family as follows:

> While the older people were drinking mate through a *bombilla,* the younger generation drank cups of Chinese tea, [a product] whose consumption has been propagated for some years through the influence of foreigners. (Silva Vargas 1992, 319)

One may speculate on the rise of the coffeehouse but not the teahouse: the greater availability of models of coffeehouses in Europe and elsewhere in Latin America; the economies of scale in toasting and grinding coffee beans; the somewhat feminine character of tea that rendered it less appropriate to public places. Whatever the differences, both coffee and tea increased in popularity.

Rumbold's claims about the "lower orders" are difficult to substantiate, though it seems plausible that the large increases in consumption in the decades after 1870 were due to an increase in the proportion of coffee and tea drinkers in the population as well as an increase in the per capita consumption among the established drinkers. Coffee does seem to have been widely consumed in the mining camps and northern mining ports by the 1870s. The first accounts of coffee consumption among the working poor in Santiago appear in the first decades of the twentieth century. Reports in the Boletín de la Oficina del Trabajo detailed the food expenditures of 94 working-class families between 1912 and 1925, and listed coffee as a frequently consumed item (DeShazo 1983, 64–67). Apparently many of them were making purchases, presumably small ones, of ground coffee, since a newspaper article reports that coffee was sometimes adulterated with sawdust (DeShazo 1983, 67).

Rumbold's claims about the class basis of the third beverage, at least, are indisputable. His associations of yerba mate consumption with "forefathers" and with rudeness are substantiated by many accounts. For the question of the forefathers, at least, we can note that the habits of mate drinking were essentially unchanged from Graham's visit over fifty years earlier and, indeed, from patterns of the colonial period; we can even trace the pre-Columbian origins of these customs. Yerba mate or Paraguayan tea (*Ilex paraguensis*), a member of the holly genus, is native to the fluvial reaches of the Río de la Plata. Central to ceremonial practice of the pre-Hispanic Guaraní, its use spread after the conquest through the mestizo and white population fanning outward to Brazil, the Andean region, and Argentina. Promoted in the seventeenth century by the Jesuits, ever eager for revenue to support their educational and missionary enterprise, merchants carried tons of mate on mule back across the Andes into Chile, where it had been previously unknown (Garavaglia 1983, 35). Although now and then taken as a cold *refresco* or drunk in cups (the so-called Jesuit tea), mate is characteristically prepared in the *honda de la calabaza* or gourd and then sipped through the *bombilla* (usually a reed straw or silver tube, with a filter at one end, though *bombillas* made of wood and even bird bone are also recorded). Mate might be drunk several times during the day but especially with breakfast and again in the late afternoon. From its distant indigenous origin, mate was an intensely convivial or communitarian drink. Rarely consumed in public places—there were no mate cafés or mate-houses—small groups of people passed the gourd among themselves and took sips from the same bombilla.

Everyone who writes about mate consumption underlines this feature:

> It is difficult to transmit, to those who do not enjoy mate, the deep feelings shared in passing the bowl from hand to hand, a feeling accentuated by using always a common straw. (Garavaglia 1983, 47)

This practice also commonly cut across class lines; the foremost modern writer on mate believes that the drink had the effect of subverting the barriers of colonial society, "of uniting people beyond their differences" (Garavaglia 1983, 47). In Chile it became, in effect, the national hot drink by the end of the colonial regime, with the wealthy using elegant objects made of silver, the poor more ordinary ones of plant material.

This very feature, however, offended most of the foreign visitors who poured into Chile after Independence and made it difficult for them to associate with Chileans who regularly consumed mate. Maria Graham, generally open to new experience, was repelled. "I'm attracted very little," she sniffed, "at the idea of using the same tube that has served a dozen other people" (1824, 119). The very communitarian ritual practice that helps explain its widespread popular use and its persistence well into the twentieth century was also difficult to accept by those Chileans who sought "to acquire more European, or more modern, forms of behavior" (Silva Vargas 1992, 319–20).

Rumbold erred only in believing that the rural populations were "being gradually weaned" from the custom. The descriptive sources on rural Chilean life are unanimous on the great frequency of mate drinking among rural populations well into the 1950s and 1960s and indeed up to the present. We do not have precise quantitative figures to separate urban and rural consumption of this drink in the period from 1870 to 1930. However, a number of factors suggest that the very gradual overall decline in per capita consumption reflects a combination of a sharper decline in urban consumption and an increase in rural consumption. The virtually complete silence on the consumption of yerba mate by urban workers in the 1910s and 1920s, for example, suggests that this class, like the urban wealthy, consumed much less of this beverage than of coffee.[4]

One detailed source suggests the relative importance of these three beverages among the wealthy. Describing imports of hardware into Chile in 1915, Havens (1916, 134–35) discusses, among other items, what he calls "the finer decorated class of enameled ware"—a set of goods that are "purchased only by people with a reasonable amount of money," and can afford these items that are "generally expensive, but [whose] appearance and presentation are excellent." He notes

> a considerable quantity is also sold of series of covered cans or boxes of cylindrical form, which come in sets, nested together, each having lettering on the outside indicating what should be put in it: "Café" (Coffee), "Té" (Tea), "Azúcar" (Sugar), "Sal" (Salt), "Pimienta" (Pepper), "Ají" (Red pepper), "Yerba" (paraguay tea), and "Comino" (Cumin seed).

To the manufacturers, nested canisters are convenient to ship, since they take up far less volume than other items that cannot be packed one inside another. They may also suggest a change in the patterns of storage of some foodstuffs and condiments—no longer kept in a kitchen or storeroom off a back patio, but now inside the main house itself. The German manufacturers of the fine enamelware, who took care to tailor their production to the requirements of specific markets,[5] chose a specific ordering of these items, including the three substances for hot drinks. Coffee and tea are the first ones, probably because they were consumed in larger quantities and because they were associated as more modern. Mate occurs far down on the list; to the families that used this sort of canister, it would be an item that they would want to have in their kitchens, but one that they used no more of than they would of the spices that flavored their dishes.

Matters of price offer a partial explanation for the retention of yerba mate among the rural poor. The price data indicate that tea and coffee were generally more expensive than yerba mate, on a price per unit weight basis. (These figures also explain the more rapid growth of tea consumption in the first half of the period, and of coffee in the second; both spread more rapidly during periods of slower price increases.) Moreover, we may infer that yerba mate was even more inexpensive when one calculates the cost per drink, since the British travelers—familiar with tea-drinking and, one may assume, attuned to variations in its preparation—comment that hot water was poured repeatedly on yerba mate leaves and make no similar comment for tea. However, the matter of price does not explain the switch from yerba mate to coffee among the urban working poor, who were heavily constrained by low wages, and who often mobilized politically to keep basic foodstuffs at affordable levels. For the rural poor, mate's appeal may have lain in its familiarity and for the air of sociability that it established, both among the more settled service tenant (*inquilino*) and the more mobile day-worker (*peón*) populations.

For the urban working poor, at least, an explanation of their consumption could include the question of status emulation—the imitation of

TABLE 5.2. **Price of Selected Hot Beverages in Chile (in pesos per kilo)**

Year	Coffee	Tea	Yerba Mate
1871	0.31	1.10	0.15
1880	0.44	1.96	0.20
1890	0.40	1.50	0.20
1900	1.43	2.00	0.49
1910	0.59	1.50	0.40
1920	1.24	2.77	0.91
1930	1.91	5.31	1.21

Source: Chile, Oficina Central de Estadística. Estadística Comercial de Chile.

people higher up the social hierarchy. Most of the wealthy abandoned yerba mate early, attracted to coffee and tea for their associations with European customs, to tea for its association with British civility and gentility, and to coffee, if Silva Vargas's account is correct (1992, 334–43), for the freedom of conversation in the coffeehouses. The "rudeness" that Rumbold mentions may also have been a factor; the passing around of the gourd and bombilla may have been seen as inelegant and somewhat rustic. In this sense, a theme of refinement and decency can be noted, following closely Norbert Elias's notion of the "civilizing process" as a gradual increase of constraint on bodily functions. Much as it became more elegant in Chile to serve wine in small bottles rather than large jugs, to live in houses in which rooms had clearly defined functions and in which animals were more clearly removed from the spaces of human habitation, so too the drinking of hot beverages entailed the serving of individual portions in cups, rather than circulating a common drinking device.

What makes so great a difference between drinking coffee and drinking yerba mate? Both were imported into Chile. Only a few hundred kilometers separated the Brazilian estates where the trees were grown whose berries are used for the former from the Paraguayan and Argentine estates where the trees were grown whose leaves were used for the latter. They were used to produce similar beverages—bitter hot drinks containing caffeine. Nonetheless, the appeal of foreign goods—the central theme of this chapter and this volume—lay at the heart of the attractiveness of coffee and, to turn once more to Rumbold, the "rudeness" of *yerba mate*. Coffee, and tea as well, were new, and seen as new, while yerba mate was old. Coffee and tea were urban, linked to the coffeehouse and the parlor, while yerba mate acquired a rural tone, even in the few instances when it was detached from the gourd and *bombilla*. As with the differences between varieties of wine, then, the relative Europeanness of these hot beverages was constructed, rather than innate.

IV.   Houses

Of the consequences that the import boom in the belle epoque brought to Latin America, none have been as well described, both by contemporary observers and by historians of later eras, as the transformations of national capitals from small provincial towns into large elegant cities. Gas lighting, streetcars, fancy new theaters, and large mansions, whose arrivals have been described for Rio de Janeiro, Buenos Aires, Lima, Mexico City, and even smaller cities such as San José, came to Santiago as well, altering not only the city itself, but, by rapidly shifting the contrasts between the housing of the elite and the poor, the urban and the rural dwellers, changing the social significance of space in the entire nation.

The houses of the wealthy in Santiago, well-described in memoirs and in travelers' accounts, are also illustrated in many sketchbooks and books of engravings. Through the 1850s, the rich lived close to the center of town in large houses. These houses fronted directly on the street. Their entrances, typically consisting of a pair of huge wooden doors, would open onto a large patio, from which a number of rooms could be reached. Lying further back from the street would be a second and perhaps even third patio, surrounded, like the first, by rooms. Some of the houses had second stories, reached from exterior staircases within the patios; galleries running around the interiors of the patios gave access to these rooms. Coming off the first patio might be a few larger and better furnished rooms, a living room and a dining room, but most of the rooms were simply rooms, not dignified with any specific name, shifting in use from sleeping quarters to kitchens to storage. A surprising feature of these houses was their accessibility. When the main doors to the street were opened, many different sorts of people could walk in and proceed to the appropriate portion of the house: genteel visitors usually arrived by coach and would go to the living room off the first patio, while the interior patios were the destination of those of lower classes—vendors and peddlers, domestic servants, workers from estates owned by the family who brought wagons of produce.

The great houses on the rural estates themselves were generally similar, a series of rooms, one little different from another except for a larger living room and dining room. At most the configuration of the rooms might be different—the rooms forming an L or an H rather than a series of enclosed patios with only one entrance (Pereira de Correa 1992). Here, too, the dependent workers had access to many of the rooms in the house.

This lack of contrast between urban and rural houses that we have noted for the rich also characterized the poor, who lived in small shacks of one or two rooms, made often of wood, sometimes of adobe, usually with porches to provide protection from the sun and rain and with outbuildings for cooking and storage. These poorer houses had literally a marginal setting, located at some distance from the centers of towns or from the larger houses of the estate owners. Accessible to rich and poor alike were the public spaces. All classes would gather for masses on saint's day celebration in the churches—often large, and located on squares, in town; and usually small, and adjacent to the main hacienda house, in rural areas. There were other broad open areas—in Santiago, the Alameda, a wide tree-lined avenue where different social classes strolled on Sundays, or gathered for the eighteenth of September, Independence Day; on the estates, the large empty fields at some distance from the main house where workers and owners would gather for the threshing of wheat or the annual roundup and branding of cattle and for the festivities that followed. In this fashion, the houses of the rich and the poor, along with the public areas, formed single social and spatial units.

The new houses that began to appear in Santiago in the 1860s brought sharp discontinuities with this pattern of similarity between urban and rural houses and this characteristic mixing of social classes. Though these houses differed somewhat by period, they shared a number of features. Many were freestanding, usually two or three stories high, and frequently with mansard roofs. Although they were not literally imported from Europe, they nonetheless succeeded in replicating the houses that Chileans, beginning to travel abroad more frequently in the 1850s, had seen there. Often designed by French architects, they followed French styles and incorporated many imported elements, from pianos to doorknobs and hinges. The dozens of private residences illustrated in Tornero (1872) with engravings based directly on photographs show the sharp differences between the new and the old. In this case, quantitative data on imports are more difficult to follow, since they tend to be reported in kilograms—a less useful measure of consumption for pianos or sofas than for wine or coffee.

A detailed account written in 1916 by an American commercial attaché, however, does document the importance of French styles in architecture. The author, Havens, sought to find markets for American hardware in Chile. Though the United States already dominated the market for goods as diverse as hammers, pitchforks, coffee grinders, and sandpaper, and might have expanded its market in others, he was pessimistic about wresting the monopoly of goods associated with architecture from the French:

> The owner seeks the assistance of an architect for all the work to be done. If the owner is wealthy or a member of one of the leading families, he has probably traveled in Europe; in any event, his ancestors and relatives, because of their European origin, have followed the European styles in house construction. The architect has, ordinarily, obtained his higher training in France, and has returned from the

country imbued with ideas wholly French. Although he would not be likely to buy in France because of sentiment, he, and the owner also, might naturally be inclined to favor the French design. It should be clearly understood that a century of training, even in the matter of door knobs, is not easily overcome. . . . One of the notable features about Chilean buildings is that the windows, being of the French type, generally open like a door. In order to close them, a vertical bolt is required and in this article there is some unimportant local competition. The shutters are on the inside, almost universally of solid wood, and have little latches and hinges. . . . Most doors leading from a corridor to an apartment or suite of rooms, as well as many inner ones, are double, opening like the French windows and having panels of glass covered by wooden blinds on the inside. It is not unusual, then, for an important door or window to have 2 door bolt sockets, 18 to 24 hinges of various sizes, 4 complete latches and catches, the locking up-and-down bolt, and the transom locks, besides the door locks—with the possible addition of a chain with hooks for more secure fastening. The system is very expensive, highly unsatisfactory, exceedingly impractical, but the people like it. This is the only (although an entirely sufficient) reason for its existence. (114–15)

These houses were more removed from the public world of the street— set back from the sidewalk at some distance, often behind wrought-iron fences. Much greater scrutiny was applied to visitors, who now needed to walk down a path and pass through a semiprivate space before arriving at the front door, if they were of the same class as the owner, or who came to a rear entrance, if they were not. Moreover, because of their location in a newer part of town near the Club Hípico, they were somewhat further from the central squares and principal churches. Indeed, these new French-style houses were so different from the older ones that the grander ones were described by a new term. No longer "houses" (*casas*), by the 1890s they began to be called "palaces" (*palacios*).

As the wealthy moved from the center of town, they often rented their former houses to the poor. Demand for housing was high, as the population of Santiago grew more rapidly than that of the country as a whole. Entire families moved into single rooms, so that dozens of families might live in a house that had once been the residence of a single wealthy family and their dependents. These converted mansions became known ironically as *conventillos*, "little convents." Other districts of rough one- and two-room houses for the poor began to appear on the edge of town, especially to the south and west.

This spatial segregation was rendered sharper by the shift of the wealthy to less public forms of social activity. Though saints' day celebrations continued to have some importance well into the twentieth century, the weight of the church as a center of public social activity began to decline, especially after the expansion of public education in the 1870s and the rise of civil marriages and lay cemeteries in the 1880s. The shift from religious to secular institutions was paralleled by the growth of public places for which admission fees were charged. The Teatro Municipal, destroyed by fire in 1870, was rebuilt along plans designed by a French architect in 1873. Though the noise from the conversation often made it difficult to hear the actors' lines and the cigar smoke created enough haze to impede the view of the stage, it was a popular spot for socializing—women, girls, and young boys visited each other in their boxes (*palcos*), while the men and older boys would congregate in the bar and café (Subercaseaux 1936, 64–65). Social clubs and cafés also grew in popularity, while the elite began to take their strolls not in the more mixed-class Alameda but in the Cerro Santa Lucía, the hill on the edge of town whose rough slopes had been rebuilt in the form of walks and grottoes. There was a shift in marketing as well. Covered arcades with stores were established in the final years of the nineteenth century, and the first department store, Gath Chavez, was opened in 1910 (Commercial Encyclopedia 1922, 830). It became acceptable for women to stroll through the arcades or to go out shopping in the department stores, reflecting both a relaxation of the strict standards that had governed upper-class female comportment and a more effective class segregation of public space. These new social spaces allowed for separation not only of rich and poor, but also among the rich themselves, highly conscious of distinctions between old and new money, between the genuinely elegant and the boorish parvenus who could not always buy their way into social clubs or who might not know which café was the truly fashionable one.

The hacienda houses continued relatively unchanged: the covered arcade that ran the length of the house might be enclosed, or an area in front of the house might have a garden planted in it, but the sprawling one-story form of the house remained the same. If anything, these houses were used less frequently, as the social life in Santiago gained in appeal. The horse races in the countryside, a form of popular and elite entertainment for the first two-thirds of the nineteenth century, took on a more rustic quality after European-style racetracks were opened close to Santiago, starting with the Club Hípico in 1869. The major exceptions were houses on haciendas close to Santiago, especially those that produced French grapes. Otherwise, older architectural patterns continued, as Havens noted. Familiar with the American pattern, in which farmers sought to improve their houses and barns, he was struck with the fixity of rural architecture. He mentioned that the American-style barn, stable, and garage doors, mounted with pulleys or rollers on horizontal tracks, were

> not in general use. The small consumption is in club stables, riding clubs, army stables, and storage buildings. The greatest demands is in the ports, where material is held in stock, where carts go in and out, or on the properties of foreign mining companies. Practically all stores [in large towns] use vertical roller doors [made locally with imported wheels, chains, and axles] in place of the sliding door, and in rural districts swing doors are common. The nitrate companies of the north use a few sliding-door fixtures, and a small quantity is sold throughout the country, but nothing at all comparable to the amount that the same population would require in the United States. . . . [E]ducation will be required before the old Spanish practice of making swinging doors of enormous size can be abolished. This education will hardly come through distribution of catalogues or advertising matter, since the numerical majority of consumers are not those reached by such means. It will rather come with the general development of American trade and the American entrance into mining, agriculture, and retail business. . . . An enormous advantage might be secured for the use of many articles of American hardware by locating a farm manager on large Chilean properties, where the wealthier class might desire to take advantage of the excellent training young men receive in modern farming in the United States. (1916, 128)

While the urban poor began a new mode of housing in the *conventillos,* the rural poor continued to live in simple shacks. These, too, were not called houses (*casas*) but rather shacks (*ranchos* or *chozas*). Their crowded squalor attracted attention from foreign visitors, struck by the contrasts of wealth.

While descriptions of Santiago such as Graham's in the 1820s and Gilliss's in the 1850s noted the relatively homogenous character of architectures in the city, Rumbold in 1876 commented that the city seemed "like slices of Paris dropped down here and there in the midst of a huge, straggling Indian village" (366). Once again, he demonstrated a kind of prescience. The economic expansion of the following decades did not lead this contrast between rich and poor to diminish; if anything, it grew as the elite withdrew from some public spaces into their increasingly ostentatious palaces.

In 1908, Orrego Luco wrote a novel to demonstrate the decadence of the upper classes. His main characters, idle rich, were filled with the desire for foreign goods. Eager to attend clubs and parties, they neglected their families and eventually succumbed to physical and moral decay. He titled this novel *Casa grande,* Big House, the houses serving as a metonym for the class whose materialism, emptiness, foreignness, and inauthenticity he sought to indict. This book created a stir in Santiago; Orrego Lugo describes how many of his former friends and associates snubbed him in the streets after its publication. Whatever the accuracy of his portrayal of a class, he seems to have been right on the mark in his choice of using houses to stand for classes.

V.   Conclusions

The three sets of goods that we have examined in detail allow us to make some tentative conclusions regarding the consumption of imports in Chile in the nineteenth and early twentieth centuries. We wish to stress three features of the spread of these foreign goods.

First, the demand for these goods was *early,* in the sense that it appeared before (rather than with, or after) the expansion of mining and the growth of exports. The appetite for European goods came into being well before the mining booms after 1870 that financed the expansion of imports through an increase in income and a strengthening of the national currency. To take only two examples, many Chileans eagerly visited the cafés that opened in the first decades after Independence, and they made considerable effort to obtain French wines and French grape rootstock in the 1850s.

Second, the demand for these goods was *broad,* in the sense that it touched, to some degree or another, a large proportion of the population of Chile. To offer two examples again, foreign cloth virtually eliminated homespun cloth in much of the core region of the central valley by 1895, even among the poorest categories of agricultural workers, and greatly reduced it even in the more remote regions further south. Coffee also reached a wide proportion of the population, including most of the working poor in the cities.

Third, the demand for these goods was *uneven,* in the sense that it affected different social classes and groupings in Chile to widely varying degrees. Chilean households ranged from the wealthy aristocracy in the cities, who prided themselves on the virtual absence of Chilean goods from their French-style mansions, to the rural poor, who might have only some imported cloth or tools (English hoes were especially popular [Havens 1916, 105]). In between these extremes lay a vast number of different positions. Lacking detailed household inventories, we are unable to map out precisely the distribution of foreign goods in the intermediate sectors, but we note, for example, that some urban middle classes could afford the "French" wines produced in Chile. This group probably overlapped considerably with the one-seventh of the population in whose bathrooms towels hung from French or German towel racks (126), as opposed to the other six-sevenths who hung towels from nails, or who lacked towels, or who lacked bathrooms. It may also have included those who developed new ways to use these expensive foreign goods: "Practically no child has two roller skates, generally using one to ride on and pushing with the other foot" (153). A bit lower down the social hierarchy were the "[estate] foremen, who "like[d] a[n imported German pocket]knife with tools in it—such as a corkscrew, saw, file, hoof cleaver, and that sort of thing—of ordinary quality, and the cheaper the better" (109). Still other intermediate positions undoubtedly existed.

The patterning of goods demonstrates the importance of market forces—the shifts in the price of goods and the income of different classes of Chileans. Indeed, there seems to be an association between the relative price of a good, the timing of its arrival, and the extent of its spread. The great increase of global coffee production in the nineteenth century brought that beverage below a threshold of affordability for wide segments of Chilean society, whose incomes seem to have risen somewhat during the economic expansion of the late nineteenth and early twentieth centuries. Coffeehouses were common in Santiago in the 1840s, while tea became popular as an evening drink for the elite at the same time or even earlier. Coffee and tea spread throughout the society and became strongly rooted in the habits of the population; coffee consumption did not fall off sharply with the advent of the Depression. The "French" wines, requiring greater investment in production and processing facilities, remained somewhat more expensive, within the reach only of upper and middle sectors. These wines entered a bit later, becoming popular around the 1850s, and did not spread as widely. Though the unaged *chichas* and *chacolies* declined in popularity, the bulk of the population continued to drink "country" wines—crude jug wines, rather than expensive "French" wines of named varieties sold in bottles. The fashion of European-style houses began even later, around the 1860s, and remained restricted to the narrow sector of the urban elite who could afford the French-style "palaces." The cheapest goods came in first and spread most widely through the society.

Nonetheless, social, cultural, and political forces can complement and expand these economic arguments. We have already noted that the market forces do not offer a full account of the arrival of imported goods in Chile. We also suggest that the use of imported goods did not merely reflect already existing divisions between rich and poor and between the city and the countryside. Since the patterns of use made these divisions more evident and impeded social interaction across them, it seems fair to say that imported goods widened the gaps between groups that had already existed. In the first decades after Independence, most Chileans drank some sort of fermented juice of local grapes, whether aged wine for the rich or *chicha* for the poor; they drank *yerba mate,* though the rich might have fancy silver *bombillas* while the poor used crude ones made from straws. It was only in the 1850s that the expansion of European and European-style wines led to a devaluation of the "country" wines in relation to "French" wines, much as the new consumption of coffee and tea led yerba mate to become a rustic old-fashioned beverage, rather than an unproblematic everyday drink. Even in housing, where there had already been greater differences in the styles (the rich living in large houses built around one or more patios, the poor in one- or two- room shacks), the introduction of French-style mansions led to greater spatial segregation of rich and poor. It seems difficult to claim that these widening gaps in the daily lives and social identities of Chileans were merely a consequence of increasing income differentials.

Many other studies have demonstrated the ways that consumption is an active sphere in social and economic systems, tied as it is to public display, to the routines, rituals, and crises of daily life, to the human body itself. We seek to explain, though, not merely why goods played so active a role in marking and shaping social difference, but also why this role fell largely to foreign goods. In our view, the critical link is the one that conjoins this import boom with Chilean independence from Spain. We recognize the importance of the other themes in nineteenth-century history (the growing prosperity, the loosening of caste-like identities with the expansion of the market economy and salaried work, the extension of political participation to broadening sectors of society with the expansion of unions and of political parties with ties to middle and working classes). Nonetheless, the foreign goods were not fashionable merely because they were new or relatively scarce. Their foreignness itself granted them a special allure. Through their use of foreign goods, the elites after the 1860s or so marked themselves not merely as wealthy (as earlier elites had done through the size of their houses and through the abundant use of silver in *bombillas,* in the trappings of their horses, and in many other items) but also as sophisticated. To the elites of Chile, like those of the other newly independent nations of Latin America, no internal source of signs of sophistication could be as effective as those that came from abroad. To lead their new nations, in cultural as well as political and economic terms, these elites had to demonstrate their differences from the masses as well as their connections with them. The public and private display of foreign goods carried this message of differences from the mass of fellow citizens for the Chilean elites, who, by mid-century, lacked the hierarchical underpinnings implicit in the corporate religious ideologies of Spanish imperial rule, and who lacked even the striking differences in color or language that separated elites and masses elsewhere in Latin America.

Foreignness and newness seemed linked in another way. The Independence that had granted Chile autonomy as a nation had also bestowed upon it a position in a world concerned with progress. This theme of modernity overlay an element of temporality on the theme of status distinctions. Country wines, yerba mate, the urban houses with multiple patios—displaced by French wines, coffee, and freestanding mansions— became not merely unfashionable, but also old-fashioned. This world of newness and progress seems largely to have bypassed the countryside— with the exception of a few outposts of urban life in the fancy vineyards and estates near Santiago. In the cities, it offered an ambivalent message: even the working poor could now drink coffee, and they might drink wine rather than *chicha* or *chacolí.* But this wine would be of the wrong sort, and there would be other signs of backwardness as well—in their simple houses, in their dress, in their exclusion from the new European-style social clubs and department stores.

In this world of social distinctions, such a concern with fashion was able to feed upon itself and grow. As sociologists of fashion have argued, a multiplicity of goods and social positions creates a great awareness of the nuances of taste and fashion. Unlike their antecedents in earlier decades, late-nineteenth-century memoirs include references to the gauche errors of the nouveaux riches (Orrego Luco 1984, 6). To the list of urban social types depicted in the lithographs and watercolors of the 1830s (Rugendas [1838] 1973; Villalobos 1973)—the effete *lacho* or dandy, the *aguatero* or water-vendor, about to whip the old horse he rides, the sullen unkempt *carretero* or ox-cart driver, goad in hand, Tornero in 1872—using engravings now as a means of illustration—added those defined as social climbers, such as the *siúticos* who pretend to have more, or better, or newer foreign goods than they really do, and the *niñas de medio pelo* (461), given to name-dropping and other pretensions, and who "sing and play instruments divinely, the piano of course, because the guitar, well that is for the more common people" (Tornero 1872, 465). His readers did not need to be told that all pianos were imported, while many guitars were locally made.

If this concern with imported goods fed on itself, it also undermined itself by creating a nationalist reaction. The urban working classes could recognize not only that some foreign goods were within their reach, but also that other such goods were not; the opulent displays of the wealthy seem to have given some force to the claims of unions and poor neighborhood groups of their rights to basic necessities. The doubts about the primacy of imported goods affected other classes as well. There had long been scattered references to the absurdity of those who aped foreign fashions (Subercaseaux notes that in the 1860s, his friends—members of the best families of Santiago—would joke about those who returned from Europe "and about their clothes which they would show off, with all the folds and wrinkles from having been packed in a trunk [for such a long time on the ocean voyage from Europe to Chile]" (1936, 86). More systematic analyses soon appeared. Cruchaga, writing in 1878, complained of the ways in which conspicuous consumption weakened the development of agriculture and industry, a point echoed by Manuel González in his 1889 essay "Luxury, Our Enemy" and by Encina in his 1911 book *Our Economic Inferiority: Its Causes, Its Consequences,* in which he criticizes "the thirst for luxury, to build mansions, to spend on carriages and jewels." This concern also took literary form as well, as in Orrego Luco's already-mentioned 1908 novel *Casa grande.* By the first decades of the twentieth century, then, this nationalist critique of foreign-oriented conspicuous consumption was already in place, and became one of the central themes of the often strident class tensions in Chile in this century—as seen in Allende's simple nationalist phrasing of his vision of well-being as "a Chile of meat pies and red wine" (*un Chile de empanadas y vino tinto*). In recent years, there has been considerable enthusiasm over the economic expansion brought to Chile by an opening to export-oriented agriculture, mining, forestry, fishing, and manufacture and by the greatly expanded availability of foreign consumer goods; this enthusiasm, however, has been tempered by the recognition of continuing gaps in living standards, a recognition stimulated by the dramatic evidence of the limitations to the circulation of foreign goods within Chilean society.

In sum, we have seen the growth of the appeal of foreign goods in Chile. We find evidence of the spendthrift class, the *clase derrochadora,* the champagne-drinking set who lived in fancy mansions—and of other consumers of imported goods as well. It is this multiplicity of goods and of consumers that we wish to stress. The line separating foreign and Chilean goods appeared again and again for many Chileans, at many points in their daily lives and at many special occasions as well. These foreign goods expressed and intensified the ambivalent relation between nationhood and modernity—a dilemma that appears far from resolved.

NOTES

1. We wish to note that in countries with marked ethnic and racial stratification, such as Peru and Brazil, elites also were eager to use imported goods as a way to confirm their distance from the lower classes. Krügeller's chapter in this book discusses such a case in detail.

2. The type of rootstock does not affect the quality of the grapes which grow on the grafted vine.

3. To calculate these rates, we took five-year averages for 1871–1875 and assigned that rate to the year 1872.5; we performed similar operations for the periods 1898–1902 (to assign a figure to 1900) and 1926–1930 (for the year 1927.5).

4. To take a modest hypothetical situation, if the per capita consumption of yerba mate is assumed to have been equal in urban and rural areas in Chile in 1870, and if urban rates fell by half between 1870 and 1930, then rural per capita consumption would have grown by an annual rate of 0.6 percent. More realistic rates of decline in urban consumption would give higher rates of growth of rural consumption.

5. Havens notes that the Germans oriented specific lines of goods to national markets smaller than Chile, such as Bolivia, and even to regional markets within these nations.

Chapter 6

Imports and Standards of Justice on the Mexico–United States Border

Josiah McC. Heyman

Introduction

Imports from the United States pervade Mexico's northern border regions. Northern Sonora offers no exception, whether we look at goods themselves, such as pick-up trucks and televisions, or we focus on contexts of imports, such as mine company stores and everyday cross-border shopping. Do the social and political meanings of Mexican border imports emphasize Mexico's profound—and profoundly unequal—relationship with the United States? Are imports used to embrace the United States, to resist the United States, to accommodate to the United States? We cannot dismiss these questions. However, if we concentrate too quickly on the United States, we risk excluding issues internal to Mexico itself. What do some Sonorans think of other Sonorans' wealth and their shopping trips across the border? Which women and which men in the household buy American goods, and who possesses and uses them?

We may proceed with both sets of questions by linking two levels of analysis. Imports form part of major world economic transformations. Since many imports are visibly from outside the country in which they are consumed, broad social collectivities—nations, regions, classes—may use imports to represent and communicate aspects of these global processes. At the same time, imports are used inside household production and reproduction both for practical and communicative purposes. Imports thus enter into the relationships and conflicts between generations and genders. Changes in domestic economies, as part of global changes, force householders to acquire and use specific imported goods to survive and thrive. The use of goods thus entails locally common sense notions of adequacy and fairness.

Concepts such as adequacy, fairness, and the like refer to evaluations added on top of the quantities of goods; in this manner, Sidney Mintz's argument about rural proletarian class consciousness, here applied to material culture, remains illuminating: "it is important to understand how populations come to the recognition that their felt oppression is not merely a matter of *poor* times, but of *evil* times—when, in short, they question the *legitimacy* of an existing allocation of power, rather than the terms of that allocation" (1979, 191; emphasis in the original). Two prongs arise in Mintz's argument: the material conditions of daily life; and the moral weighing of those conditions, as a whole and with reference to varied items. Ideas of justice may be complex, and focused on highly specific goods; hence, the judgments rendered must be understood within the conditions of imports in particular local circumstances and relations. But insofar as the goods at issue are imported, debate over just access to (or rejection of) imports becomes a crucial opportunity for people to speak about and try to alter their immediate position in the global economy.

The moralization of goods is not transparent from their places in the national and international economies. Benjamin Orlove and Henry Rutz (1989), for example, envision consumption as a complex process in which people act on and through material culture, rather than a final, passive using up of goods. James Carrier (1994) argues against a tendency to attribute public meanings to goods without considering how people acquire and use them. The way people appropriate (buy, give, use, and discard) goods stands between the public symbols conveyed as goods are sold, and their meanings—including the evaluation of justice—to the person, family, and social-political coalition.

For border Sonora, we should ask to whom and what ideas of justice refer. Two sets of questions occur. First, as part of wrenching proletarianization, U.S. immigration and return, and urbanization, Sonorans have undergone a profound shift in their self-provisioning: they have gone from a fairly sparse, but locally made and relatively little commoditized material culture to an extensive reliance on manufactured food and goods. Foreign goods, mostly of U.S. origin, played a central role in this change. (A few external commodities, including a scattering of European imports, did reach northern Sonora before this epoch.) One set of evaluations, then, focuses on U.S. importation as the visible carrier of social changes involving material culture changes. Put more simply, what do border Sonorans think of becoming consumers? Second, we may envision the situation once it is already thoroughly commoditized. People evaluate the visible goods of their neighbors, the private choices of their spouses and children. In a commoditized situation, one way people think and enact their social relations is through commodities (Miller 1987; 1995). As we envision life in border Mexico, we can venture to identify two rough domains of social relations that might be expressed in the idiom of imports. What role do imports play in relations between Mexicans? Mexico has engaged in a series of ideological and economic projects, responding in part to its seemingly perpetual imbalance with the United States: the investment-opening Porfirian 1880s and 1890s, the nationalist and populist 1930s, and the neo-Porfirian North American Free Trade Agreement (NAFTA) of the 1990s. How do national projects refract in a particularly import-dependent northern region? Then, crossing the border, we can ask what border folk think of their intimate relationship with America, seen specifically in terms of U.S. goods. The virtue of this framework is that we consider each ramification of imported goods before we engage in the deceptively obvious question of the Mexican identity vis-à-vis the United States.

Of course, it does matter that northern Sonora is close to the U.S. border. Importing clearly implies some notion of crossing social boundaries, and the Mexico-U.S. border may be thought of as an epitome of this more general activity. Still, it behooves us to consider the specific geography of the Mexico-U.S. borderlands. Households quite readily cross the border to earn money, learn information, and buy goods within the foreign country itself. The act of border-crossing decontextualizes the goods from the Mexican social structure. Imported goods may, then, be associated with a novel option to walk away, as it were, from intra-Mexican inequalities and invidious rankings.[1] (The international migration from nonborder locations requires an analysis of imports strongly reminiscent of the one here.) We may contrast this with an importation process that subdues the "border" quality of the imports. Goods are imported and sold through a domestic commercial system. This implies a recontextualization of the foreign good into one or several social structures, a pattern we can by no means neglect for the northern Mexican borderlands.

The general period of this study begins in the mid-1880s, the start of extensive U.S. imports in conjunction with the advent of industrial and agro-industrial capitalism, and it ends a century later with the completion of my main fieldwork in 1986. My first topic is the shift from local material culture to manufactures. This process has continued through this entire period, partly because different American manufactures have reshaped Sonoran material culture at different dates (cast-iron stoves earlier, for example, and refrigerators later), and partly because the basic commoditization varies according to the local penetration of the cash economy and migration. On the latter topic, an oral history of childhood in a mine center of the 1920s might report a conceptually parallel shift to manufactures as reported by a 1980s border city migrant from an isolated peasant village. In this chapter, however, my informants moved from agro-pastoral towns to either substantial mine cities, border cities, or the United States (often, a mixture of several of those) in the 1910s, 1920s, and 1930s. This locates the section entitled "Becoming Consumers" to persons who physically moved to the urban working class during that particular apogee of Sonoran capitalist transformation.

My second section, "Imports in a Time of Nationalism," concentrates on American-owned company towns, and in particular their company stores. Industrial-scale copper mining in northern Sonora has endured from the 1880s to the present, with periods of boom alternating with periods of mass layoffs. The 1920s through the early 1940s are particularly interesting, however, for during this time militant nationalism among Mexicans generally, and copper workers specifically, confronted the fact of company store reliance on U.S. imports. The people I worked with most closely had moved into mine cities by the 1920s, while they were forced to depart these places for the border cities during two outbursts of mine closures in the 1930s Depression and in the post–World War II slump in copper mining. My third section, "The Border City: Import Boom and Crisis," follows the same population to Agua Prieta (on Sonora's northeastern boundary with Arizona). It therefore looks at the role of goods that were readily purchased right across the border. Border cities have had this unusual relationship with U.S. imports the full length of their existence (in Agua Prieta's case, since 1900). However, Mexican border cities entered in an unprecedented period of growth after 1940, and it makes particular sense to focus the border section on this period when large numbers of resettling households were equipping themselves with U.S. goods. While the initial part of the border city story discusses prosperity, from 1982 on, Mexico's foreign debt payments to U.S. banks forced a series of drastic devaluations of the peso against the dollar. This hit hard at border city residents, peso-bearing buyers of dollarized goods, and thus the theme of the Agua Prieta segment is the political dimensions of a rapid shift from acquisition to deprivation of imports. My observations of, and data on, peso devaluations were collected from 1984 to 1986, supplemented by return visits to my friends' (that is, informants') households in 1992; but the devaluations I observed then have recurred with equal ferocity in the mid-1990s, and, what is more important, the mid-1980s material is contextually useful in understanding Mexican politics in the ongoing process of structural adjustment and NAFTA. In this regard, my research in Sonora is especially germane to the present conjuncture because Agua Prieta has been a free trade zone throughout the century; because of this status, it anticipates NAFTA in both the legal openness to U.S. imports and the economic realities of whether or not common Mexicans can afford them.

This framework develops several interesting ways of addressing my argument that moral evaluations of imports are embedded in particular paths of material culture in household and community, rather than being readily deduced from the Mexico-United States relationship. In particular, the Sonoran material permits us to compare two very different understandings of importation: in the company town, with a nationalist context, and in the complex city, with a free-market adjustment context. And in each of those cases, the framework requires us to surround the immediate political meanings of imports with the broader process and meaning of being a consumer that differentially affects women and men, and older and younger generations.

Becoming Consumers

Although consumption change may appear conceptually distinct, in fact it cannot realistically be divided from importation in the northern Mexican borderlands. To the people of Agua Prieta (the collective noun in Spanish is *Aguapretense*), an opinion about the whole phenomenon of novel goods and consumerism is an opinion about the impact of U.S. goods on their lives, so pervasive has been the influence of America on their home region of northern Sonora. The most interesting issue in all of consumption, as far as urban *Aguapretense* were concerned, was a poignant nostalgia for simpler, self-made rural technologies and self-provided and processed rural foods. This rested uneasily with their simultaneously deep interest in and appreciation of American consumer goods and skills. I regard this complicated discussion as a subtle attempt by Sonorans to weigh out their moral valuation of an extremely comprehensive and radical transformation of their technologies, their knowledge base, and their work, both paid and unpaid. And we must examine, in fairly complex detail, the interconnected effects of capitalist material culture and household economic organization in order to consider the benefits and burdens Sonorans weigh.

Sonorans have witnessed in the last one hundred years a dramatic rearrangement of everyday life. The regional material culture certainly had undergone important alterations prior to industrialization (the introduction of European technologies and animals, for instance), but it is reasonable to characterize this frontier state as possessing a fairly self-enclosed subsistence circuit by the early 1880s, with but a few selected imports. Households used locally available materials, such as leather, wood, clay, and palm fronds, to house the family, to chill food and water against the desert heat, to bake bread and heat tortillas, to store corn, beans, and chiles, and to shoe feet. Such items and processes were gradually replaced as a cash-based commercial economy introduced de-regionalized manufactures such as roofing metal, canvas shoes, and powered refrigerators. Household material items changed by virtue of streams of importation and goods transfer grounded in broader economic processes: temporary labor migration in the United States; urbanization, wage labor, and working-class formation in Sonora; the closure of resources in the countryside; and the commercialization and capitalist "rationalization" of the cattle-raising economy. Here, I focus on the first manifestations of commoditization, associated with the rise and the consolidation of an industrial working class from the late 1880s through the 1930s. Looking at that epoch, the key bearers of goods were Sonoran peddlers and merchants crossing through border ports of trade, mining companies that stocked proprietary stores, and, above all, Mexican households that readily moved back and forth between Sonora, Arizona, and California.

Manuel Gamio (1930) assembled Mexican government statistics for 1927 on goods migrants brought back from the United States, presented in table 6.1. The date of Gamio's information is fortuitous, since it permits us to view the goods of householders—rather than merchants—at a moment when critical tendencies toward working class formation, binational migration, and commoditization of material culture had reached full development, shortly before the interruption posed by the Great Depression. Gamio's data, delineating specific items, permit us to explore the impact of concrete goods in transforming household production rather than just speaking of general consumerism. The figures on table 6.1 are presented as numbers of items per one hundred persons reentering Mexico to facilitate easy reading of the table. We do not know the average returning household size, but we know that migration during this period involved whole households as well as isolated men (Heyman 1991, 63–65). It is reasonable to argue that items with reported frequencies as high as or higher than 20 per 100 returning persons were, in fact, goods that many or most returnee households did possess. I have therefore presented all items and sets of related items that occur more frequently than 10 per 100 entrants (e.g., stoves). I also present items less frequent than 10 per 100 entrants that are of interest either because they are traditional rural Mexican material culture that was in fact not frequent (e.g., *metates*) or because they represent new items not yet of great interest to returning Mexicans, though they would be so later (e.g., sofas). I portray the specific situation for northern Sonora through the combined data for the Agua Prieta and Naco ports of entry (data was missing for Nogales), and I add the aggregate data for the entire Mexico–United States border for comparison.

The change in goods—the replacement of 1880s wood, clay, and leather by the imported manufactures in the 1927 Gamio list—were not simply a passing of traditional technologies or a rearrangement of domestic items, but rather a transformation from "flow-conserving households" to "flow-through households" involving interconnected shifts in time, productivity, durability, and cash rather than in-kind incomes. Table 6.1 shows that virtually every household function was affected: sewing; food storage and cooking; heating; clothing; shoes and hats; sleep; housing; transportation; and music and storytelling. (For a longer discussion of my typology of households and of consumer proletarianization, as well as an item-by-item review of changes in material culture, see Heyman 1994a.) Focusing on our theme of moral evaluation, people were ambivalent about these changes. They did present de-skilling, dependency, and a kind of consumer "speed-up." The capitalist transformation of Sonora deprived rural and new working class Sonorans of critical commons resources needed for their self-made, relatively self-sufficient material culture. New material culture filled the gap when Sonorans were excluded from more localized alternatives. Migration placed Sonorans in cities and indeed, in a foreign country, where their older technologies could not be made. Furthermore, new jobs and replacement goods contributed to the decline of skills that had been transmitted across generations. I term this forced change *consumer proletarianization*. Thus new goods could bear the symbolism for a whole lost, indeed, seized rural world.

As manufactures entered people's lives, they introduced new constraints: a gradual shift toward dependence on purchased energy and repair parts; a gradual shift toward dependence on and interest in extraregional inputs of style and knowledge; and a locational bias against the countryside that took the form of a disdain of rural backwardness. Certain

TABLE 6.1. Objects Brought into Mexico by Persons Returning from the United States, 1927ª

Item	All Mexico–U.S. Border 2,104 Entrants	Northern Sonoran Ports 95 Entrants
Women's Tools and Related Items:		
Clothes (trunks, suitcases, bundles)	176.8	158.9
Kitchen utensils	78.0	83.1
Stoves	27.6	31.6
Sewing machines	16.6	47.4
Buckets	17.1	27.4
Laundry sets and washing machines	14.1	23.2
Wash tubs	12.2	17.9
Irons	5.1	14.7
Refrigerators	3.8	14.7
Corn mills	2.3	3.6
Dining utensils (sets)	1.7	6.3
Metates	0.8	0.0
Men's Tools:		
Tires, wheels, inner tubes	67.7	30.5
Cars, trucks, motorcycles	37.8	43.2
Agricultural tools	29.0	15.8
Shop tools (hand powered)	16.7	17.9
Axes, machetes, picks, shovels	14.8	2.0
Carriages	6.4	1.0
Auto tools	5.3	0.0
Bicycles	2.5	2.1
Motors and powered tools	0.2	3.1
Household Items:		
Chairs	124.8	216.8
Beds and bedsteads	89.9	109.5
Pillows and bedclothes (bundles)	80.2	35.8
Mattresses	70.5	72.3
Tables	31.6	109.5
Bathtubs	10.4	61.2
Mirrors	7.0	7.4
Bedroom furniture	5.9	10.5
Oil lamps	5.4	2.1
Chests of drawers	2.5	22.1
Rugs	4.8	32.6
Chifferobes	4.7	4.2
Cradles	2.5	4.2
Curtains (sets)	3.0	10.5
Dining room sets	1.9	0.0
Clocks	1.0	4.2
Parlor furniture	0.6	1.0
Sofas	0.4	4.2

TABLE 6.1.—*Continued*

Item	All Mexico–U.S. Border 2,104 Entrants	Northern Sonoran Ports 95 Entrants
Media:		
Records	128.6	202.1
Photograph frames	21.0	41.1
Phonographs	12.8	23.2
Musical instruments	8.1	9.5
Books (boxes)	3.1	18.9
Typewriters	1.4	7.4
Radios	0.2	0.0
Miscellaneous:		
Chickens	123.1	12.6
Larger animals	37.7	15.8
Food (bundles)	23.2	15.8
Shoes (bundles)	6.9	2.1
Toys	4.1	13.7

Source: Gamio 1930, 224–29.

[a]Frequency per 100 persons entering Mexico.

consumer goods, the tools we call appliances and cars, were important in this transformative process because they provisioned the household rather than just being used up. But the major household machines are expensive, on the whole. They were afforded only by wage labor, intermittent or permanent, or by prosperous commercial peasants under the relatively uncommon circumstance that they possess sufficient land.[2] In exchange for new goods, however, male workers in mines, in day and construction labor, and in the United States, and women who work in factories and as domestics were subject to rigid work disciplines. They experienced altogether new ways (as opposed to rural inequities) to occupy the bottom of society in terms of power and respect. In turn, household members with outside cash incomes were pushed through family ideologies to buy major durable, or "collective" goods enjoyed by the whole household (Wilk 1989). Thus, with consumerism an arena of domestic disputes opened.

Working (and school-attending) husbands, sons, and daughters had less time in Sonora for use-value production inside the household. The burden of filling this deficit shifted to married women. New appliances, derived for the most part from U.S. sources, enabled housewives to compensate for proletarianization with great skill and productivity (Simonelli 1985; Heyman 1991, 139–41). Indeed, time allocations became increasingly specialized for all household members since their time allocations now divided segments of paid and "house" work rather than constantly interweaving in-kind, subsistence, and salable commodity production. In summary, the organizational demands of the flow-through economy required reformulating and juggling a series of intra- and extrahousehold roles such that imports complicated life and engendered interpersonal tensions.

Importantly, however, Sonorans experienced this consumer transformation as filled with new opportunities, not just constraints (for an extended treatment, see Heyman 1991, 80–109). Married women had, through their vital tool set (stoves, sewing machines, and the like), special claim on their husband's and children's incomes through the ideal of collective consumption. Furthermore, women's tools were turned into income-generating trades (seamstress work, restaurants). Appliances in the early consumer era became women's insurance against widowhood and the misbehavior of men. Purchased tools gave men a way to exit the seemingly hopeless rural Sonoran extremes of wealth and poverty. One example will suffice. Inequality in the Sonoran countryside is represented by the male horse rider. The horse retains the colonial imagery of being wealthy and white as opposed to the earthbound, poor ex-Indian man, or woman or child leading a *burro* (Owen 1959, 26; Pennington 1979, 240–41; Sheridan 1988, 89). However, owning or operating a truck is a reasonable, though high, aspiration for Sonoran working man with experience in the mines, sawmills, or the United States (in addition to Heyman, above, see Alvarez and Collier 1994). In the same way, for working children houses, appliances, and other collective goods also provided new claims that permit the youth to lighten previously strict, inheritance-based obligations to the older generation (Heyman 1990).

Finally, working Sonorans find deep satisfaction and interest in new manufacture-based skills that engage their intellects and dexterity. Mechanized sewing, for example, provided particular pleasure to the older women I knew. Fabric and needles had long been "imported" into Sonora, though the sources shifted from central Mexico and overseas manufacturers to U.S. goods brought over the land border. More important, the production of clothing was made more efficient and more elaborate by two imports. An American sewing machine was an expensive, durable, and universal item in every mine worker and middle class family where I had interviewed a woman who had grown up before 1940. More importantly, women mastered imported information about styles of clothing based on

Euro-American fashions. Specifically, they drew on the Sears catalog (mentioned in oral histories as early as the 1920s, and probably predating that), as well as storefronts in U.S. border towns and the largest Sonoran mine cities. Sewing also supported widows, and it exemplifies the role of manufactures in women's new opportunities inside and outside the home (Heyman 1991, 104–5; 1994a, 192–95; Owen 1959, 31; Ruiz 1988, 123–25, 129–30). In summary, the pleasure in consumer goods is sustained because common border folk are still poor enough to be incompletely commoditized (when, for example, they repair old manufactures rather than buying new ones).

The processes by which Sonorans became consumers, then, associate imports with an ambivalent gains and losses. Rural nostalgia is the strongest theme. Urban informants, most of whom had rural pasts or connections,[3] depict life in the countryside as healthy (*sano*), clean or unspoiled (*puro*), and simple or devoid of conflicts and pressures (*una vida sencilla*). They note that it involved extensive sharing.[4] Rural nostalgia themes are framed by discussions of specific material culture changes away from older rural life; informants imply that consumer change has caused the loss of these values. I therefore regard rural nostalgia as a commentary, by inversion, on the problems that people perceive in their current working and consuming lives. Rural nostalgia, however, stands inconsistently alongside modernization, a quite different discourse about consumer goods. This discourse sees consumer goods as vital, positive aspects of a linear progression from the backward (*atrasado*) to the advanced (*avanzado* or *moderno*). The United States, associated with its material products, clearly stands toward the advanced end of modernization. The ideology of modernization is an alignment of ideas applied at the national level (for it has long been the ideology of Mexican elite developmentalism), while rural nostalgia is a localizing discourse. Yet both patterns of propositions are spoken by the same persons. I suggest that this contradiction makes sense in terms of a material culture transformation that both shattered old bonds (modernization) and introduced new conflicts in need of resolution (rural nostalgia).

To illustrate these ideas, I examine the views of one Aguapretense, Florencio Galván,[5] born in 1916 in the highland town of Villa Hidalgo, Sonora. His father was a sharecropper,[6] and he recalls his childhood as bitterly impoverished. The rich, he recalls, rode well-equipped horses, while the poor had but a burro, worth no more than 50 cents. However, Galván grew up with stories of the United States, for his father had worked as a musician in the mine city of Bisbee, Arizona (quite near the Sonoran border). After his father became ill and elderly, the brothers moved their family to the small border city of Agua Prieta. There, they settled on the *ejido* (collective farm) of Agua Prieta and eked out livings by small gardening and by construction labor. Galván saw freedom from rural poverty and disrespect in new job opportunities and new U.S. border goods. He conveys the modernization side through his discussion of shoes at the border, as well as his admiration for U.S.-influenced construction techniques. However, houses also represent the breakdown of cooperative labor, and he explicitly calls for a return to values of social solidarity (*solidaridad*)[7] in a city life he sees as alienating and conflictual.

Galván conveys the escape from rural landlessness through shoes laden with the meaning of European domination over indigenous traditions. In rural Sonora, the common people made their own footwear, a leather moccasin called a *tegua,* while the rich and white families purchased shoes. Yet America, its jobs and its stores, could provide shoes even for the humble folk:

> This is an important thing. We poor people didn't have shoes [in Villa Hidalgo]. Certain families were able to have shoes for their children because these families had someone working in the United States, and they sent shoes from here [the border] to there [Villa Hidalgo]. Here in Mexico there were shoes, very good shoes, but we couldn't afford them. Instead we used a shoe that my own father made for us—people made it for themselves—the famous *tegua*. Who knows if you have heard of it, but it's famous here in Sonora . . .

After discussing old and new style shoes for a while, Galván turns to the irony that today *teguas* are soaked in rural nostalgia. Now rich people own *teguas,* and even he has a pair of crude, rawhide *teguas*—ironically made in Douglas, Arizona!

In Agua Prieta, Florencio made his way from construction labor to skilled carpentry. I had concentrated on recording his knowledge of changes in techniques and materials of house construction (see Heyman 1994b). He loved U.S.-influenced construction techniques, and spoke several times with real pleasure of his work with unusual architectural styles and novel, imported materials. In one interview I had been asking about adobe and stone walls, and tile or dirt and cane roofs—that is, older rural house styles—and I then turned to a question about whether people had shared the work of house building in his natal town. He enthusiastically launched on a sustained rural nostalgia narrative, portions of which I present here:

> That's exactly it, how people pulled together [*se solidarizaba*], one family with the others. Better said, in these little villages you could see something that you don't see any more, which is that if there was a single family that lacked something, even if they had a different last name, well tell my child's godmother [*comadre*][8] to send this and nobody would say "no" . . . The solidarity of the village was like that. . . .
>
> Well, like I said, there was solidarity with people that didn't have a house. Like, "today I don't have any time but look, we'll begin tomorrow morning." Then, we get together 20 persons, they help to make adobes, . . . and the women together make food so everyone can eat. This is something that I have not seen again until recently when I went to Safford, Arizona, to see the Catholic Action group there. They met together, 110 members, to make the house of one person. They were the catechists doing it. I think that all religions ought to be this way, or at least everyone where the people have a good heart.

Galván projects nostalgia onto the countryside in order to recuperate these values in the present. Galván led the volunteers who built a modern-style, brick Catholic church in his working-class neighborhood. The idea of social solidarity clearly appeals to him, as does the rejection of power and status. Galván has been a lifelong political outsider. In the years before my interview he significantly influenced neighborhood dissent against the Mexican government when he was affiliated with the Catholic-oriented, right-wing National Action Party (PAN). If commoditization strains daily life, then Galván seeks to repair the bonds of trust and love with bucolic ideals. Yet, within his own life, shaped by relocation to the border, he discovers in imported technologies and skills the right to demand as much of life as the rich.

Florencio Galván is an unusual person, but the theme of rural nostalgia is not. The juxtaposition of ideologies of the modern and ideals of the countryside is a recurrent result of a century-long displacement of Mexico from a rural to an urban nation. Mexicans like Galván find in material culture an important and palpable manner to comment on their uprooting and replanting. Sonorans' moral evaluations of imports relate to more widely shared evaluations of what it feels like to become a consumer, cast in terms specifically influenced by the United States as a source of these transformations.

Once household material provisioning was commoditized and delocalized, the consumer framework was set in place. We now turn to a second phase—the development of interests, preferences, and evaluations within this new material culture. We may think of the first process as the making of needs for purchased goods, and of the latter process as the making of "needs within needs," including for imports. Needs within needs are sensitive to local contexts, commercial systems, and social relations, and to claims of just and unjust access to goods within them. Ideals of justice in particular rest on claims that common Mexicans should have access to historically appropriate standards of decent living. Decencies are neither strict necessities nor luxuries; people can reasonably be expected to own them at some point during a lifetime; and they convey to the household a standing above abject poverty but below ostentation (Heyman 1991, 175, drawing on Schneider 1980, 328). We will explore the reinterpretation of remarkably continuous needs for specific household goods, in the 1930s as a nationalistic Mexican labor issue and in the 1980s as an inwardly focused dispute over forced austerity. People have changed crucially the way they think *access* to imports should be achieved.

Imports in a Time of Nationalism

Most of Mexico's industrial-scale copper mining is located in northern Sonora, relatively close to the U.S. border. Sonoran industrial miners are full-time wage workers, urban residents, and thus fully proletarianized consumers.[9] From the late 1880s until the late 1940s, miners probably represented the largest U.S. import market in northern Sonora (and perhaps at times in the whole state); remarkably, that period coincided with the birth, development, and florescence of militant unionism and Mexican nationalism, cut short by mine decline and closure. My elderly interviewees all formed households during the decades of the 1930s and 1940s when these two tendencies—consumer formation and nationalism—peaked and then collapsed. My informants had undergone, of course, the usual complicated lives, so that their individual household histories cannot be reduced to an archetypal "mine" experience, but it is reasonable to summarize their formative years as fitting two circumstances conveying roughly similar consequences for consumption. One group had been Sonoran miners, who mainly shopped at U.S.-owned company stores. A second group had been young men or members of entire households who had worked in the United States, most often in Arizona copper mining and smelting. Company stores were also found in those places (as well as similar patterns of segregation and inequality between Mexicans and Anglo Americans). In the 1920s, the United States exercised minimal Mexican border control, and consequently both legal and undocumented Mexican immigration were very high in that decade. Upon the advent of the Great Depression, Mexicans were particularly targeted for blame, and many persons were driven out of the United States by application of unemployment relief or immigration laws. Others left voluntarily, upon losing their jobs. Collectively, both groups were termed *repatriates*. The possessions of Sonoran miners and repatriates, taken together, provide the best evidence I have about formative working-class ideas of a decent standard of living.

Table 6.2 shows major, enduring pieces of household equipment for four households around 1940, as reconstructed from oral history. The Córdoba household supported itself by full-time mine employment in Sonora, as did the Aguirres. The Hernández household had been repatriated from a U.S. border copper smelter city (Douglas, Arizona) to rural Sonora; they rebounded to the border city of Agua Prieta (across from Douglas) by 1940. The Durazo household was founded by a Mexican migrant worker in the United States who returned in 1930 to his home in the mine city of Nacozari, Sonora.

Around 1940 the decent standard of living required a cast-iron firewood stove, a pedal-driven sewing machine, a bed, box spring, and mattress. All of these items were U.S. imports for these households. Trucks were also brought from the United States, but they were not necessities (except for the Durazo household that combined trucking with a succession of small stores). The sources of furniture, other than beds and mattresses, were difficult to determine from oral history; people bought trunks, dressers, dish cabinets, tables, and chairs from stores in Mexico, but they may well have been originally made north of the border. U.S. radios were, again, an optional but not obligatory element of "decent" material culture. Other, less durable goods do not appear in table 6.2, but oral history indicates the importance of manufactured fabric, garments, and manufactured dishes. Cloth may have either been imported or brought from central Mexico. Women home-sewed some women's and children's garments. But men's clothing, especially the decent, denim work-style clothing, was (according to oral history) almost entirely American. Dishes were likewise bought from U.S.-operated company stores or imported and sold by peddlers. The two largest U.S. company stores (Cananea and Nacozari) supplied inexpensive meat from nearby company-affiliated ranches in Mexico. By oral report, their lard and wheat flour was imported, but this remains uncertain, while beans were brought from local farms. Firewood was cut locally, and hence it does not count as an import, even though it was often harvested on lands controlled by U.S. corporations. Imported goods, then, composed much of the 1940 decent standard of living. Furthermore, relying so heavily on the U.S.-owned company store caused a merger in memories, and probably in the experience of the time, of goods of Sonoran provenance with imported items. It therefore behooves us to examine the institution of the company store in its social context.

A. L. Epstein (1958), discussing the Zambian (then Rhodesian) Copperbelt, argues that mine-company towns have a "unitary structure." Epstein notes that analytically diverse aspects of daily life overlap, including occupational rank, work relations, class experience, race experience, housing, gender relations, and consumption, forming a single pattern of unequal relations determined by the structure of the large corporate enterprise. In Sonoran mines, for example, the very active and radical Mexican labor movement faced not only a U.S.-owned corporation, but also segre-

TABLE 6.2. **Possessions of Four Households, circa 1940**

Item	Household Name			
	Córdoba	Aguirre	Durazo	Hernández
Wood stove (cast-iron)	US/USCom	US/MexDom$_1$	Mex/MexCom	US/USCom
Sewing machine (pedal)	US/MexDom$_3$	US/MexDom$_3$	US/MexCom	US/USCom
Truck	None	None	US/USCom	US/USCom
Bed/mattress	US/USCom	?/MexCom	?/MexCom	US/USCom
Trunk(s)	US/USCom	?/? (Yes)	?/? (Yes)	US/USCom
Table	US/USCom	Mex/MexDom$_2$	?/MexCom	US/USCom
Chairs	?/? (Yes)	Mex/MexDom$_2$	?/? (Yes)	US/USCom
Dish cabinet	US/USCom	None	None	None
Radio	US/MexCom	None	US/MexCom	None

Summary: Imported goods = 19; Mexican goods = 3; obtained from U.S. commerce = 13; obtained all other ways = 12.

Note: For all possessed items: [nation of origin]/[context of acquisition].

Nation of origin: US = imported from U.S.; Mex = made in Mexico.

Context of acquisition: USCom = purchased in U.S. (commercial setting); USDom$_1$ = purchased in U.S. (kin or acquaintance); USDom$_2$ = gift or inheritance from kin in U.S.; MexCom = purchased in Mexico (commercial setting); MexDom$_1$ = purchased in Mexico (kin or acquaintance); MexDom$_2$ = self-made; MexDom$_3$ = gift or inheritance from kin in Mexico; (Yes) = possessed this item, no other information available; None = did not possess this item.

gated workplaces (in which American engineers and managers outranked Mexican foremen and miners), segregated housing areas, and a U.S.-owned company store with differential lines of credit allocated by income (implicitly valuing better-paid Americans over lower-paid Mexicans). Class, national, and race relations were inseparable.

The predominant source of goods in the mine city was the company store. The larger mine cities such as Nacozari or Cananea had independent commercial houses, while smaller mine towns and camps lacked them. In all cases, however, the company store was several times larger than the nearest Mexican-owned competitor.[10] Company stores sold consumable, bulk goods—meat, flour, lard, wood, fabric, dishes—while Mexican stores sold the expensive durables that appear in the material culture histories of table 6.3. The company store operated on a wage-scale credit, payroll deduction system. Workers (who were men) were allocated credit according to their earnings levels. Wives or mothers of workers shopped during the week on this line of credit. Those purchases were deducted weekly from the paycheck.[11] Men got their drinking and music money—or what they brought home—from the cash that was left over.

The company store credit and deduction system affected relations of husbands and wives. (Women were, in the vast majority of cases I have been able to reconstruct, housewives while married; some unmarried daughters worked for American managers as domestics; while widows carried on small businesses.) The types of tools (sewing machines, stoves, beds) and inputs (fabric, dishes) that households bought in the 1930s shows the relative power of housewives in this contest of domestic influence. Internally, women and men might have split, but externally they joined as a class, for they both faced one unified corporation that was supplier of consumer goods and enforcer of labor duties.

Working people, whether women or men, recall the company store system in two principal manners. On the one hand, the company store reminded every person interviewed that they had little real cash; that they survived very close to the line of weekly credit. Angelita Aguirre, the stepdaughter and wife of miners, explained to me that "with our small family, a little remained of the pay, but families with many children lived on pure credit; not much cash was handled then, like it is today." Or, as a son of another miner put it to me, "we were yoked, like oxen," a pungent Mexican metaphor playing on the negative sexual innuendo of the word *buey* (ox). On the other hand, the mine store was a bountiful source of good consumer items, especially marked (in people's minds) as coming from the

TABLE 6.3. Possessions of Eight Households, 1986

Item	Córdoba	Aguirre	Durazo, Sr.	Durazo, Jr.	Islava (Hernández Da.)	Gamez (Hernández DaDa.)	Valenzuela	Rojas
Gas stove (range)	US/MexDom$_1$	US/MexDom$_1$	US/USCom	US/USCom	US/MexDom$_1$	US/USDom$_1$	US/USDom$_1$	Mex/MexCom
Wood stove	Mex/MexCom	Mex/MexDom$_1$	None	None	Mex/MexDom$_3$	None	US/MexDom$_3$	Mex/MexCom
Refrigerator	US/USCom	US/USCom	US/USCom	US/USDom$_1$	US/MexDom$_1$	Mex/MexCom	US/MexDom$_1$	US/USDom$_2$
Sewing machine (electric)	US/MexCom	US/USCom	US/USCom	None	US/MexCom	None	None	None
Bedroom (sets or beds)	US/MexDom$_1$	US/USCom	US/USCom	US/USDom$_1$; Mex/MexDom$_1$	US&Mex/MexCom	Mex/MexCom	US/MexDom$_3$	US/MexDom$_1$
Living room set or sofa	US/MexDom$_1$	US/USCom	US/USCom	US/USCom	US/USDom$_1$	None	?/MexDom$_3$	US/MexDom$_1$
Dish cabinet	Mex?/MexCom	None	None	US/USCom	None	None	None	None
Table	US/MexDom$_1$	US/MexCom	?/? (Yes)	US/USCom	?/? (Yes)	Mex/MexCom	?/? (Yes)	US/USDom$_3$
Television	US/MexDom$_3$	US/USCom	US/MexDom$_3$	US/USCom	US/USCom	US/MexDom$_3$	US/MexDom$_3$	US/USDom$_3$
Radio	?/? (Yes)	?/? (Yes)	US/USCom	US/USCom	US/USCom	US/MexDom$_3$	?/MexDom$_3$	?/MexDom$_1$
Truck/car	US/MexDom$_1$	US/MexCom	None	Mex/MexCom	None	?/? (Yes)	None	None

Note: For all possessed items: [nation of origin]/[context of acquisition].

Nation of origin: US = imported from U.S.; Mex = made in Mexico.

Context of acquisition: USCom = purchased in U.S. (commercial setting); USDom$_1$ = purchased in U.S. (kin or acquaintance); USDom$_2$ = gift or inheritance from kin in U.S.; MexCom = purchased in Mexico (commercial setting); MexDom$_1$ = purchased in Mexico (kin or acquaintance); MexDom$_2$ = self-made; MexDom$_3$ = gift or inheritance from kin in Mexico; (Yes) = possessed this item, no other information available; None = did not possess this item.

United States. Aguirre likewise recalled the company store in a medium-sized U.S.-owned mine as dealing in "exclusively (*puros*) American goods," using the expressive word *puro* with respect to her viewpoint in 1985 after a series of brusque devaluations had cut Angelita off from her favored U.S. stores. Ramón Barrios, a former miner, commented "the company store gave credit by the level of pay, but it was always sufficient to live" (implying that to live was to live a decent life). However, he continued, "now, if you want to wear clothes, you can't eat, and if you want to eat, you can't wear clothes." My informants thus looked back on the 1930s and 1940s mines, an era of rapidly rising real wages (Heyman 1991, 44), through nostalgic intertemporal comparisons.

The company store was thus one of several connected points of contention between the Sonoran miners and the American corporation. The specific role of imported goods in this particular conflict merits particular attention, because of the interaction of regional, national, and international dynamics. National sentiment was galvanized in 1938 by Mexico's expropriation of the foreign oil industry. The miners were particularly militant. They demanded the parallel expropriation of the Mexican mining industry. This thrust was blunted by mine companies and the central government. However, the miners obtained the conversion of company stores into union cooperatives as part of the culmination of their unionization struggles. This measure was seen as a means to increase the real buying power of union members (Bernstein 1964, 192–99; Besserer, Novelo, and Sariego 1983, 32–37). In a survey of Mexican consumer cooperatives made in 1942, Cananea (with 3,120 members and \$M607,000 pesos capital) and Nacozari (with 1,254 members and \$M137,498 pesos capital) were the largest and the third largest cooperatives in the republic (Instituto de Investigaciones Económicas 1944). They continued to function for many years as cooperative stores, faltering after these mines either closed or made basic changes in their organization.

Reduction in imported goods was not an agenda involved in the expropriation of the company stores. Import substitution, which was beginning in central Mexico, had not yet reached northern Sonora, and in fact few domestic alternatives would arrive before adequate roads were built in the 1970s. My informants who experienced the transfer of the company store told me that the store itself, its goods and policies, changed little (I do not doubt this, though commercial records would provide stronger proof). More important for my argument, 1930s Mexican nationalism in border Sonora was compatible with desire and admiration for U.S. goods, as the interviews above make abundantly clear. This makes sense if we envision the lives of the Sonoran workers in that epoch. They could not do without imported U.S. goods, for their household production required them. Therefore justice involved a fairer and more secure claim to income and imports. Security came with mine union reforms of production contracts, seniority, and employment rights. Fairer access, however, emerged by nationalizing the previously racist unitary structure, including the company store.[12] In fact, one could hardly accuse the company store of prejudice (no interviewee did). But it was one company-owned institution that working people, men and women alike, thought about on a daily and weekly basis, and one that the mine union did deliver as a fairer deal to Mexican workers. The idea of a just claim on imported goods arose from household organization. It was channeled by the peculiar company town class relations, into the overall state-building project of Cárdenas, through a Mexican nationalist criticism of North American domination. That ideas about similar goods may flow down different streams, on quite different hills, is shown by the Mexican border of the 1980s.

The Border City: Import Boom and Crisis

Beginning around 1940, and accelerating during the 1950s and 1960s, a stream of displaced miners and land-short peasants filled Agua Prieta. Families landed in relatives' homes or cramped rental apartments, but they soon stripped the brush land around the border city for new house lots. The new homes had to be furnished, partly with old sewing machines and other goods they brought along, but usually with new versions of the familiar furniture and appliances. This "settlement process" took place during an unprecedentedly long rise in real wages and purchasing power for Mexican working and middle classes, lasting from 1948 to 1976, and perhaps through 1981. At the border, the rise was accentuated by access to commuting jobs and dollar-earning businesses (Heyman 1991, 44, 128–31). Consumption of imports was vital to survival and reconstruction. This consumption gave rise to a strongly import-oriented border city style, with some continuities and some differences from the earlier mining town period.

In the same period householders rearranged income, domestic power, age, and gender roles in the context of a diversified border city economy. The *maquiladora* program involves foreign-owned (mostly U.S.) subsidiaries or linked subcontractors bringing U.S. electronic, garment, and auto parts into Mexico, assembling them there at low wage costs, and returning them to the U.S. market. It has grown from a scattering of factories in 1965 (1967 in Agua Prieta) to a massive border-long industrial strip. The *maquiladoras* in Agua Prieta employed over 6,400 workers in 1986 from an active labor force of about 18,000 persons. A majority of *maquiladora* workers are women in their late teens and early twenties; a substantial minority are young men (Fernández-Kelly 1983; Heyman 1991, 42, 178–84). As well as *maquiladoras,* however, a variety of occupations exist for young and older men, such as work in construction and repair shops, and for young women, store clerking and domestic positions. Both women and men commute extensively to work in the United States, legally and extralegally (sheltered under a U.S. legal fiction, an important segment of people on the border hold U.S. "legal permanent residence" status—and thus can cross daily without hindrance to work—but continue to live in Mexico). These types of employment existed before the advent of the factories in 1967. The wage work roles of young women and men thus predates the *maquiladoras,* and formed an important part in the emergence of border consumption patterns.

The border towns differ from the mine centers because of the multiplicity of employers, income sources, and household budgeting patterns. No single employer dominates the city. The *maquiladoras* are many factories even though they form one sector. Several income streams flow into most households. Young people do not give all their earnings to their parents. Women and men, younger and older, negotiate how much money goes to the collectivity and how much is retained by the individual (Heyman 1991, 178–88). Furthermore, household members—specifically non-employed mothers—manage money and even contribute cash by shopping carefully, playing currency exchange with dollars (if possible), and buying, holding, and reselling durable consumer goods.

Vendors on the border are equally diverse. They divide most obviously by nation, and secondarily by level of prices and provision of credit. In other words, vendors are not "unitary" as in the company store/town. Finally, in residential terms, families bought house lots helter-skelter when they settled down. Neighborhoods are quite mixed, and residential status groups emerged only in the weak sense that some areas are more or less stylish. Households thus stand alone with their private standard of living, either in the sense of invidious comparison to others or in the sense, closer to how people evaluate themselves, of achieved and disappointed decencies. Larger social coalitions, such as national identity or factory labor, go against the grain of the border city (though perhaps they will not prove impossible). Instead, unity of wives and husbands, sons and daughters, revolves around household well-being, especially consumer well-being.

Mexico's northern border is well known for commercial dependence on the American side. In fact, Agua Prieta provided the study that epitomized this pattern. Jerry Ladman and Mark Poulson (1972) found that *maquiladora* operatives spent 39 percent of their earnings in the United States; they estimated that indirect flows brought U.S.-side expenditures to 52 percent of the factory wage bill. Their survey was collected prior to the numerous devaluations of the peso that began in 1976 and accelerated after 1982, which assuredly reduced U.S. expenditures, but the 1972 numbers indicate the context of Sonoran border reliance on U.S.-side shopping, even for the poorer working folk. This reflects, in part, the extensive possession of U.S. Immigration and Naturalization Service "border crossing cards" among established border city residents; such cards permit the bearer and listed family members to enter the United States for up to 72 hours and 25 miles, allowing them to visit relatives and to shop, but not to earn money.

The U.S. side provides a steady supply of used furniture, used and new appliances, and used automobiles. (According to my interviews with owners of secondhand stores in Mexico, American merchandise was easily brought into Agua Prieta when that city had free-trade perimeter status before 1980.) Because used goods are far less expensive, the prices are more in line with Mexican household buying power. Used durables are sold both in both nations. The secondhand trade included used construction materials, such as roofing metal, wiring, plumbing, windows, and doors. Agua Prieta neighborhood grocery stores relied on U.S. canned goods prior to the 1982 devaluation, as well as Mexican flour, beans, cheese, and eggs. U.S.-side grocery stores have long supplied fresh milk and chickens to Agua Prieta, since these items are unavailable there. *Aguapretense* shopped for new American clothes in Douglas while they bought used American clothes from peddlers and stores on the Mexican side (again, new garments from central Mexico began to be sold in this border extremity after 1982). A similar pattern holds for shoes: Douglas stores sold desired, inexpensive shoes to northern Sonorans. Now, better-quality boots are vended in Agua Prieta, but as of 1986 cheap Asian sneakers were still mostly sold in the United States.

U.S. bank and store credit for working-class Mexicans was one of the remarkable ways that imports were promoted on the border. Florencio

Galván told me that he repaid five loans from the Valley National Bank of Douglas, including money used for the funeral of his brother, for a washing machine, for house materials, and for a car. Florencio experienced the United States through its commerce as unprejudiced:[13]

> It was very easy for us [Mexicans]. All they did was collect the number of your local border crossing card and your address. It was Varela's Furniture Store [in Douglas] that first connected me to Valley National Bank. The wife [*vieja,* literally "old lady"] and I went to Varela's. She told me that she liked this one washing machine a lot (we had a little old one and she wanted a new one, and I was working at that time). So Mr. Varela told me, pay $25 and you can take the machine; I'll prepare all the loan papers for the bank, with a little interest, of course. Well, the papers turned out very easily for me, and I was able to pay off the [$225 U.S.] loan in 10 months.

On the other hand, Florencio found that Mexican banks were prejudiced by class:

> I have never been able to mortgage anything. I went to banks, specifically to finish my house I asked for $2,000 pesos [$160 U.S.] to the National Bank of Mexico. I believe that it was very difficult for them to loan money to someone who is seen as poor and humble. They complicate the matter; . . . one had to do vast amounts of paperwork to borrow almost nothing. . . . I went to the Commercial Bank with the priest [of the church Galván worked on], to ask for a loan. The manager was very friendly, a man of honey, but after everything, he told me no. He could see unmistakably that I could make money. Perhaps I am a person [*un tipo,* "a social figure"] very inferior to them; only they can make money.

This differential experience of prejudice in the commercial world set up the ideal of U.S. consumption as a critical vantage point against Mexican internal power and political. (After the devaluation of the peso, many Sonorans could not pay their dollar-denominated debts, so that U.S. credit increasingly was offered only to the most obviously prosperous applicants.)

Douglas's downtown commercial street has been and still is lined with relatively inexpensive retail outlets, including old-style department stores, that cater to Aguapretense who walk the half-mile from the border port or the boundary fence hole. New retail chains—K-Mart, Wal-Mart—on the edges of Douglas and similar cities like Nogales, Arizona, attract those Mexican shoppers who can afford cars and pick-up trucks. U.S. shopping, then, is a pleasurable form of recreation, a break from dusty Agua Prieta. (We can contrast this with the routineness of the company store.) The pleasure in U.S. shopping was strongest for women with household provisioning responsibilities, though its attractions to men are not to be ignored. Mercedes Romero de Hernández calmly evaluates U.S. shopping: "I bought everything over there [in Douglas] because everything was cheaper. The meat was better there; I can never figure out why people come over here [to Mexico] to buy meat because meat here is very bad, very hard, and there soft, fine in quality.[14] . . . Clothing, shoes, fabric, we bought it all over there because it was cheaper, better." Mercedes, we must understand, had a steady stream of dollars with which to shop. Her husband, one of the legally admissible commuters described above, worked in a series of mining, construction, and harvest jobs. He remitted part of his earnings to Mercedes, and thus she had substantial control over the use of household income. For Mercedes, and for several other key women interviewees, shopping in the United States merged the experiences of prosperity and women's power.

On the other hand, we should not exaggerate U.S.-side purchasing. Aguapretense acquire U.S. goods in more prosaic, less exciting contexts on the Mexican side. Table 6.3, as we shall see, demonstrates more U.S.-source goods than U.S.-bought goods: in other words, Agua Prieta households obtained American goods through intranational relationships. The original material culture histories show many U.S. goods entering Mexican households through personalized transactions ranging across both nations: gifts and subsidies from brothers, sisters, or children living in the United States; items sold by persons moving from Mexico to the United States; or the seemingly endless transfer of American furniture and appliances by sale and gift among acquaintances, friends, and kin inside Mexico. Given this complex picture, we can hardly reduce the border Mexicans' experience of imports simply to their ideas about the United States, but rather can only distinguish that element in certain appropriate contexts among greater concerns focused on Mexico.

Table 6.3 summarizes the possessions in early 1986 of eight diverse households. The Córdoba, Aguirre, and Durazo Sr., are three households enduring from 1940 (table 6.2).[15] Earnings from the father's machine shop and the wages of two children working in *maquiladoras* support the Córdoba household, while the Aguirre and Durazo households are sustained by nonresident children and small rental properties. Durazo Jr., a son of the elderly Durazos, is a very prosperous truck and construction equipment owner-operator, though not at a scale where he has employees. Valenzuela, a very poor former miner, owns a backyard blacksmith/mechanical shop, while a daughter is a factory worker. Rojas, a blind widow, is supported by a resident brother who works in a broom straw factory, a son who cuts firewood, and a *maquiladora*-laboring daughter. Islava and Gamez are daughter and granddaughter of table 6.2's Hernández household. The husband in the Islava household was a postman, and the wife had a home-based cooking and sewing business; the wife in the Gamez household had worked as a factory operative and shop clerk, while the husband was a construction laborer. These tables therefore represent a range of ages and buying powers, and yet they are remarkably consistent.

The Gamez household holds particular interest because it was formed in 1984, and deliberately stocked by kin with most of its goods. It thus indicates what Aguapretense today regard as the minimum required set of household equipment. The newest and the poorest households (Gamez, Rojas) as well as the most prosperous (Durazo Jr., Aguirre) held in common the following items: a gas stove, a refrigerator, a washing machine, beds and mattresses, living room (public area) furniture such as a sofa (except Gamez), several tables, a television, and a radio. This last item is particularly important, since employers announce job openings by radio. Sewing machines are mostly owned by older women, and trucks or cars are not universal. I argue that this list approximates the decent standard of living for border Sonorans as of 1986.[16] Table 6.3 by comparison with table 6.2 demonstrates a gradual Mexicanization of products bought in Agua Prieta, occurring mostly since the late 1970s, but imports in 1986 were still essential to assembling a decent standard of living.

Those standards were brutally assaulted after 1982. In September of that year, Mexico's government announced that it could not meet the payments for its debt to foreign, principally U.S., banks. Mexico continued to pay interest on the debt, while it agreed with the U.S. Federal Reserve and other bankers to make extreme rearrangements in Mexico's domestic economy. Almost all of these actions reduced the real buying power of common Mexicans. The devaluation of the peso against the dollar hurt border residents the most, for American-origin goods (bought in either nation) are ultimately priced in dollars, and thus they became suddenly expensive. Forty-eight and a half pesos bought a dollar in the summer of 1982; by

1986, 500 pesos obtained a dollar, and by late 1987, 2,250 pesos. By the early 1990s, Mexico had renumerated its currency (turning thousands into single digits), and appeared to have stabilized both its inflation rate and its currency, when the realities of bank debts, capital flight, and import dependence overtook its economic strategy. With the unexpected devaluation of late 1994 and the subsequent national consumption collapse of 1995, it is now clear that the evidence I present from 1986—especially the role of imports—represents one side of a consistent process in the Mexican political economy. Export expansion is the other side. The export economy (facilitated by 1993's NAFTA) is Mexico's long-term direction, or perhaps long-term stagnation, for even now export earnings go right out of the country in endless debt payments. This was already manifest in the mid-1980s at the border, where cheaper peso paychecks led American corporations to increase rapidly *maquiladora* jobs (in Agua Prieta, up by over 2,000 in the four years after the 1982 devaluation). At the same time, even with added jobs, my *minimum* estimate of the four-year decline (1982–1986) was 34 percent in total household purchasing power for 63 households in two working-class neighborhoods.[17] The decline of household incomes against the more severe standard of dollar-purchasing power was 55 percent.

People had to curtail shopping in the United States, however much they liked it. In 1982, 41 percent of surveyed households had spent dollars in the past week; in spring 1986, 21 percent had spent such dollars, including shopping trips made for the special occasion of *Semana Santa* (Easter week).[18] Credit in the United States had dried up; no household reported new U.S. loans (though some had lingering ones), while credit inside Mexico had changed very little in per-household frequency. Meanwhile, used goods dealers inside Agua Prieta told me that rapid devaluations essentially put them out of that business (a sixty-dollar used stove from the United States, for example, at one time a very affordable expense, was now an entire week's income for a Sonoran household). The Mexican economic crisis of the 1980s did not halt Mexican border shopping in the United States, but it created a situation in which U.S. shopping and imports were harder, more infrequent, and, most important, restricted to wealthy or migrant-remittance–based households rather than open to nearly everyone as it had been.

The border imports crisis especially hurt women for whom Douglas was a sign of power and pleasure. From 1947 to the early 1970s, Angelita Aguirre had operated a home-based sewing business, making girls' and women's dresses for private orders. Her machine was a Singer, her fabric

American, and her sources of patterns the Sears Catalog and the window displays in Douglas store windows that she surveyed. Even after Angelita slowed her sewing business, she enjoyed visiting U.S. stores with her border crossing card. It took the devaluation, Angelita wistfully told me, to "discover Mexican goods" because before then "I was so used to American goods, we only knew their qualities."

While the devaluations hurt women most, men also suffered. Let us examine the economics of Juan Bautista Valenzuela's one-man mechanical shop. He billed clients by the cost of materials plus hours of labor, at roughly twice the going factory wage. When prices of items bought in dollars rose, Valenzuela likewise had to increase his charges, but because his was a miniature enterprise in a saturated, competitive market, he often could not increase total bills proportionately. Therefore he tended to undercharge for his own labor, the only cost under his control. Among the shops I frequented, Valenzuela was the most self-sufficient and least dependent on dollars—indeed, he had built his own drill press instead of buying a used U.S. one. Still, his key inputs were American. He paid $1.00 U.S. per welding rod, so that he easily billed as much for welding rods as for his own labor (the value of his labor was roughly equivalent to $1.00 U.S. an hour). Valenzuela bought oxygen and acetylene tanks in the United States ($100 for two tanks) as well as used grinding wheels at $1.00 U.S. each. All of this explains Valenzuela's reaction to the Mexican economic crisis of the 1980s. Mexico was corrupt, he explained to me, a country where the poor had no chance against the rich (the term *los pobres* typically encompasses diverse peasant, working, and lower middle classes). Valenzuela dramatically told me that *General Dolar manda todo* (General Dollar orders everything around).

We might read Valenzuela's pithy saying as a criticism of the economic domination of Mexico by the United States through austerity programs. Aguapretense, being border people, indeed understood the inequality of global power very well. Yet this awareness remained at the level of everyday resistance, as James Scott (1985) delineates it, at the level of critical thoughts rather than political mobilization. The themes of consumption, imports, and the peso-dollar exchange rate were not raised in order to mobilize political resistance to debt payments to the United States; they served instead to criticize Mexico's ruling party, the PRI, and its government. In two years I witnessed one consumer protest in Agua Prieta, a demonstration organized by housewives from Galván's church parish, with some supportive husbands, against a 50 percent increase in household electric bills. This protest targeted the Federal Mexican Electric Utility. The demonstration, which succeeded in having certain extreme bills reviewed for inequities, was aimed where organized protest could have effect rather than ultimate sources. It was internal to Mexico, and it focused on an arena of state controlled "collective consumption" (Castells 1983).

Principally, the economic crisis in Agua Prieta, as on much of the northern border, added support to the opposition right-wing and Catholic-oriented PAN party. The PAN is led, locally and nationally, by extremely wealthy elites; its platforms call for policies no different than the PRI's austerity regime (if anything, more severe); and it has had nothing to say about devaluation or debts. It is the opposite of a working-class party. However, the PAN was very strong in working-class neighborhoods, for example appealing to the class-sensitive (but also very Catholic) Florencio Galván. The PAN repeated a simple formula, rally after rally. Mexico was corrupt and had no democracy; the PAN was the party of the people. The PAN appealed, just in itself, as an anti-PRI alternative. The PAN proposed that it would cut *prices* rather than raise *wages*. Prices conjoined opposition to political corruption. Wages (for one could imagine a maquiladora-based border labor movement) were negated as a political option.[19]

Consumption brought Agua Prieta households together—far more so than jobs. Signs of wealth in the border city were desocialized relative to their clearer attribution in the mining town. They peaked at the relatively low level of the co-resident family, shown in the quality of their sofa and their television, or the front of their house. In the mining town, work, wages, and the ability to own were clearly shaped by race and position in a common economic structure, the mine enterprise. In Agua Prieta, on the other hand, the ability to own was detached from visible structures external to the household, except for government utilities. The market is simply too variegated and amorphous to be visible. Thus, class was privatized. This provides a fertile realm for right-wing populism. The privatization makes economic action seem less possible and less efficacious, though it sustains a party coalition around individual political rights (e.g., the PAN's call to vote freely and at one's own discretion, not that of PRI bosses).[20]

I observed consumer discontent on the Mexican border, then, to have the following characteristics. Though one might have imagined that political meanings at Mexico's northern border would be characteristically transnational, they were not. An economic crisis explicitly felt through the reduction of U.S. imports did not lead to reflection on and political mobilization around the Mexico-U.S. relation. Instead, discontent focused on issues, largely electoral (though some consumption) in the relations of Mexican people with the Mexican state. The highly nationalistic tradition of northern Sonoran resistance to U.S. domination did not transfer from the mine cities to the border city, though these were exactly the same people, in the same intercommunicating regional network of Sonorans. Particular local alignments of social structure are more powerful than political traditions. However, it merits saying that Aguapretense, such as Florencio Galván (see note 13), criticize unequal U.S. over Mexican power in immigration policy, a domain where they see more direct U.S. coercion in their lives. We must understand the multiple concerns and arrangements of Mexican border people, rather than assuming domination and resistance aimed only at the United States.

We may place Agua Prieta's local political meanings within a broader crisis of legitimacy of the Mexican government. It is engaged in a new and extreme political-economic project, that of debt-driven export capitalism. In national terms, this has meant dissolution of state enterprises, reductions in tariffs protecting national producers, and the opening of Mexico's domestic market to foreign imports, especially of consumer goods. At the border, however, an area where imports were always predominant, this project has meant working harder at making export goods, goods for others, in exchange for declining rewards. The new Mexican project has, in the realm of ideas, promoted overt display of wealth as a sign of supposed market merit. It contrasts with an earlier project that swaddled very severe inequalities of wealth in PRI-style populism.

The fact is that the PRI has presided over both projects, and it loses face for both. The situation in mid-1980s Agua Prieta, added to that in many other places in Mexico, amounted to a legitimation crisis of the Mexican state and elite. Even the supporters of the PRI in Agua Prieta accorded no trust to the government. The nationalistic project of the 1930s, seen in the mine cities, carried little weight in urban Mexican contexts of the 1980s. At the same time, a new means of revaluing wealthy families (and their American consumer style) has yet to be forged completely.[21] Indeed, very stylish imports were quite popular in 1992, when I revisited Agua Prieta—but only for those persons with the wherewithal to afford them. K-Mart and Wal-Mart are new American-side border meccas. It takes a car or truck to get to them because of their location away from the pedestrian entrance to Douglas. The majority (62 percent) of families I surveyed in 1986 did not own a car or truck, and for those who did, gasoline was expensive (an average of 16.9 percent of incomes of households with vehicles). For decades and decades in the rise of the border city, U.S. items were egalitarian—even the carpenter, even the mechanic, even the housewife could shop in downtown Douglas. Now, American goods—and the enduring admiration they command—are a powerful stratifying force on the border.

Toward Wider Comparisons

Given no choice by their manufacture-dependent production process, working people claimed a just standard of goods. Yet their demands were not, in any simple sense, the frustration of an endless spiral of desire set against the capitalist "reality" of economic setbacks. First, Sonorans, in a fundamental sense, morally questioned the very presence of consumer needs and dependence. They did this through the contradictory idioms of rural nostalgia and progress. They recognized the difficulties of their own material culture change, embracing both the ideology of capitalism and the romance of self-production rather than taking a simple, single-sided stance. I expect that anthropologists listening throughout the world will hear similar discussions about becoming a consumer, for this is a process based on convergence, on the stunning delocalization of material culture, and the weaving of global dependence on cash and energy.

Entrapped by consumption dependence, Sonorans, secondly, evaluated the morality of their access to "needs within needs." Their principal concern was the sufficiency of a household balance; their ideas of justice focused on a right to, or control over, *access* to consumer goods, in particular imports. Access was governed by distinct local class relations, and thus the ideas and the application of justice were markedly contextual. Foreign control over the company store, though not the foreignness of the goods themselves, was rejected by a strongly nationalistic mineworkers' movement. Border-city Sonorans, in terms of consumption, have viewed the United States favorably, while they have used import-dependence, part of a general sense of consumer malaise, to criticize or support internal Mexican concerns. One finds both national ideological currents and distinctive local social settings that differ impressively: the nationalization of the company store is an expectable outcome of the unitary structure that makes consumption a labor issue; the privatization of consumer suffering on the border is an expectable outcome of a loose urban social structure where households face diverse goods and labor markets with minimal mediation. Neither the meaning of "nationhood" nor of "import" is constant. As expressed through imports, Mexican oppositional national identity (vis-à-vis the United States) differs dramatically between the mines and the border cities. Indeed, I expect that the political meanings of standards of living will vary greatly in comparative perspective, shaped by the immediate contexts for providing and depriving persons of their needs within needs.

NOTES

1. The northern borderlands of Mexico are notable in Latin America, though not unique, for the early and rapid decline of personalized systems of class control, such as sharecropping and indebted contract labor. This occurred because migrant work in the United States served northern Mexicans as an easily accessible alternative to local labor regimes (Katz 1981, 12–14).

2. Thomas Sheridan found in 1981 that the median household in the northern Sonoran municipality of Cucurpe did not have sufficient access to land and livestock to make a living without access to external or local wage income (1988, 124).

3. My material comes from oral histories and kitchen conversations recorded inside the city of Agua Prieta. Most Aguapretense were still close to the consumer transformation. First, most of them had lived through major changes, though for older persons this may have been decades before. Second, the rural immigration to Agua Prieta from the highland northeast has been steady for fifty years (Heyman 1991, 38–39), and most Aguapretense have close personal and visiting connections back to the countryside. The comparison of rural folkways and modern goods was a topic of marked interest.

4. Older material culture supported cooperation and sharing in at least some domains. In rural Sonora prior to the advent of refrigerators, meat was almost never eaten except at parties where it was distributed on kin and friendship lines (Sheridan 1988, 212). Material culture change did indeed reduce this pattern of sociability. I found that, with refrigeration in Agua Prieta, meat was a part of daily diet at a remarkably high frequency (48 percent ate meat in a 24-hour meal recall). However, it was consumed inside the home rather than in extrahousehold events, though with the exception that life-cycle and other festivals continue to offer meat dishes. Likewise, with reference to house construction (Galván's chosen topic), I suspect that the increases in purchased electrical and plumbing systems, as well as other changes in construction, have gradually favored paid specialist labor in conjunction with unpaid household labor, rather than the widespread exchange of unpaid labor facilitated by the simple adobe-wall, dirt-floor house construction technology.

5. This is a pseudonym, as are all subsequent names of interviewees.

6. His father, Florencio recalls, received half the crop because he did not own tools and the landlord had to provide tools and seed.

7. This interview took place in 1985, and the term *solidarity* was not yet associated with the highly politicized development grant program of the Salinas administration (1988–94).

8. A *comadre* is the mother of one's godchild or the godmother of one's child. It is an important relationship, and when used by Galván, it indicates that people responded to their social obligations.

9. A variety of smaller mines in Sonora extract specialty minerals and employ commuting peasants and floating proletarians. However, full-time labor, full consumer-good dependency has been more common in northern Sonoran mines.

10. Héctor Aguilar Camín (1977, 114–15) demonstrates this for the period before 1910. The oral histories I collected indicates that this situation was likely to have been the same in the 1930s and 1940s.

11. I have argued elsewhere (Heyman 1991; 1994a) that the mine corporation had two rationales for the company store credit system. First, and perhaps most importantly, corporations reduced their cash flow by keeping ranching, payroll, and shopping inside the firm. Second, by keeping credit levels high, and by facilitating continuing consumer needs and flows, workers were tied down to jobs within a fluid regional labor market that included mine and smelter jobs in Arizona as well as Sonora. Meat was a memorable example of a company store good that attracted experienced miners and their families, since it was sold cheaply based on mine-affiliated ranches. However, I also argue that companies did not extend so much credit that workers accumulated large debts. I asked about debt and credits extensively, but recollections by miners and their wives simply did not mention burdensome, lengthy, or inescapable debts to the corporations. Debt peonage did not function so close to an open U.S. border (see note 1).

12. The unions likewise added to the basic fairness of the mines by "Mexicanizing" (that is, opening up from segregation) various upper-tier managerial, engineering, office, and craft trades in this epoch, resembling the process of nationalizing the company store without really changing it.

13. Galván expressed considerable resentment over what he viewed, probably justifiably, as very harsh undocumented migrant work experiences in the United States. Galván not only worked hard there, he was deported several times. That is, he was expelled through a legal process after spending time in detention, rather than the milder treatment of exiting soon after signing a voluntary departure form. At least one time, according to Galván, two INS officers threatened him with jail. Galván thus has reason to look on the United States as a source of disruption of social relations, a disruption to be assuaged by a rural ideal.

14. This discussion is informed by the change in meat cooking styles and qualities in Sonora. Stringy, lean, range-fed beef (often dried, shredded, and recooked in the form called *machaca*) is suited for lengthy stewing; this would have been characteristic of rural meat use and is a quality subject to rural nostalgia. Mercedes here prefers U.S., feedlot-raised, heavily marbled, soft beef, suited for pan-cooking and clearly associated with the idea of imported flavors and styles.

15. The Hernández household from table 6.2 still existed in 1940, but I could not usefully reconstruct the sources of many of their household items, because the elderly informants gave me incomplete information.

16. Mitchell Seligson and Edward Williams (1981, 52–53) provide extensive evidence on appliance and car ownership both for Agua Prieta and for the border

generally, which corroborates my development of a list of standard material culture for border working-class families. For some inexplicable reason, I neglected washing machines in my material culture surveys so that they are absent from table 6.3, but I know that all these homes had washing machines except Gamez (the wife used her mother's, next door), Valenzuela, and Rojas.

17. For information on this figure, and other higher estimates, including the nature of the survey conducted by James Greenberg (in 1982) and myself (in 1986), and the ways to deflate nominal income into real buying power, see Heyman (1991, 177–78; 1994a, 223, 234).

18. I cannot calculate the 1982–86 decline in average amounts spent in the United States because my informants reported U.S. shopping, done irregularly on holidays such as Christmas and Easter, in a manner that did not allow construction of uniform time units for expenditure amounts.

19. The maquiladora managements use economic need and the household-income generating role of young workers to exercise work discipline and, I suspect, reduce labor militancy. For details, see Heyman (1991, 188–92).

20. I thank James Carrier for helping me clarify my ideas in particular in this passage.

21. Indeed, in my opinion, American imports in 1980s Agua Prieta cast a patina of admiration not only on the wealth from overt enterprises but also wealth from drug smuggling and similar extralegal businesses.

Chapter 7

Building from Migration: Imported Design and Everyday Use of Migrant Houses in Mexico

Peri L. Fletcher

For many residents of Napízaro, a rural village in central Mexico, migration to the United States provides the opportunity to build what one migrant calls his *casa de sueños,* or house of dreams. The community of eight hundred residents has relied on migrant remittances to supplement agricultural subsistence since the 1950s. More recently, migrant remittances have been at the center of a construction boom of new and remodeled houses. House building takes place within a conjunction of historical forces: declining subsistence and increased marginalization within Mexico, new sources of income through migration, and a widespread exposure to mass media and availability of mass-produced consumer items. Migrant houses embody many of the contradictions and paradoxes inherent in the incorporation of a small rural village into the global economy and the huge dislocations of rural farmers who became transnational labor migrants.

In this village, where most men and many women spend years laboring in the United States, the distinction between modernity and tradition is as problematic as the distinction between rural and urban, smallholder and proletarian, Mexico and the United States. In many cases, the built environment bridges the gap between the present and the past, even as modernization produces new meanings. Houses are part of a larger sphere of consumption and identity where old practices and new are sometimes contested, sometimes co-opted. As Mintz (1985) has shown in his work on sugar, and Weismantel (1989) and others for subsistence foods, consumption involves multiple intersections of taste and social identity within a complex world of producers and consumers, rich and poor, powerful and

185

exploited. Consumption and identity become intertwined with new roles, new aspirations, and new gender and generational relationships (Orlove and Rutz 1989; Weismantel 1989; Mintz 1985). These are reflected in the proliferation of new houses being built using designs, ideas, and appliances imported from the United States (see Pader 1993 and Heyman 1994). The new designs shape the spatial ordering of everyday life and are part of the re-creation of social space in a changing economic and moral landscape.

Many villagers point to their houses as one of the main benefits of migrating two thousand miles to labor in California, and building a house is one of the main incentives to migrate. The new houses break with tradition in many ways (in terms of design, materials, and use of space), but at the same time they represent a continuity with the past. Not only do they link migrants to the village, but they also carry on a tradition of the house and family as the center of everyday life. While in many ways new houses are built to U.S. specifications, they are modified to accommodate a rural Mexican lifestyle. Migrants speak of having the comforts of the United States, but in the village, and of "raising themselves up" through migration. Migration is seen both as bringing unwelcome changes, reflected in anxiety about the future, and as opening up possibilities. By working in the United States to build elaborate houses in Mexico, Napizareños are both breaking with tradition and building on the past.

Bourdieu has argued that the house is a reduced image of the world. Houses both reflect social structure and are a spatial objectification of cultural meanings. Bourdieu (1977, 1980, 1990) shows how the built environment reinforces social relations but is maintained through the everyday actions of human actors. The geographer David Harvey argues, however, that in the context of capitalism, Bourdieu's reading of the spatial environment is overly determined and static. For Harvey, "modernization entails the disruption of temporal and spatial rhythms, [as] modernism takes as one of its missions the production of space and time in a world of ephemerality and fragmentation" (Harvey 1989, 216).

In this paper, I argue that, although houses reinforce and reflect social relations and structure everyday behavior, these relationships are increasingly problematic in the context of the high rates of social mobility and heterogeneity found in a transnational migrant community. The house and daily lives of household members reflect the realities of a transnational existence: lives and families and work spread out across a multiplicity of locales and involving a diversity of identities (Marcus 1986; Jameson 1985; Rouse 1989). Despite a growing dependence on migrant remittances, most villagers continue to pursue agricultural activities, but these activities are often difficult to carry out in houses built to U.S. standards. Village moral standards of behavior between genders and generations are at odds with some of the new house designs and reflect a growing division between and within families as their lives become increasingly fragmented. Large new houses may represent a migrant's success in the United States but also are displays of conspicuous consumption incompatible with the village ethic of equality.

These contradictions raise questions about how social relations are reproduced by a built environment that is in constant flux, when members of the same family live in radically different houses, and when within a single generation the built environment has changed profoundly. How do people "fit" their new houses, with designs and spatial relationships imported from the United States, into the existing social context? How are the subtle lessons about social relationships and propriety transmitted to youngsters who live in houses completely unlike the ones in which their parents were raised? Houses are the intimate sites of family life, and they are also the sites of these radical changes. The everyday experience of living in migrant houses at times both creates practical problems and produces profound disjunctures between tradition and modernity.

Migration and Houses

Napízaro is famous in the Pátzcuaro region for its high rates of migration, its new church built by migrant remittances, and its proliferation of new houses. The village, which is located in a mountainous region of the state of Michoacán, is situated on the shores of Lake Pátzcuaro, a large fresh water lake surrounded by high peaks. At 2,050 meters above sea level, it is in the *tierra templada,* or cool country. Like other communities around the lake, Napízaro is an *ejido.*[1] Villagers rely on the traditional *milpa* (maize, beans, and squash) grown on rain-fed lands of relatively poor quality.[2]

A small village in a rural region of subsistence farmers, Napízaro is far from national or even state centers of power. A one-lane paved road connecting Napízaro to the *cabecera municipal* (analogous to a county seat, the nearest town) was completed only in 1990. However, Napízaro's seeming isolation is illusory. Like other rural areas throughout the world, Napízaro is increasingly integrated with national and international markets for commodities and labor. As in many communities in Mexico, migration represents the key mode in which villagers in Napízaro are brought into an international economic system.

Villagers from Napízaro have been involved in labor migration to the United States since the late 1940s. During the Bracero program about half of the married village men migrated.[3] Once a short-term means of pursuing modest goals within a peasant *ejido* economy, today migration is a source of long-term employment and is viewed as a permanent part of the fabric of village economy, society, and culture. Income remitted by migrants represents a significant component of the village economy. In 1989, 88 percent of households in the village received remittances from migrants in the United States. On average, remittances comprised one-third of these households' total income.[4]

A larger share of village households are landless than in the past due to a substantial increase in population since the land distributions of the 1930s and 1940s. The village is no longer comprised solely of subsistence-based family farms. Only half now belong to the *ejido;* the rest control no land, though they may sharecrop, rent fields, or have access to *ejido* land through family members. Increasing numbers of households today are dependent on migrant remittance income.

Money earned in the United States is necessary to maintain even a fairly modest life style. In the past ten years, certain levels of material living have become viewed as the minimum. Houses ideally should be at least somewhat modernized (*mejoradas,* literally, "improved"), with cement floors, electricity, and brick or concrete walls. For a small-holding farmer, to live in a modest house and meet even the basic needs of a varied diet and medical care requires extending household activity into labor markets outside the village.

Mexico's economic crisis in the mid-1980s and a lack of urban employment opportunities in Mexico meant an increased involvement in wage labor in the United States. This activity, however, comes into conflict with other values and ideals, especially in terms of family unity. The original aim of the migrants—to supplement subsistence in the village—is often sidetracked by new goals, expectations, and complications arising from migrants' experience in the United States. The undertaking of constructing a modern house prolongs many migrants' sojourns in the United States. The paradoxical result is that, although families are spread over two countries, much of their effort goes toward building a family home in the village, in which they may not be able to live.

The house itself, inextricably tied to place, retains a great symbolic and material significance. Despite Napizareños' reliance on migrant remittances, the small-holding farm unit is still of central importance economically. Although their activities take place within much larger spheres—the village, region, Mexico and the global economy—it is through the house that people, money, and goods flow and resources are allocated. The importance of the house has its roots in the traditional economic practices of smallholding. The centrality of the house is evoked in villagers' discourse about economics and agricultural activity. Expenditures are referred to as *gastos de la casa* (expenditures of the house), while household income is called *ingreso de la casa* (income of the house).[5] Houses are also at the center of family life in Napízaro and are where much of everyday life is transacted. It is within the house that people are nourished, raised, and taught in the ways of life. Houses also have sacred qualities. Most contain an altar, and new construction is blessed by the priest and adorned with a cross.

Overwhelmingly, the main project funded by migrant earnings is house improvement and construction. Most of the new additions are of brick, locally produced and laid by masons from the nearby village of Puácuaro. Some of the newest houses are built of reinforced cement. New houses are built by young couples on the husband's parents' *solar* (house plot) or on land deeded by the *ejido*. House improvements are almost always paid for by remittances, and, when asked, villagers give the cost of construction in dollars. Houses are a visual record of a family's migration history. They tell much of the story: the dutiful children who have paid to add a brick second story to their parents' old adobe, the successful migrant who builds a new concrete home in anticipation of marriage, and the larger unfinished homes of migrants who now only dream of retiring in Napízaro.

House building in Napízaro is not a new activity. At the time of the revolution most people lived in small one- or two-room stone houses with dirt floors and wooden roofs. They were built of local materials with family and kin labor. The first large wave of house improvement came during the late 1940s and 1950s, when braceros first began migrating to the United States. Many men migrated for the purpose of saving money to build a house and get married. The stone houses were replaced by small adobe structures with clay tile roofs, and eventually concrete floors. The greatest change in this period was in the number of houses. Young men were much less likely to bring their new wife home to live with their parents, and a new, modest adobe house became almost a prerequisite for marriage. House construction sped up in the late 1970s and 1980s, reflecting a new surge in migration from the village, increased remittances sent home for house improvements, and return migrants embarking on ambitious new-house construction. Migrant households prospered relative to nonmigrant ones. Table 7.1 compares U.S. migrant and nonmigrant household incomes. In 1989, the average income of households with migrants in the United States was double that of households without U.S. migrants. Average remittances to U.S. migrant households were $1,372 (not counting remittances in kind). The average number of U.S. migrants per U.S. migrant household rose from 2.8 to 4.3 between 1982 and 1989.

Migrant houses, already larger than those of nonmigrants in the early 1980s, became more so by the end of the decade (table 7.1, bottom panel). In 1982, the average number of rooms (excluding kitchens) in houses without migrants was 1.5; in houses with migrants, it was 2.8. By 1989, while nonmigrant houses stayed the same size, the average migrant house expanded to 3.6 rooms. This number includes new migrants who had just started to improve their houses; some families with a longer history of migration had as many as ten rooms.[6]

New houses signaled a break in the relationship between house and environment. Thick, insulating adobe walls made of local material gave way to houses of brick, concrete, and rebar. For the first time, concrete two-story additions appeared, often connected to old adobe structures

TABLE 7.1.   Comparison of U.S. Migrant and Nonmigrant Incomes and Houses

	U.S. Migrant Households		Nonmigrant Households[a]		All Households	
1989						
Income	$4,479		$2,285		$4,127	
Remittances from						
U.S. migrants	$1,372		$287		$1,198	
Year:	1982	1989	1982	1989	1982	1989
U.S. migrants						
per household	2.8	4.3	—	—	1.8	3.6
Number of rooms						
per house	2.7	3.6	1.5	1.5	2.6	3.3
Share with some brick						
and concrete walls	9.5%	52%	0%	0%	8%	44%

[a]Include households with rural-to-urban migrants in Mexico.

reinforced with steel and concrete. No nonmigrant houses have brick or concrete construction, and only 10 percent of migrant houses did in 1982. By 1989, however, 52 percent of families with migrants had some brick or concrete walls in their house. New houses, built entirely from brick and concrete, incorporated design elements new to Napízaro such as glass windows set into steel frames, interior staircases, dining and living rooms, and modern interior kitchens. Today, most construction in Napízaro is a hodgepodge of additions to existing adobe structures, one wall or room at a time. The most common house comprises two or three rooms built in a row along a *corredor* (porch). The kitchen is usually joined to these rooms, but it may be a small separate outbuilding in the traditional style.

Houses built in Napízaro since the mid-1980s reflect the suburban styles of southern California as much as the middle-class urban style of Mexico. Most migrants went to suburban Los Angeles, where they lived in apartments or in rented houses. The suburban houses in which migrants lived were built around the concept of the working man, housewife, and children. As Hayden (1984) has noted, suburban houses are empty boxes meant to be filled with consumer items. New houses in Napízaro share many features with suburban California housing: downstairs living, dining, and cooking spaces open to each other, with bedrooms removed from view either upstairs or down a hallway.[7] While not all of Napízaro houses are *mejoradas,* they illustrate the transnational lives of their occupants in other ways. Images of the United States adorn the walls: calendars, postcards, posters, and photographs of children at Disneyland. Almost all migrant homes have television sets, and many have VCRs. Boxes of clothes sent from the United States are stored along with maize. Other manufactured items have been purchased in the town of Pátzcuaro: mattresses, acrylic blankets, some furniture items, china, pots and pans, blenders, and plastic buckets and dishes. These replace sleeping *metates* (reed mats), rough wooden tables and chairs, earthenware dishes and cooking pots, and stone mortars and pestles, all produced locally and available in the Erongarícuaro market.

House Design, Economic Space, and Consumption

In the transnational context the built environment is separated from its role in the reproduction of social relations. The house, in particular, is increasingly linked to individual consumption choices, influenced by U.S. styles and the invasion of consumer images through the media, on the one hand, and new sources of income, on the other. Paying attention to the everyday practices of consumption is critical to understanding both daily life and larger social transformations. In this sense, houses are central as the locus of growing consumerism, as consumer items in themselves, and as goods saturated with meaning.

Houses as Consumer Goods

Wilk (1989) has pointed out the importance of understanding houses as consumer goods in themselves. Decisions about house construction involve the allocation of resources, but they also are a reflection of identity and position within the community and activities and dynamics within the household.[8] Thus, while house construction involves consumption decisions about cost, style, size, and materials, these decisions are made within the context of village opinions and values, as well as family dynamics. The role of houses as consumer goods also becomes more pronounced as house building becomes a means of self-expression. Consumption and identity are intertwined with new aspirations and desires, shaped both by migrants' experience in the United States and by exposure to consumer goods through the new proliferation of televisions in the village. Differences in housing, in a village much more homogeneous in the past, is a striking reminder of the disparities in income and life-styles being introduced by remittance income.

In the past, the social landscape was more fixed, and Napizareños' houses looked like rural peasant houses throughout the region: small one-room adobe or stone houses with clay tile roofs. As ejidal small-holding farmers on marginal lands, far from urban centers of power and influence, consumption levels were relatively static and low. In that landscape, houses were, among other things, a reflection of the marginal position of Napízaro in the social hierarchy of Mexico. Napizareños identity was tied to region, ethnicity, and occupation.

Migration introduces a confusion and multiplication of acceptable identities. Consumption becomes a means of self-expression that is manifested not only in house styles, but in other ways; for example, in the widely divergent styles of dress now worn in the village. Several new homes are overtly oriented toward display, with televisions and other consumer goods displayed in large picture windows that defy the convention of private interiors found throughout Latin America.

Houses as the Locus of Consumption

Houses in Napízaro are increasingly the locus of consumption and reproduction, with productive activities carried on as wage labor elsewhere. While families still engage in the daily routines of agricultural labor, more of their income comes from livestock, remittances and other activities than from the traditional *milpa* farming, which in 1989 only accounted for 8 percent of the average composition of household incomes. (This figure includes the implicit value of subsistence production.) The other 92 percent was divided almost equally among livestock, remittances, and "other," which includes handicrafts, fishing, and local wage labor. Consumption takes on a whole new meaning, as it is no longer tied to subsistence production but is underwritten by cash remittances and includes a vast new world of consumer goods that are increasingly available in rural Mexico as well as purchased by migrants in the United States. Houses demonstrate this new consumption orientation; they are less and less suited to accommodate traditional production activities.

The adobe houses that dominated the village until the 1980s were the center of many agricultural production activities: from growing and preparing foods to raising animals and storing and repairing equipment. In traditional houses, chickens roam freely on dirt patios, and rabbit hutches often occupy a shady corner. Pigs are kept in pens adjacent to the yard. These animals are fed scraps from the day's meals. Porches and patios are areas where tasks are performed, from repairing plows and fishing nets to shelling beans. Donkeys are often brought into the patio in the evening, and households with a horse usually have a small stable in the yard.

The new houses reflect the commodification of houses and of the daily lives of people within them (Evers, Claus, and Wong, 1984), as the new designs reflect the loss of productive activities. New styles are not suited to an agricultural way of life. Yards are planted with rose bushes, and, in one case, a grass lawn. What is missing in the new houses is as telling as what is added: often the special area for storing maize in the rafters, the *tapanco,* is absent, as poured-concrete roofs eliminate this space entirely from most new houses. Small stables have been converted into garages for trucks and tractors. Not all the improvements find an easy fit in the rural setting, however. Chickens roost on television sets. Toilets sit in sheds, unusable without sewers or septic systems; burros and horses are stabled in carports. Gas stoves sometimes go unused, as women continue to prepare tortillas over wood fires.

Kitchens are now being brought into the house, as cooking departs from a subsistence-based diet of beans and tortillas. Beans are usually cooked in clay pots over small, wood-burning fires that burn all day in the old kitchens, situated away from the house and often rather smoky. In traditional kitchens, tile roofs allow smoke from wood burning stoves to escape through their many cracks and gaps while helping to reduce spoilage of maize stored in the rafters. In the new homes, kitchens have low, flat, plaster and concrete ceilings. Because of this, women often still prepare tortillas and beans in separate, traditional kitchens, using old wood-burning stoves, or *paranguas* (an arrangement of cooking pots on three stones over a small open fire). In houses with two kitchens, new gas stoves, paid for by migrant remittances, may be used to cook some dishes, but it is commonly believed by both men and women that beans and tortillas taste better when prepared over a wood fire. Gas stoves also represent more commitment to a cash economy, as gas must be purchased from vendors outside the village. This is in contrast to firewood, which is gathered in the nearby mountains.

Now cooking is more of a purely consumptive activity as people with remittance income eat more purchased foods that entail less preparation. This suggests changes in women's activities, which are becoming more oriented toward consumption and reproduction and less to production. Women previously worked long hours turning products of the land into food. Now more and more women buy prepared foods, especially bread and in some cases corn flour for tortillas, and families with remittances eat beans less often.

The shift away from household production in the village is nowhere more evident than in houses built by migrants who are unwilling or unable to keep their families in the village. These houses are built entirely for consumption and recreation and are often oriented toward a view of the lake, as retired migrants use their earnings to consume landscapes as well as "village life." The houses are empty because migrants do not have the means to support themselves in the village. They are usually unfinished because even successful migrants do not earn much money. These houses are the most poignant reminders of the contradictions of a transnational existence. While they embody migrants' commitment to life in the village, they also entail an ongoing engagement in waged labor. Years spent in the United States often bring on further complications, such as marriage to a nonvillager and the arrival of children who do not wish to return to the village.

House Design, Social Space, and Social Relations

I have noted some of the disjunctures between agricultural pursuits and modern houses. There are other more personal ways in which the organization of household space evokes the uneasy balance between tradition and modernity, migrant and nonmigrant, Mexico and the United States. Both household activities and social relationships are reconfigured in the new house designs.

Relationships within the Household

The organization of household space structures and reflects activity, but sometimes in an uneasy mix. Houses in rural Mexico traditionally have reinforced notions of propriety and patriarchal hierarchy. They are women's domain. Women and children are expected to remain within the house, except for short purposeful expeditions to the church or *tienda* (store) or to visit female relatives. (One of the most frequent criticisms of migrants' children, especially teenage girls, is that they are in the street for no purpose.) Notions of male and female both constrain and are constrained by the use of space, and this tension is reflected in people's apparent unease with the changes in floor plans.

Older houses do not have a living room at all. Guests are entertained on the *corredor,* the covered porch found on most adobes, or in the patio. Porches and patios are transitional zones between the house and yard. The interior rooms (usually two *recámaras* and sometimes a kitchen) are more private, although friends may be invited into a kitchen if it is part of the house and a place where the family takes its meal.[9] Only during the worst weather are nonfamily members invited inside a *recámara.* Normally, the only place where unrelated men and women visit is on the patio or *corredor.* Usually, the woman is engaged in some other activity, such as washing or sewing clothes or shucking corn.

In the new homes, men and women are less segregated. There is no *corredor* and often no patio, and in a departure from cultural norms visitors are invited into the house. Many of the newest homes are built on an "open plan," with rooms, including the kitchen, situated off a central living room. Women are no longer out of sight in a separate kitchen or in the private space of the bedroom. This often means women must retire into a bedroom when their husbands entertain guests in the living room or else violate a code of separation of unrelated men and women. Migrant families find that their children who have spent years in the United States now demand privacy and independence, including rooms, stereos, and televisions of their own. Pader (1993) argues that such conflicting conceptual and spatial frameworks are a means by which changing attitudes about the roles of individuals are mediated. I turn now to one family whose experiences building a suburban style house illustrate some of the negotiations and accommodations made by migrant families in the village.

Samuel and Marta's house is the end product of fifteen years spent laboring in the United States. The youngest son in a large family, Samuel had no hope of inheriting land, and at eighteen he left the village to begin his long sojourn as a transnational migrant. During this time his aspirations shifted away from the hope of returning to the village, and he, in his own words, decided to better himself. He learned fluent English, rose to the position of production manager, and eventually became legalized. After marrying a migrant from the village, he and his wife began to save to buy a house in California, where they could raise their children in a better environment than in the crowded apartment complex where they lived. But they were impeded by California's real estate boom in the 1980s and found that the $25,000 they had saved could not help them buy even a modest home.

Samuel and Marta decided instead to use the money to build what Samuel calls his *casa de sueños,* or dream house, in the village. For $75.00 they purchased plans from a contractor for a tract-style home in a California suburb. Over three years, Samuel spent summer vacations supervising work on his large two-story house. The house is built on an open plan, with kitchen, dining room, and living room all connected. The living room furniture is laid out around a large Zenith console television, which is centered in the picture window.

While building a house is a family project, the design and use of space raises conflicts between individuals and between older notions of propriety, privacy, and function. Of the three bedrooms upstairs, one was to be for visiting relatives, but to Samuel's surprise each of his two daughters insisted on having her own room. He spoke often of how he wanted his children to have everything in the village they had in the United States. However, he had not counted on their newly acquired desire for individual space and privacy. He, his wife, and their youngest daughter continue to share a room. The house does not have a patio. Visitors invited into the house sit in the living room, from which Marta can be seen cooking at the kitchen stove, although she often retires upstairs when friends of Samuel stop by. The oldest daughter resents being told to go upstairs when she is watching television. Samuel's house lacks an altar, and he says he feels the lack but he did not know quite where to put it, in the largest house in the village. He explains that it would look strange in the new house.

Although their savings covered the cost of building the house, Samuel was not able to join his family in Mexico until almost three years after they returned to the village. He continued to work, to purchase the furnishings and appliances needed to fill the large house. His last major purchase before he quit his job to return permanently to Mexico was a large satellite dish, the village's first and, in 1991, only. His wife had hoped for a washing machine. He and his daughters campaigned for the highly visible satellite dish, so that they could watch shows from the United States. However, it turned out that only religious shows from the United States travel the distance, and so his children watch Mexican television and his wife continues to wash clothes by hand in a cement basin in the yard.

Despite the perception that the new houses are more comfortable and modern, they are not easier to maintain than traditional houses. Marta now spends less time cooking but more time cleaning and maintaining the large house: hauling water to the upstairs bathroom, still without working plumbing; trying to keep mud from the street off her white tile floors; hauling laundry upstairs from the back yard to hang out to dry on a small roof area; traveling to market in Erongarícuaro to buy food.

Relations within the Village

Modern house designs encourage new types of social interaction between villagers as well as between family members. One example is the way villagers socialize and visit. The new living rooms with comfortable chairs may seem more conducive to visiting. However, their formality discourages the kind of casual visiting done in traditional homes, where a visitor may sit on a stool or wooden chair while his or her host continues to shuck corn or repair a fishing net. Consumption goods, which were formerly kept in the more private *recámaras,* become public, as visitors sit surrounded by goods purchased in the United States (television sets, stereos, VCRs, and appliances). Furthermore, not everyone is invited in, so what may have been a brief visit on someone's patio becomes an awkward discussion at the front door.

The houses themselves are a socially acceptable form of consumption. They are less threatening to other villagers than investment in productive activities might be—there is a sense that investment in cattle depletes village resources, for example. Investment in houses signals a commitment to the village, and most people are pleased by the aesthetics of the new concrete structures. Houses are a socially preferred consumption good partly because they reflect values within the community; they are the center of family life. However, Samuel's house and satellite dish are the subject of veiled but significant criticism. The satellite dish, visible throughout the village, is thought to *chupar las ondas* (suck the airwaves) from the other villagers' more modest antennas. A television and an antenna have been the mark of the successful migrant, and now their achievement is eclipsed if not negated by the new satellite dish. While people aspire to live in a new house, or at least an "improved" house, conspicuous consumption such as Samuel's challenges a village ethic of equality, reflected in the popular refrains *todos somos iguales aquí* (we are all equal here) and *somos pobres juntos* (we are poor together).[10]

Samuel's *casa de sueños* is not just a symbol of his aspirations to be middle class or North American. As he explains it, it is his life achievement, following a new route to success now available to a landless young man with no prospects in Mexico. But his somewhat uncomfortable position in the village reflects how Samuel is representative of something most villagers dread—the demise of their way of life, the erosion of subsistence farming, and a new class division. During his fifteen-year absence Samuel did not continue to participate in village life as much as most migrants. He paid his *cooperación* (contribution) for the church and the annual fiestas, but he did not maintain extensive *compadrazgo* (fictive-kinship) relationships. Even now, when *ejido* reforms make some land available to migrants, he disdains the life of a farmer. Instead, after returning from the United States, he lived off of savings until he finally found a job in the nearby *cabecera municipal.*[11] In the past migrants used their remittances to invest in an agricultural way of life, to build a house, buy animals, seed, fertilizer, and possibly a tractor or truck. Samuel's level of consumption, the size of his suburban style house, filled with imported goods such as a refrigerator from Sears and a VCR, mark a new level in the scale of consumption.

Samuel's house, which used to be an anomaly, now appears to be the harbinger of the future. Another village migrant has hired Samuel's bricklayer and is building a copy of his house. This upsets Samuel and Marta greatly, as they feel their house is a reflection of themselves. The other village tract house sits empty and unfinished. The owner sends money to his father, who oversees the construction.

Conclusion

Empty, unfinished houses scattered around the village of Napízaro illustrate the way an agricultural life has been preempted by the experience of migration. That they are even being built is testimony to migrants' sense of commitment and their reluctance to abandon their sense of who they are. Migrants retain an enduring sense of identity with the village. At the same time, however, they entail a prolonged engagement in proletarian labor.

The new houses, financed by migrants and based on designs imported from the United States, are increasingly centered around consumption, not production. The house is losing its role as the center of productive activities, as the household is increasingly drawn into market relations, especially wage labor. This is part of a historical process throughout the world, with the workplace of labor far removed from the site of reproduction. As houses in Napízaro lose their productive function (in terms of subsistence agriculture), they increasingly serve reproductive functions by creating new laborers for distant markets. In this way, the house is at the center of the transformation of an agricultural community into a source of labor for transnational labor markets and a market for manufactured goods. New houses as a repository of consumer goods signal a growing commitment to a cash economy, entailing an ongoing need for migrant remittances.

The new designs also both reflect and restructure social relationships. In some cases the houses are modified (for example, Samuel stores corn in a small room originally intended for the TV); in others, domestic social relations are renegotiated within the new spatial arrangements. (By the end of my fieldwork, for example, Samuel's daughter had won the right to remain in the living room when guests arrived.) The acceptance of these new styles in the village is changing, as well, and what was once controversial is becoming the norm. By 1992 virtually every family received some remittance income, many more house projects were underway, and another family had set up a satellite dish.

It is tempting to view these new ranch-style houses with their large picture windows as markers of rural Mexican villagers' aspirations to be more modern or to embrace U.S. culture. There may be some truth in this reading, but as anthropologists come to a new understanding of the complex interweaving of cultural identity and consumption, we need to look more closely at these interrelationships (Weismantel 1989). For some migrants, new houses reflect aspirations, for others they are markers of real achievements. But they also call into question power and identity. To some villagers they pose a threat. What is at stake is not simply a question of consumption and different house styles, but the loss of a rural way of life.

Migrants initially go to the United States for village-centered reasons such as to build a house for marriage. But as complications arise in their lives in California, some find it difficult to return to live in these houses. Others who do return find themselves increasingly drawn back to the United States as their new houses, appliances, and lifestyles demand a continual influx of cash. For many migrants, building a house remains proof of a commitment to the community. Whether lived in or not, the houses tie migrants to the village and provide a way for them to bridge the gap between their lives in the United States and their lives in Mexico.

The new migrant houses should be seen not only within the context of global labor and commodity markets, but also within the context of changing spatial relationships that reflect an overall reworking of the village economy and social structure. The village map is changing, with new houses, a new church financed by remittances, and a road that now links Napízaro with the outside world, significantly paving the way for an influx of consumer goods. A new landscape is wrought by declining agricultural yields, the *milpa* giving way to monocropping, and hill lands turned to pasture. Increasing numbers of landless villagers either migrate to the United States or labor on the lands of those who use remittances to pay them. While the new houses themselves are not a cause of the demise of the subsistence economy, they are visible markers of new class differences dividing the village and a reminder that to pursue agriculture in the village is to remain poor.

NOTES

An earlier version of this paper was presented at the American Ethnological Society Meetings in Santa Fe in 1993. This paper is based on research conducted in Los Angeles and Mexico in 1983, 1989, 1990, and 1992, supported in part by a research grant from the Johns Hopkins University, Department of Anthropology. Additional support was provided in 1992 by a National Science Foundation Grant for a larger project undertaken by Benjamin Orlove, J. Edward Taylor, and myself. I would like to thank both Benjamin Orlove and Edward Taylor for their insightful comments on this paper.

1. *Ejidos* are communities granted land during reforms after the Revolution of 1910, and especially during the presidency of Cárdenas in the 1940s; they are currently undergoing a massive reorganization, though this process began largely after the fieldwork reported here. *Ejido* also refers to the plots of land themselves.

Ejidatarios are granted use rights to the land, which is held corporately by the community, not the individual. Contrary to law, much *ejido* land is rented and sharecropped.

2. Productivity in this region is lower than average for Mexico: less than one metric ton of corn per hectare. Ejidal holdings in Napízaro are 9 hectares each.

3. What is commonly referred to as the Bracero program was a series of bilateral agreements between the United States and Mexico that brought short-term contract workers from Mexico to the United States from 1917 to 1964.

4. Some households have been able to use remittances to accumulate livestock, which have become the largest single source of income in the village. The rapid growth of this local income source is due to remittances from U.S. migrants. It illustrates the way in which Napízaro's economy has been transformed by migration indirectly.

5. See Gudeman and Rivera (1990) for their concept of the house economy, based on folk concepts, metaphors, and practices in Colombia.

6. All figures in this chapter were compiled from data collected in Napízaro village surveys carried out in the summers of 1983 and 1989. Thirty households were randomly selected for the 1983 survey and reinterviewed in 1989. The surveys gathered information on household income from all activities inside and outside the village, including migration; household assets; and work by all family members during the year preceding the survey.

7. See Pader 1993 for a discussion on the separation of rooms and on distinctions between the areas allocated to family and guests in new homes built with migrant earnings in Jalisco, Mexico.

8. Colloredo-Mansfeld also shows how villagers in an Andean community use new houses to affirm their social position and to legitimize new forms of wealth (1994, 845).

9. *Recámaras* are multipurpose rooms. They serve as bedrooms (shared by several family members), storerooms, and a place to eat and relax in cold weather. They often contain both a television set and an altar.

10. Unequal land distribution due to population increase after the initial land redistribution in the 1940s led to differences in income levels. However, the increased dependence by some families on remittances and the investment of remittances in livestock production have led to an acceleration of income differences in the last decade. For example, the coefficient of variation of household incomes (the standard deviation divided by the mean) rose from 0.86 in 1982 to 1.27 in 1988.

11. Samuel is one of only a handful of villagers who have found employment in the nearby *cabecera municipal* (the local seat of government) of Erongarícuaro.

Bibliography

Acción Cultural Loyola and Corporación de Desarrollo de Chuquisaca. 1979. *Estudio socioeconómico de la Provincia Hernando Siles.* 2d ed. Sucre: n.p.

Ades, Dawn. 1989. *Art in Latin America.* New Haven: Yale University Press.

Aguilar Camín, Héctor. 1977. *La frontera nómada: Sonora y la revolución mexicana.* México, DF: Siglo Veintiuno Editores.

Alberti, Giorgio, and Enrique Mayer, comp. 1974. *Reciprocidad e intercambio en los Andes Peruanos.* Lima: IEP.

Alberti, Giorgio, and Rodrigo Sánchez. 1974. *Poder y conflicto social en el Valle del Mantaro (1900–1974).* Lima: IEP.

Alvarenga, Patricia. 1986. Las explotaciones agropecuarias en los albores de la expansión cafetalera. *Revista de Historia* 14:115–32.

Alvarez, Robert R., and George A. Collier. 1994. The Long Haul in Mexican Trucking: Traversing the Borderlands of the North and the South. *American Ethnologist* 21:606–27.

Anderson, Benedict. 1983. *Imagined Communities: Reflections on the Origin and Spread of Nationalism.* London: Verso.

Anderson, Eugene N. 1988. *The Food of China.* New Haven: Yale University Press.

Appadurai, Arjun, ed. 1986. *The Social Life of Things: Commodities in Cultural Perspective.* Cambridge and New York: Cambridge University Press.

Barber, Benjamin R. 1995. *Jihad vs. McWorld.* New York: Times Books.

Beezley, William. 1987. *Judas at the Jockey Club and Other Episodes of Porfirian History.* Lincoln: University of Nebraska Press.

Bernstein, Marvin D. 1964. *The Mexican Mining Industry, 1890–1950.* Albany: State University of New York Press.

Besserer, Frederico, Victoria Novelo, and Juan Luís Sariego. 1983. *El sindicalismo minero en México, 1900–1952.* México, DF: Ediciones Era.

Bhabha, Homi. 1977. Of Mimicry and Man: The Ambivalence of Colonial Discourse. *October* 3–4: 125–33.

Bloch, Maurice, ed. 1975. *Political Language and Oratory in Traditional Society.* New York: Academic Press.

Bonilla, Heraclio, comp. 1977. "Charles Milner Ricketts and George Canning," December 27, 1826. *Gran Bretaña,* 17–83, 69. Lima: IEP.

———. comp. 1977. Los mecanismos de un control económico. *Gran Bretaña y el Perú: Informes de los cónsules británicos.* 5 Vols. Lima: IEP.

Bonilla, Heraclio, Lía del Río, and Pilar Ortiz de Zevallos. 1978. Comercio libre y crisis de la economía andina: El caso del Cuzco. *Histórica* 2 (1): 1–25.

Borja y Borja, Ramiro. 1988. Los regimenes de la representación política en Latinoamérica. *Revista de Historia de las Ideas* 9 (second series): 173–207.

Bourdieu, Pierre. 1977. *Outline of a Theory of Practice.* Cambridge: Cambridge University Press.

———. 1980. The Production of Belief: Contribution to an Economy of Symbolic Goods. *Media, Culture and Society* 2 (3): 261–93.

———. [1980] 1990. *The Logic of Practice,* trans. R. Nice. Cambridge: Polity.

Braudel, Fernand. 1973. *Capitalism and Material Life,* trans. Miriam Kochan. New York: Harper and Row.

Breckenridge, Carol A., ed. 1995. *Consuming Modernity: Public Culture in a South Asian World.* Minneapolis: University of Minnesota Press.

Brenneis, Donald Lawrence, and Fred R. Myers. 1984. *Dangerous Words: Language and Politics in the Pacific.* New York: New York University Press.

Burga, Manuel, and Wilson Reátegui. 1981. *Lanas y capital mercantil en el sur: la Casa Ricketts, 1895–1935.* Lima: Instituto de Estudios Peruanos.

Calderón, Fernando. 1988. *Imágenes desconocidas: La modernidad en la encrucijada postmoderna.* Biblioteca de Ciencias Sociales, Buenos Aires: Consejo Latinoamericano de Ciencias Sociales.

Calzavarini, Lorenzo G. 1980. *Nación chiriguana: Grandeza y ocaso.* La Paz: Los Amigos del Libro.

Carballo Vega, José Luís. 1982. *Hacia una interpretación del desarrollo costarricense: Ensayo sociológico.* San José: Editorial Porvenir.

Cardoso, Ciro. 1976. La formación de la hacienda cafetalera en Costa Rica (siglo XIX). In *Avances de investigación. Proyecto de historia social y económica de Costa Rica (1821–1845).* 4: 21.

Carrier, James G. 1994. *Gifts and Commodities: Exchange and Western Capitalism since 1770.* London: Routledge.

Castells, Manuel. 1983. *The City and the Grassroots: A Cross-Cultural Theory of Urban Social Movements.* Berkeley and Los Angeles: University of California Press.

Chervin, Arthur. 1908. *Anthropologie Bolivienne.* Vol. 1 Paris: Imprimie Nationale.

Chile. 1915. *Chile in 1915.* Santiago: Published by the Chilean Government.

Chirot, Daniel. 1976. *Social Change in a Peripheral Society: The Creation of a Balkan Colony.* New York: Academic Press.

———. ed. 1989. *The Origins of Backwardness in Eastern Europe: Economics and Politics from the Middle Ages until the Early Twentieth Century.* Berkeley and Los Angeles: University of California Press.

Chocano, Magdalena. 1983. Circuitos comerciales y auge minero en la Sierra Central a fines de la época colonial. *Allpanchis* 19 (21): 3–26.

Clastres, Pierre. 1977. *Society Against the State.* Oxford: Mole Editions.

Cochran, Sherman. 1980. *Big Business in China: Sino-Foreign Rivalry in the Cigarette Industry, 1890–1930.* Harvard Studies in Business History. Cambridge: Harvard University Press.

Cohen, Ronald, and Elman R. Service, eds. 1978. *Origins of the State: The Anthropology of Political Issues.* Philadelphia: Institute for the Study of Human Issues.

Colloredo-Mansfeld, Rudolf. 1994. Architectural Conspicuous Consumption and Economic Change in the Andes. *American Anthropologist* 96 (4): 845–65.

Combès, Isabelle, and Thierry Saignes. 1991. *Alter Ego: Naissance de l'Identité Chiriguano.* Paris: Ecole des Hautes Etudes en Sciences Sociales.

Commercial Encyclopedia. 1922. Argentina Brazil Chile Peru Uruguay. *British and Latin American Chamber of Commerce Sole Official Annual and/or Biennial Organ.* Comp. and pub. W. H. Morton-Cameron. London: Globe Encyclopedia Company.

Corrado, Alejandro M. [1884] 1990. *El Colegio Franciscano de Tarija y sus misiones.* 2d ed. Tarija: Editorial Offset Franciscana.

Cortés, Ramón E., and José Manuel Padilla. 1927. "Estadística de la Provincia del Azero año 1927." *Informe Prefectural: Departamento de Chuquisaca,* Eulogio Ostria Reyes. Sucre: ANB.

Cruchaga, Miguel. 1878. *Estudio sobre la organización económica i la hacienda pública en Chile.* Santiago: Imprenta de "Los Tiempos."

Curtin, Philip D. 1984. *Cross-Cultural Trade in World History.* Cambridge: Cambridge University Press.

Custred, Glynn, and Benjamin S. Orlove. 1980. The Alternative Model of Agrarian Society in the Andes: Households, Networks, and Corporate Groups. In *Land and Power in Latin America: Agrarian Economies and Social Processes in the Andes,* ed. Glynn Custred and Benjamin S. Orlove. New York: Holmes and Meier Publishers.

Dalence, José María. 1975. *Bosquejo estadístico de Bolivia.* La Paz: UMSA.

De la Cadena, Marisol. 1994. Decencia y cultura política: Los indigenistas del Cuzco en los años veinte. *Revista Andina* 1:79–122.

Delaney, Carol. 1991. *The Seed and the Soil: Gender and Cosmology in Turkish Village Society.* Berkeley and Los Angeles: University of California Press.

de Nino, Bernardino. 1912. *Etnografía chiriguana.* La Paz: Tipografía Comercial de Ismael Argote.

———. 1918. *Misiones franciscanas del Colegio de Propaganda Fide de Potosí.* La Paz: Tipo-Litografía "Marinoni."

DeShazo, Peter. 1983. *Urban Workers and Labor Unions in Chile 1902–1927.* Madison: University of Wisconsin Press.

Dirlik, Arik. 1994. The Postcolonial Aura: Third World Criticism in the Age of Global Capitalism. *Critical Inquiry* 20 (2): 328–56.

Earle, Timothy K., and Jonathon E. Ericson. 1977. *Exchange Systems in Prehistory.* Studies in Archeology. New York: Academic Press.

Eastman, Lloyd A. 1988. *Family, Fields, and Ancestors: Constancy and Change in China's Social and Economic History, 1550–1949.* New York and Oxford: Oxford University Press.

Edwards Bello, Joaquín. 1994. [1934]. *La chica del Crillón.* 10th ed. Santiago: Editorial Universitaria.

Encina, Francisco Antonio. 1912. *Nuestra inferioridad económica, sus causas, sus consecuencias.* Santiago: Imprenta Universitaria.

Epstein, A. L. 1958. *Politics in an Urban African Community.* Manchester: Manchester University Press.

Evers, H., W. Clauss, and D. Wong. 1984. Subsistence Reproduction: A Framework for Analysis. In *Households and the World Economy,* ed. J. Smith, I. Wallerstein, and H. Evers, 23–36. Beverly Hills: Sage Publications.

Fernández, Hernando Sanabria. 1972. *Apiaguaiqui Tumpa.* La Paz: Los Amigos del Libro.

Fernández-Kelly, María Patricia. 1983. *For We Are Sold, I and My People: Women and Industry in Mexico's Frontier.* Albany: State University of New York Press.

Fernández Guardia, Ricardo. 1982. *Costa Rica en el siglo XIX. Antología de Viajeros.* San José: Editorial Universitaria Costa Rica.

Figueroa, Adolfo. 1984. *Capitalist Development and the Peasant Economy in Peru.* Cambridge: Cambridge University Press.

Fisher, John R. 1970. *Government and Society in Colonial Peru: The Intendent System, 1784–1814.* London: University of London, Athlone Press.

Flannery, Kent V. 1976. *The Early Mesoamerican Village.* New York: Academic Press.

Flores-Galindo, Alberto. 1977. *Arequipa y el sur andino: Ensayo de historia regional, siglos XVIII–XX.* Lima: Editorial Horizonte.

Gal, Susan. 1991. Bartók's Funeral: Representations of Europe in Hungarian Political Rhetoric. *American Ethnologist* 18:440–58.

Gamio, Manuel. 1930. *Mexican Immigration to the United States.* Chicago: University of Chicago Press.

Garavaglia, Juan Carlos. 1983. *Mercado interno y economía colonial.* Mexico: Grijalbo.

Gerstäcker, Friedrich. 1973. *Viaje por el Perú.* Lima: Biblioteca Nacional.

Gilliss, J. M. 1855. *The U.S. Naval Expedition to the Southern Hemisphere during the Years 1849 – '50 – '51 – '52.* Washington, DC: A. O. P. Nicholson.

Glade, William. 1989. Latin America in the International Economy, 1874–1914. *The Cambridge History of Latin America,* ed. Leslie Bethell. Cambridge and New York: Cambridge University Press.

Golte, Jürgen. 1974. *Reparto y rebeliones, Túpac Amaru y las contradicciones de la economía colonial.* Lima: IEP.

Goñi, Rafael A. 1986–1987. Arqueología de sitios tardíos en el Valle del Río Malleo, Provincia del Neuquén. *Relaciones de la Sociedad Argentina de Antropología,* 37–66.

González, Manuel. 1889. Nuestro enemigo el lujo. *Estudios económicos,* 429–62.

Goody, Jack. 1982. *Cooking, Cuisine, and Class: A Study in Comparative Sociology.* Cambridge and New York: Cambridge University Press.

Gootenberg, Paul. 1981. Artisans and Merchants: The Making of an Open Economy in Lima, Peru, 1830 to 1860. Ph.D. diss., University of Oxford.

———. 1989a. *Between Silver and Guano. Commercial Policy and the State in Post-Independence Peru.* Princeton: Princeton University Press.

———. 1989b. *Tejidos, harinas, corazones y mentes: El imperialismo norteamericano de libre comercio en el Perú, 1825–1840.* Lima: Instituto de Estudios Peruanos.

———. 1990. Carneros y Chuño: Price Levels in Nineteenth-Century Peru. *Hispanic American Historical Review* 70 (1).

———. 1993. *Imagining Development: Economic Ideas in Peru's "Fictitious Pros-*

perity" of Guano, 1840–1880. Berkeley and Los Angeles: University of California Press.

Graham, Maria. 1823. *Journal of a Residence in Chile During the Year 1822 and a Voyage From Chile to Brazil in 1823*. London: Longman, Hurst, Rees, Orme, Brown and Green.

Gudeman, Stephen, and Alberto Rivera. 1990. *Conversations in Colombia: The Domestic Economy in Life and Text*. Cambridge: Cambridge University Press.

Gunst, Péter. 1989. Agrarian Systems of Central and Eastern Europe. In *The Origins and Backwardness in Eastern Europe: Economics and Politics From the Middle Ages Until the Early Twentieth Century*, ed. Daniel Chirot, 53–91. Berkeley and Los Angeles: University of California Press.

Haas, Jonathan. 1982. *The Evolution of the Prehistoric State*. New York: Columbia University Press.

Haas, Jonathan, Shelia Pozorski, and Thomas Pozorski, eds. 1987. *The Origins and Development of the Andean State*. Cambridge and New York: Cambridge University Press.

Haigh, Samuel. 1829. *Sketches of Buenos Aires, Chile, and Peru*. London: J. Carpenter and Son.

Hall, Carolyn. 1976. *El café y el desarrollo histórico-geográfico de Costa Rica*. San José: Editorial Costa Rica.

Hamilton, Gary G. 1977. Chinese Consumption of Foreign Commodities: A Comparative Perspective. *American Sociological Review* 42:877–91.

Harvey, David. 1989. *The Condition of Postmodernity*. Cambridge: Basil Blackwell.

Havens, Verne L. 1916. *Markets for American Hardware in Chile and Bolivia*. Washington, DC: U.S. Department of Commerce, Government Printing Office.

Hayden, Dolores. 1984. *Redesigning the American Dream: The Future of Housing, Work and Family Life*. New York: W. W. Norton.

Healy, Kevin. 1982. *Caciques y patrones: Una experiencia de desarrollo rural en el sud de Bolivia*. Cochabamba: Imprente El Bruite.

Herndon, William, and Lardner Gibbon. 1853. *Exploration of the Valley of the Amazon Made Under the Direction of the Navy Department*, Exec. Nr. 36. House of Representatives, 32d Congress, 2d Session, Washington, DC.

Heyman, Josiah McC. 1990. The Emergence of the Waged Life Course on the United States–Mexico Border. *American Ethnologist* 17:348–59.

———. 1991. *Life and Labor on the Border: Working People of Northeastern Sonora, Mexico, 1886–1986*. Tucson: University of Arizona Press.

———. 1994a. The Organizational Logic of Capitalist Consumption on the Mexico–United States Border. *Research in Economic Anthropology* 15:175–238.

———. 1994b. Changes in House Construction Materials in Border Mexico: Four Research Propositions About Commoditization. *Human Organization* 53:132–42.

Hirsch, Silvia. 1989. Mbaporenda: El lugar donde hay trabajo. Migraciones chiriguanas al noroeste argentino. *Primer Congreso Internacional de Etnohistoria*, Buenos Aires.

Hoodfar, Homa. 1997. *Between Marriage and the Market: Intimate Politics and Survival in Cairo*. Berkeley and Los Angeles: University of California Press.

Hoskins, Janet. 1993. *The Play of Time: Kodi Perspectives on Calendars, History, and Exchange.* Berkeley and Los Angeles: University of California Press.

Hurtado Ruíz-Tagle, Carlos. 1966. *Concentración de población y desarrollo económico—el caso chileno.* Santiago: Universidad de Chile, Instituto de Economía.

Jacobsen, Nils. 1988. Free Trade, Regional Elites, and the Internal Market in Southern Peru, 1895–1932. In *Guiding the Invisible Hand: Economic Liberalism and the State in Latin American History,* ed. Joseph. L. Love and Nils Jacobsen. New York: Praeger.

———. 1993. *Mirages of Transition: The Peruvian Altiplano, 1780–1930.* Berkeley and Los Angeles: University of California Press.

Jacoby, Russell. 1995. Marginal Returns. *Lingua Franca* 5 (6): 30–37.

Jameson, F. 1985. Post-Modernism, or the Cultural Logic of Late Capitalism. *New Left Review* 146: 53–92.

Janos, Andrew C. 1982. *The Politics of Backwardness in Hungary, 1825–1945.* Princeton: Princeton University Press.

Jiménez, Michael F. 1995. From Plantation to Cup: Coffee and Capitalism in the United States, 1830–1930. In *Coffee, Society, and Power in Latin America,* ed. W. Roseberry, L. Gudmundson, and M. S. Kutschbach, 38–64.

Jones, Kristine L. 1984. Conflict and Adaptation in the Argentine Pampas. Ph.D. diss., University of Chicago.

Katz, Friedrich. 1981. *The Secret War in Mexico: Europe, the United States, and the Mexican Revolution.* Chicago: University of Chicago Press.

Kerrigan, Anthony. 1950. *Partisan Review* 17 (2): 143–51.

Kierszenson Rochwerger, Frida. 1986. Historia del monopolio de licores (1821–1859). Ph.D. diss., University of Costa Rica.

Kochanowicz, Jacek. 1989. The Polish Economy and the Evolution of Dependency. In *The Origins of Backwardness in Eastern Europe,* ed. Daniel Chirot, 104–43. Berkeley and Los Angeles: University of California Press.

Krüggeler, Thomas. 1993. Unreliable Drunkards or Honorable Citizens? Artisans in Search of Their Place in the Cuzco Society (1825–1930). Ph.D. diss., University of Illinois at Urbana-Champaign.

Kula, Witold. 1976. *An Economic Theory of the Feudal System: Towards a Model of the Polish Economy, 1500–1800,* trans. Lawrence Garner. New ed. London: N.L.B.

Ladman, Jerry R., and Mark O. Poulson. 1972. *The Economic Impact of the Mexican Border Industrialization Program: Agua Prieta, Sonora.* Special Study no. 10. Tempe: Center for Latin American Studies, Arizona State University.

Langer, Erick D. 1987. Franciscan Missions and Chiriguano Workers: Colonization, Acculturation, and Indian Labor in Southeastern Bolivia. *The Americas* 42 (1).

———. 1989. *Economic Change and Rural Resistance in Southern Bolivia 1880–1930.* Stanford: Stanford University Press.

———. 1995. Missions and the Frontier Economy: The Case of the Franciscan Missions Among the Chiriguanos (1845–1930). In *The New Latin American*

Mission History, eds. Erick D. Langer and Robert H. Jackson, 49–76. Lincoln: University of Nebraska Press.

Langer, Erick D., and Zulema Bass Werner de Ruíz, eds. 1988. *Historia de Tarija: Corpus documental.* Tarija: Universidad Juan Misael Saracho.

Langer, Erick D., and Gina Hames. 1994. Commerce and Credit on the Periphery: Tarija Merchants, 1830–1914. *Hispanic American Historical Review* 74 (2): 285–316, 302–3.

Larson, Brooke. 1988. *Colonialism and Agrarian Transformation in Bolivia: Cochabamba, 1550–1900.* Princeton: Princeton University Press.

Las cooperativas de consumo organizados sindicalmente en México. 1944. *Instituto de Investigaciones Económicas, Universidad Nacional Autónoma de México.* México, DF: Ediciones Minerva.

Lehmann, David. 1982. Introduction: Andean Societies and the Theory of Peasant Economy. In *Ecology and Exchange in the Andes,* ed. David Lehmann, 1–26. Cambridge: Cambridge University Press.

León, Víctor. 1947. *Uvas y vinos de Chile, Santiago.* Santiago: Sindicato Nacional Vitivinícola.

Lever, Janet. 1983. *Soccer Madness.* Chicago: University of Chicago Press.

Lloyd, Reginald, editor-in-chief. 1915. *Twentieth Century Impressions of Chile. Its History, People, Commerce, Industries, and Resources.* London: Jas. Truscott and Sons.

Long, Norman, and Bryan Roberts, eds. 1984. *Miners, Peasants and Entrepreneurs. Regional Development in the Central Highlands of Peru.* Cambridge: Cambridge University Press.

MacLachlan, Colin, and William Beezley. 1994. *El Gran Pueblo: A History of Greater Mexico.* Englewood Cliffs, NJ: Prentice-Hall.

Malinowski, Bronislaw A. 1922. *Argonauts of the Western Pacific: An Account of Native Enterprise and Adventure in the Archipelagoes of Melanesian New Guinea.* London: G. Routledge.

Mallon, Florencia E. 1983. *The Defense of Community in Peru's Central Highlands: Peasant Struggle and Capitalist Transition, 1860–1940.* Princeton: Princeton University Press.

———. 1995a. The Promise and Dilemma of Subaltern Studies: Perspectives From Latin American History. *American Historical Review.* 99 (5): 1491–515.

———. 1995b. *Peasant and Nation: The Making of Post-Colonial Mexico and Peru.* Berkeley and Los Angeles: University of California Press.

Mandrini, Raúl. 1987. La sociedad indígena de las pampas en el siglo XIX. *Antropología,* comp. Mirta Lischetti, 311–36. Buenos Aires: EUDEBA.

Manrique, Nelson. 1983. Los arrieros de la Sierra Central durante el siglo XIX. *Allpanchis* 18 (21): 27–46.

———. 1987. *Mercado interno y región. La sierra central 1820–1930.* Lima: Desco.

Marcoy, Paul Laurent de Saint Cricq. 1875. *Travels in South America. From the Pacific Ocean to the Atlantic Ocean,* Vol. 1 London: Blackie and Son.

Marcus, George. 1986. Contemporary Problems of Ethnography in the Modern World System. In *Writing Culture: The Poetics and Politics of Ethnography,* ed.

James Clifford and George Marcus. Berkeley and Los Angeles: University of California Press.

Martarelli, Angélico. 1918. *El Colegio Franciscano de Potosí y sus misiones: Noticias históricas.* 2d ed. La Paz: Tipo-Litografía Marinoni.

Mbembe, Achille. 1997. *Provisional Notes on the Post-Colony.* Berkeley and Los Angeles: University of California Press.

Meléndez, Carlos. 1977. *Costa Rica: tierra y poblamiento.* San José: Editorial Costa Rica.

Mendieta, Manuel S. 1928. *Tierra rica, pueblo pobre: Por nuestras fronteras.* Sucre: Imprenta Bolivar.

Mintz, Sidney. 1979. The Rural Proletariat and the Problem of the Rural Proletarian Consciousness. In *Peasants and Proletarians: The Struggles of Third World Workers,* ed. Robin Cohen, Peter C. W. Gutkind, and Phyllis Brazier, 173–97. New York: Monthly Review Press.

———. 1985. *Sweetness and Power: The Place of Sugar in Modern History.* New York: Viking.

Molina Jiménez, Iván. 1991. *Costa Rica (1800–1850). El legado colonial y la génesis del capitalismo.* San José, Costa Rica: Editorial Costa Rica.

Murphy, Robert F., and Julian H. Steward. 1956. Tappers and Trappers: Parallel Process of Acculturation. *Economic Development and Cultural Change* 4: 335–53.

Naylor, Robert J. 1988. *Influencia británica en el comercio centroamericano durante las primeras décadas de la independencia (1821–1851).* Guatemala: Centro de Investigaciones Regionales de Mesoamérica.

Needell, Jeffrey D. 1987. *A Tropical Belle Epoque: Elite Culture and Society in Turn-of-the-century Rio de Janeiro.* Cambridge: Cambridge University Press.

Nordenskiöld, Erland. 1913. *Indianerleben: El Gran Chaco (Südamerika).* Leipzig: Georg Merseburger.

———. 1979. *The Changes in the Material Culture of Two Indian Tribes Under the Influence of New Surroundings.* New York: AMS Press.

Obregón, Clotilde. 1982. Inicio del comercio británico en Costa Rica. *Revista de Ciencias Sociales* 24:59–69.

Orlove, Benjamin S. 1977. *Alpacas, Sheep, and Men: The Wool Export Economy and Regional Society in Southern Peru.* New York: Academic Press.

Orlove, Benjamin S., and Glynn Custred. 1980. Agrarian Economies and Social Processes in Comparative Perspective: The Agricultural Production Unit. *Land and Power in Latin America. Agrarian Economies and Social Processes in the Andes.,* editors Benjamin S. Orlove, and Glynn Custred. New York: Holmes and Meier Publishers.

Orlove, Benjamin S., and Henry J. Rutz. 1989. Thinking About Consumption: A Social Economy Approach. In *The Social Economy of Consumption,* ed. Henry J. Rutz and Benjamin S. Orlove, 1–58. Lanham, MD: University Press of America.

Orlove, Benjamin S., and Ella Schmidt. 1995. Swallowing Their Pride: Indigenous and Industrial Beer in Six Andean Regions. *Theory and Society* 24 (2): 271–98.

Orrego Luco, Luís. 1908. *Casa Grande.* Santiago: "Zig-Zag" Editores.

———. 1984. *Memorias del tiempo viejo.* Santiago: Ediciones de la Universidad de Chile.

Owen, Roger. 1981. *The Middle East in the World Economy.* London: Methuen.

Owen, Roger C. 1959. Marobavi: A Study of an Assimilated Group in Northern Sonora. *Anthropological Papers of the University of Arizona.* Tucson: University of Arizona Press.

Pader, Ellen J. 1993. Spatiality and Social Change: Domestic Space Use in Mexico and the United States. *American Ethnologist.* 20 (1): 114–37.

Palermo, Miguel A. 1988. La innovación agropecuaria entre los indígenas pampeano-patagónicos: génesis y procesos. *Anuario IEHS* 3:43–90.

Palmer, Steven. 1990. A Liberal Discipline. Inventing Nations in Guatemala and Costa Rica (1870–1900). Ph.D. diss., Columbia University.

Parama, Roy. 1991. *Indian Traffic: Subjects in Motion in British India.* Berkeley and London: University of California Press.

Pardo, Manuel. 1947. Estudios sobre la provincia de Jauja (1862). *Manuel Pardo,* comp. Jacinto López. Lima: Imp. Gil.

Parker, David S. 1992. White Collar Lima, 1910–1929: Commercial Employees and the Rise of the Peruvian Middle Class. *Hispanic American Historical Review* 72 (1): 47–72.

Peloso, Vincent C. 1985. Succulence and Sustenance: Region, Class, and Diet in Nineteenth-Century Peru. *Food, Politics, and Society in Latin America,* ed. John C. Super and Thomas C. Wright. Lincoln: University of Nebraska Press.

Pennington, Campbell W. 1979. *The Material Culture of the Pima Bajo of Central Sonora, Mexico.* Vol. 1. Salt Lake City: University of Utah Press.

Pereira de Correa, Teresa, ed. 1992. *Formas de sociabilidad en Chile 1840–1940.* Santiago: Fundación Mario Góngora.

Pereira Salas, Eugenio. 1977. *Apuntes para la historia de la cocina chilena.* Santiago: Editorial Universitaria.

Pifarré, Francisco. 1989. *Los Guaraní Chiriguano: Historia de un pueblo.,* 269–391. La Paz: CIPCA.

Pinckert Justiniano, Guillermo. 1978. *La guerra chiriguana.* Santa Cruz: Talleres Graficos "Los Huerfanos."

Polanyi, Karl, Conrad M. Arensberg, and Harry W. Pearson. 1957. *Trade and Market in Early Empires.* Glencoe, IL: Free Press.

Poole, Deborah. 1997. *Vision, Race and Modernity: The Andean Visual Economy.* Princeton and London: Princeton University Press.

Quesada Monge, Rodrigo. 1985. El comercio entre Gran Bretaña y América Central (1851–1915). *Anuario de Estudios Sociales Centroamericanoss* 11 (2): 85.

Richards, Alan, and John Waterbury. 1990. *A Political Economy of the Middle East: State, Class and Economic Development.* Boulder, CO: Westview Press.

Robinson, Richard D. 1963. *The First Turkish Republic: A Case Study in National Development.* Cambridge: Harvard University Press.

Roseberry, William, Lowell Gudmundson, and Mario Samper Kutschbach, eds. 1995. *Coffee, Society, and Power in Latin America.* Baltimore and London: The Johns Hopkins University Press.

Rouse, Roger. 1989. Mexican Migration and the Social Space of Postmodernism. *Diaspora: A Journal of Transnational Studies* 1:8–23.

Rowe, William, and Vivian Schelling. 1991. *Memory and Modernity: Popular Culture in Latin America.* London: Verso.

Rugendas, Johann Moritz. [1838] 1973. *Album de Trajes Chilenos.* Santiago: Imprenta Litográfico de J. B. Lebas.

Ruíz, Ramón Eduardo. 1988. *The People of Sonora and Yankee Capitalists.* Tucson: University of Arizona Press.

Rumbold, Horace. 1876. Report by Mr. Rumbold on the Progress and General Condition of Chile. *Reports by Her Majesty's Secretaries of Embassy and Legation on the Manufacturers, Commerce & C., of the Countries in Which They Reside.* Commercial. No. 14 (Trade Reports). London.

Sahlins, Marshall. 1972. *Stone Age Economics.* New York: Aldine Publishing.

Saignes, Thierry. 1990. *Ava y karai: Ensayos sobre la frontera chiriguano (siglos XVIXX).* La Paz: HISBOL.

Salazar, Orlando. 1990. *El apogeo de la República Liberal en Costa Rica (1870–1914).* San José: Editorial de la Universidad de Costa Rica.

Samaniego, Carlos. 1978. Peasant Movements at the Turn of the Century and the Rise of the Independent Farm. *Peasant Cooperation and Capitalist Expansion in Central Peru,* ed. Norman Long and Bryan Roberts, 143–78. Austin: University of Texas Press.

Samper, Mario. 1978. Los productores directos en el siglo del café. *Revista de Historia* 7:123–217.

———. (no date). Agricultor o jornalero? Algunos problemas de historia social agraria. *Historia,* n.s.: 1–49.

Savigliano, Marta E. 1995. *Tango and the Political Economy of Passion.* Boulder, CO: Westview Press.

Schneider, Jane. 1980. Trousseau As Treasure: Some Contradictions of Late Nineteenth Century Change in Sicily. In *Beyond the Myths of Culture,* ed. Eric Ross, 323–56. New York: Academic Press.

Scott, James C. 1985. *Weapons of the Weak: Everyday Forms of Peasant Resistance.* New Haven: Yale University Press.

Seligmann, Linda. 1989. To Be In Between: The *Cholas* As Market Women. *Comparative Studies in Society and History* 31(4): 694–712.

Seligson, Mitchell A., and Edward J. Williams. 1981. *Maquiladoras and Migration: Workers in the Mexico–United States Border Industrialization Program.* Austin: Mexico–United States Border Research Program and the University of Texas Press.

Sheridan, Thomas E. 1988. *Where the Dove Calls: The Political Ecology of a Peasant Corporate Community in Northwestern Mexico.* Tucson: University of Arizona Press.

Silva Vargas, Fernando. 1992. Los cafés en la primera mitad del siglo XIX. *Formas de sociabilidad en Chile 1840–1940,* ed. Teresa Pereira, 315–44. Santiago: Fundación Mario Góngora.

Simonelli, Jeanne. 1985. Markets, Motherhood, and Modernization: Fertility and

Economic Change in a Rural Mexican Municipio. Ph.D. diss., University of Oklahoma.

Sommer, Doris. 1991. *Foundational Fictions: The National Romances of Latin America.* Berkeley and London: University of California Press.

Spence, Jonathan D. 1990. *The Search for Modern China.* New York and London: W. W. Norton.

Stevenson, William B. 1829. *A Historical and Descriptive Narrative of Twenty Years' Residence in South America.* Vol. 2. London: Hurst, Robinson and Co.

Subercaseaux, Ramón. 1936. *Memoria de ochenta años: recuerdos personales, críticas, reminisencias históricas, viajes anécdotas.* 2 vols. Santiago: Editorial Nascimiento.

Susnik, Branislava. 1968. *Chiriguanos.* Asunción: Museo Etnográfico "Andrés Barbero."

Taylor, J. Edward. 1987. Undocumented Mexico–U.S. Migration and the Returns to Households in Rural Mexico. *American Journal of Agricultural Economics* 69:626–38.

Taylor, William. 1973. *Drinking, Homicide and Rebellion in Colonial Mexico.* Stanford: Stanford University Press.

Temple, Edmond. 1833. *Travels in Various Parts of Peru, Including a Year's Residence in Potosí.* Vol. 2 Philadelphia: E. L. Carey and A. Hart.

Tenorio, Mauricio. 1996. *Crafting a Modern Nation: Modernity and Nationalism in Mexicos Presence at Worlds Fairs, 1880s–1930s.* Berkeley and London: The University of California Press.

Thompson, E. P. 1977. *Tradicion, revuelta y conciencia de clase.* 2d ed. Barcelona: Seix Barral.

Tignor, Robert L. 1966. *Modernization and British Colonial Rule in Egypt, 1882–1914.* Princeton: Princeton University Press.

———. 1984. *State, Private Enterprise, and Economic Change in Egypt, 1918–1952.* Princeton: Princeton University Press.

Tornero, Recaredo S. 1872. *Chile ilustrado. Guia descriptivo del territorio de Chile, de las capitales de provincia i de los puertos principales.* Santiago: Librerias i ajencias del Mercurio.

Unruh, Vick. 1994. *Latin American Vanguards: The Art of Contentious Encounters.* University of California Press.

Valcárcel, Luís E. 1981. *Memorias,* ed. José Matos Mar, José Deustua C., and José Luis Rénique. Lima: IEP.

Verdery, Katherine. 1983. *Transylvanian Villagers: Three Centuries of Political, Economic, and Ethnic Change.* Berkeley and Los Angeles: University of California Press.

———. 1991. *National Ideology Under Socialism: Identity and Cultural Politics in Ceaucescu's Romania.* Berkeley and Los Angeles: University of California Press.

Vial Correa, Gonzalo. 1981. *Historia de Chile, 1891–1973.* Santiago: Editorial Santillana del Pacífico.

Villafañe, Benjamín. 1857. *Orán y Bolivia a la márjen del Bermejo.* Salta: Imprenta del Comercio.

Villalobos, Bernardo. 1981. *Bancos emisores y bancos hipotecarios (1850–1910).* San José: Editorial Costa Rica.

Villalobos, Sergio. 1973. *Imagen de Chile histórico: el album de Gay.* Santiago: Editorial Universitario.

———. 1987. *Origen y acenso de la burguesía chilena.* Santiago: Editorial Universitaria.

von Csapolvics, Johann. 1829. *Gemälde Von Ungarn.* Vol. 1. Pest: Hartleben.

von Tschudi, Johann J. 1847. *Travels in Peru During the Years 1838–42 on the Coast, in the Sierra, Across the Cordilleras and the Andes, into the Premieval Forests.* London: David Bogue.

Wagner, Moritz, and Carl Sherzer. 1974. *La República de Costa Rica en la América Central.* Vol. 1. San José: Editorial Costa Rica.

Wallerstein, Immanuel. 1979. *The Capitalist World-Economy.* Studies in Modern Capitalism. Cambridge: Cambridge University Press.

Weismantel, Mary. 1989. The Children Cry for Bread: Hegemony and the Transformation of Consumption. In *The Social Economy of Consumption,* ed. Benjamin S. Orlove and Henry J. Rutz. Lanham, MD: University Press of America.

Wilk, Richard R. 1989. Houses as Consumer Goods: Social Processes and Allocation Decisions. *The Social Economy of Consumption,* ed. Benjamin S. Orlove, and Henry J. Rutz, 297–322. Lanham, MD: University Press of America.

Wilson, Fiona. 1982. Property and Ideology: a Regional Oligarchy in the Central Andes in the Nineteenth Century. In *Ecology and Exchange in the Andes,* ed. David Lehmann. Cambridge: Cambridge University Press.

———. 1985. *Gender and Class in an Andean Town,* A.85 2. CRD-Project Papers, Copenhagen.

Wright, Marie Robinson. 1904. *The Republic of Chile. The Growth, Resources, and Industrial Conditions of a Great Nation.* Philadelphia: George Barrie and Sons.

Wright, Thomas C. 1975. Agriculture and Protectionism in Chile, 1880–1930. *Journal of Latin American Studies* 7:45–58.

Contributors

Arnold J. Bauer, professor of history at the University of California at Davis, received his Ph.D. in history from Berkeley in 1969. He has written on rural society in Latin America and, more specifically, in Chile; social and economic aspects of the Catholic Church in Latin America; and the material culture of Latin America. His works include *Chilean Rural Society from the Spanish Conquest to 1930* (1975) as well as a number of articles and essays. He is currently at work on a synthetic work on the historical development of Spanish American material culture and an interpretive study of long-term transformations of rural economy and society.

Peri L. Fletcher is a doctoral candidate in anthropology at The Johns Hopkins University. Her dissertation, entitled "Casa de Mis Sueños: Migration and Houses in a Transnational Mexican Community," explores the dilemmas of social reproduction in a migrant community that spans southern California and Michoacán, Mexico. Her previous anthropological field research, conducted in the Caribbean, focused on market women in Dominica and Guadeloupe.

Josiah McC. Heyman is associate professor of anthropology at Michigan Technological University. After receiving his Ph.D. in anthropology from City University of New York in 1989, he published *Life and Labor on the Border: Working People of Northeastern Sonora, Mexico, 1886–1986*. His continuing research on the border, focusing on the Immigration and Naturalization Service, has appeared in *Current Anthropology* and the *Journal of Political Ecology,* while his recent work on consumption features an article (with James Carrier) forthcoming in the *Journal of the Royal Anthropological Institute.*

Thomas Krüggeler is visiting professor of history at the Universidad Nacional San Antonio Abad del Cusco and associated researcher at the Centro de Estudios Regionales "Bartolomé de las Casas." He received an

215

M.A. in history from the Universität Bielefeld (Germany) in 1987 and a Ph.D. in history from the University of Illinois in 1993. Presently he is engaged in turning his dissertation "Unreliable Drunkards or Honorable Citizens? Artisans in Search of Their Place in the Cusco Society (1815–1930)" into a book manuscript.

Erick D. Langer received his Ph.D. in history from Stanford University in 1984. He is presently associate professor of history at Carnegie Mellon University. His works include *Economic Change and Rural Resistance in Southern Bolivia 1880–1930* (1989) and *The New Latin American Mission History* (1995), coedited with Robert H. Jackson. He is presently working on an ethnohistory of the Franciscan missions among the Chiriguano Indians in the nineteenth and twentieth centuries.

Benjamin Orlove received his Ph.D. in anthropology from Berkeley in 1974. He is currently professor in the Division of Environmental Studies at the University of California at Davis. He has written several books and a number of articles on the environmental, economic, and cultural anthropology and history of Latin America, with an emphasis on the Andean region. In addition, he has written a family memoir, *In My Father's Study* (1995), published in Singular Lives: The Iowa Series in North American Autobiography. He is currently working on a book on the Lake Titicaca region.

Patricia Vega Jiménez received her M.S. in history from the Universidad de Costa Rica in 1990. She has published two books, *El colegio de periodistas de Costa Rica: su historia* (1993) and *De la imprenta al periódico: los inicios de la comunicación en Costa Rica 1821–1850* (1995), as well as a number of articles in scholarly journals. She is the director of the School of Communication Sciences in the Universidad de Costa Rica. She is presently conducting a research project on consumption in Costa Rica in the late nineteenth and early twentieth centuries.

Index

Accordions, 85
Adobe, 139, 162, 189–93
Advertisements, 4, 11, 44, 57, 67–69, 71–75, 77, 79–89, 127, 143. *See also* Catalogues
Africa, 4, 8, 17–18, 24
Agriculture, 3, 17, 20, 38, 44, 71, 81, 95, 117, 143, 148–49, 199–200; agricultural activities, 187; agricultural life, 199; agricultural subsistence, 185; agricultural tools, 158
Aguardiente, 35, 39, 52
Airplanes, 9, 114
Alcohol, 50, 109, 121. *See also* Liquor
Algeria, 24
Allende, Salvador, 148
Andes, 35–36, 40–41, 43, 47, 58–59, 61–65, 94–95, 100, 104, 117, 121, 127–28, 135, 201
Anthropology, 15, 20–21, 50, 94, 112–16, 180, 199–200. *See also* Ethnography
Apothecaries, 73–75
Appadurai, Arjun, 14
Appliances, 80, 159–60, 170, 172, 174, 182, 186, 197, 200. *See also* Refrigerators; Sewing machines; Stoves; Washing machines
Architecture, 82, 140, 143; architects, 119, 140
Argentina, 10, 12, 96, 98–106, 108–10, 113, 122–23, 127–28, 130, 135, 138
Artisans, 40, 53, 55–59, 63, 65, 79, 82, 120, 133
Asia, 4, 8, 17, 172

Automobiles, 10, 12, 158–59, 173–75, 179, 182
Axes, 85, 158

Balconies, 86, 127
Banks, 26, 46, 62, 115, 154, 172–73, 176
Banquets, 114, 130, 133–34
Bargaining, 44, 78, 88
Barter, 35, 50, 80, 102
Bathrooms, 145, 197
Bathtubs, 158
Beads, 85
Beans, 4, 69–70, 114, 134, 156, 166, 172, 187, 193–94
Beds, 46, 158, 165–68, 175
Beef, 113, 182
Beer, 13, 27, 36, 41, 56, 64, 72, 112, 121–22
Belgium, 96
Benches, 67, 69, 71, 73, 75, 77, 79–81, 83, 85, 87, 89, 91
Berlin, 20
Beverages, 4, 27, 72–73, 86, 90, 131, 133, 136–38. *See also* Alcohol; Coffee; Tea
Bhabha, Homi, 9
Billiard tables, 35, 87, 133
Bloch, Marc, 106
Body, 77, 103, 138, 146
Bolivia, 13, 16, 66, 93–97, 101, 103, 105–6, 111–12, 117, 149
Books, 64–65, 86, 104, 127, 129, 139, 144, 148–49, 159
Booms, 4–5, 7, 12, 21, 28, 35, 39, 51,

Booms (*continued*)
  96, 103, 108, 120, 138, 144, 146, 154,
  170, 185, 196
Borders, 15, 22, 96, 100, 130, 151–65,
  167, 169–83
Bottles, 24, 27, 50, 69, 71–75, 85, 125,
  130, 138, 146
Bourdieu, Pierre, 186
Bourgeoisie, 89, 119
Boys, 77, 103, 142
Braceros, 189
Brazil, 4, 6–7, 135, 138, 149
Bread, 26–27, 156, 194
Brenneis, Donald, 106
Brick, 163, 188–91
Britain, 13, 21–25, 33–36, 38, 42–43,
  51, 48, 54, 58, 68, 74, 77, 80, 83, 89,
  96, 118–19
Bronze, 82
Buenos Aires, 5, 9, 11, 29, 63, 96, 111,
  138
Burro, 118, 160–61, 193
Butter, 42, 70

Cafés, 133–36, 142, 144
California, 63–64, 69, 122, 127, 156,
  186, 191, 196, 200
Candlesticks, 82, 85
Capital cities, 6–7, 12–13
Capitalism, 1, 63, 153–57, 179–80, 186
Caps, 52, 76–77, 86
Cárdenas, Lázaro, 170, 200
Caribbean, 4, 122
Carpets, 82
Carrier, James, 152, 183
Cash, 31–32, 35–37, 39, 45–47, 50–53,
  56, 61–62, 154, 157, 159, 167, 171,
  180, 182, 193–94, 199–200; economy,
  36, 51, 53, 61, 154, 194, 199
Castells, Manuel, 178
Catalogues, 143, 161, 177
Catholic Church, 163
Cattle, 21, 95–103, 108, 110, 112, 140,
  198
Ceramics, 58
Chacolí, 123–24, 128, 130, 146–47

Chairs, 36, 59, 80–81, 83, 158, 165–66,
  191, 197
Champagne, 71, 73, 114, 119, 124–25
Cheese, 69–70, 172
Chess, 87
Chests of drawers, 46, 59
Chicha, 41, 52, 64, 122–24, 128, 130,
  133, 146–47
Chickens, 48, 70, 159, 172, 193
Children, 5, 46, 75–76, 87–88, 102, 118,
  145, 153, 160, 162–65, 167, 174–75,
  182, 189, 191, 194–97. *See also* Boys;
  Girls; Youth
Chile, 8, 13–14, 16, 43, 63, 66, 68–69,
  71, 89, 100, 113–29, 131–33, 135–41,
  143–49
China, 1, 9, 11, 18, 21–24, 28, 40, 45,
  77, 134, 191
Cholera, 67
Christianity, 14, 97, 122, 183
Cigarettes, 23
Cigars, 142
Class, 2, 5, 15–17, 32–33, 37–40, 46–47,
  54, 65, 86, 114–16, 120, 135–36,
  141–44, 148–49, 152, 154, 156–57,
  160, 166–67, 170, 173, 178, 180–81,
  198, 200. *See also* Artisans; Bourgeoisie; Labor; Middle class; Peasants; Poor, the; Proletariat; Working
  class
Clocks, 80–81, 88, 158
Cloth, 7, 13, 16, 20, 23, 34–35, 37, 40,
  42, 45, 48, 52, 55–56, 58, 60, 63, 76,
  78–79, 93–103, 105–11, 144–45, 165.
  See also Cotton; Damask; Fabric;
  Lace; Leather; Linings; Ribbons;
  Silk; Wool
Clothing, 14, 26–27, 41, 48, 52, 55, 60,
  62, 66–67, 69, 72, 75–79, 85–86, 94,
  97, 99, 107, 157, 160, 165, 174. *See
  also* Caps; Coats; Collars; Corsets;
  Crinoline; Hats; Jackets; Lingerie;
  Neckties; Pants; Shawls; Shirts;
  Shoes; Stockings; Sweaters;
  Trousers; Underwear; Uniforms;
  Vests

Clubs, 6, 141, 143
Coats, 76–79
Coca, 102, 104, 109
Cocoa, 4, 68, 86
Coffee, 4–5, 14–15, 27, 67–68, 71, 74, 76, 78, 80, 82–83, 89, 102, 113–14, 121, 131, 133–34, 136–38, 140, 144–47; coffee exports, 67, 89. *See also* Cafés; Coffeehouses
Coffeehouses, 134, 138
Cognac, 72
Collars, 65, 75, 77
Collective goods, 159–60
Cologne, 44, 77, 85
Colombia, 69, 201
Colombian, 113
Commerce, 17, 23, 31, 35, 49, 51, 58, 65–66, 83–85, 93, 97, 100–102, 166, 173; commercial agents, 40; commercialization, 156. *See also* Barter; Trade
Commodities, 7, 12, 22, 24, 152–53, 156, 163, 187
Compadrazgo, 41, 198
Concrete, 4, 12, 14, 156, 188–91, 194, 198
Confucianism, 10, 22
Consumer cooperatives, 169
Consumer culture, 39, 46, 48, 52–53
Consumer goods, 32, 37, 40–41, 44, 49–50, 52–55, 57, 59, 61–63, 149, 155, 159, 161, 167, 171, 179–80, 192–93, 199–200
Consumption, 1, 4–10, 13–17, 19–20, 22–23, 25–28, 31–33, 35–41, 43–49, 51–53, 55–59, 61–65, 67, 69, 77, 81–83, 88–89, 93–94, 96, 98, 102–3, 105–6, 110, 116, 118–19, 121–23, 125, 130–31, 133–37, 140, 143–46, 148–49, 152, 155, 160, 164, 166, 170–71, 173, 176–80, 185–87, 191–94, 197–200; conspicuous, 33, 40, 62, 148, 187, 198. *See also* Consumer culture; Consumer goods
Consumption decisions, 192

Cooking, 17, 23, 27, 69, 139, 157, 175, 182, 191, 194, 196–97
Copper, 83, 113, 115, 117–18, 154, 164–65
Corsets, 88
Costa Rica, 15, 67–68, 70–74, 76–81, 84, 86, 89–91
Cotton, 25, 34–35, 46, 48, 60, 75–79, 88, 108
Cradles, 158
Credit, 67, 112, 167, 169, 171–73, 176, 182
Crinoline, 79
Culture, 16, 49, 52, 94, 103, 112, 118
Cups, 9, 85, 133–35, 138
Currency, 29, 144, 171, 176. *See also* Cash; Devaluations; Pesos
Curtains, 158
Customs duties, 96

Damask, 76
Debt, 25, 99, 103–4, 109–10, 154, 175–77, 182
Decadence, 31, 40, 64, 144
Depression, 2, 6–7, 22, 26, 113, 120, 145, 154, 156, 165
Devaluations, 146, 154–55, 169, 172–78
Development, economic, 113
Developmentalism, 62, 161
Dietary patterns, 23, 69, 116, 122, 181, 188, 194
Dish cabinets, 165, 166, 168
Dishes, 23, 70, 137, 165–68, 181, 191, 194, 197–99
Doorknobs, 140
Douglas, Mary, 162, 165, 172–74, 176–77, 179–80
Dressmakers, 40, 42

Earrings, 77–78
Economy, 2–3, 5, 18, 21, 23–24, 27–28, 32, 34, 36, 39, 48–54, 56, 59, 61, 75, 95, 100–101, 103, 105, 110, 113–15, 117, 147, 152, 154, 156, 160, 170, 175–76, 185, 188–89, 194, 199–201
Education, 26, 43, 46, 115, 142–43

Eggs, 70, 172
Egypt, 24–27
Ejidos (Mexico), 162, 187–89, 198, 200–201
Electricity, 188
Energy, 157, 180
Environment, 3, 42, 45, 185–87, 190–91, 196
Equality, 187, 198
Esthetics, 97, 198
Ethnography, 26, 94, 200
Europe, 6, 21, 25–28, 94, 102–3, 120, 125, 128, 130, 138, 143, 146–47
Everyday life, 31, 156, 186, 189
Excess, 14, 31, 113–16, 120
Expenditures, 52, 134, 172, 189
Exports, 1–4, 7, 12, 15–16, 21, 25, 29, 35, 58, 67–68, 89, 93, 113–15, 118–20, 144, 176, 179
Expositions, 97, 129–30

Fabric, 43, 46, 56, 60, 76, 88, 160, 165, 167, 174, 176, 188
Factories, 9, 13, 20, 34, 36, 40, 46, 53–54, 56, 58–59, 66, 70, 98, 171–72, 175, 177; textile, 36, 40, 54–56, 63
Fads, 10, 82
Families, 7, 13, 15, 23, 26, 36–41, 43–50, 54, 56, 58, 61–62, 80, 83, 106, 117, 127, 131, 133–34, 137, 140–41, 144, 148, 162, 167, 170–71, 179, 182–83, 186–88, 190–91, 193–94, 196, 201; daughters in, 15, 159, 167, 172, 196–97; dynamics, 192; life, 6, 187, 189, 198; sons in, 45, 159, 172. See also Households
Fashions, 6, 8, 10–11, 14, 28, 31, 37–42, 45, 55, 57, 62, 75, 79, 115, 118–20, 140, 146–48, 161; acceptability, 164, 171. See also Fads; Style
Firewood, 166
Flour, 69, 71, 87
Food, 17, 20, 23–24, 27, 31, 46, 67–69, 71, 85–86, 104, 108, 113, 131, 134, 137, 152, 155–57, 159, 163, 185, 193–94, 197. See also Banquets;

Beans; Beef; Bread; Butter; Cheese; Cocoa; Eggs; Flour; Fruit; Grain; Grapes; Ham; Herbs; Herring; Meat; Noodles; Potatoes; Restaurants; Rice; Salmon; Salt; Spices; Sugar
Foreignness, 1–6, 8, 10–14, 16, 18–29, 31–40, 42–48, 50–52, 54–60, 62–66, 68–70, 72, 74, 76, 78, 80, 82–84, 86, 88, 90, 93–112, 114–16, 118, 120–26, 128, 130, 132–36, 138, 140, 142–49, 152–54, 156–58, 160, 162, 164, 166, 169–70, 172, 174–76, 178–80, 182, 186, 188, 190, 192, 194, 196, 198, 200
Frontier, 93, 95–111, 156
Fruit, 69, 122
Furniture, 20, 27, 34, 36, 38, 45–46, 59–62, 66–67, 72, 80–81, 85–86, 119, 158, 165, 170, 172–75, 191, 196. See also Beds; Benches; Billiard tables; Carpets; Chairs; Chests of drawers; Clocks; Cradles; Dish cabinets; Lamps; Mattresses; Mirrors; Rugs; Sofas; Tables; Windows

Gardens, 82, 119, 127–28, 142
Garlic, 114
Garments, 20, 41, 42, 46, 60, 78, 88, 165, 170, 172. See also Clothing
Gasoline, 179
Generations, 22, 118, 131, 134, 151, 155, 157, 187. See also Children; Youth
Gente decente, 47
Gentility, 43, 79, 138–39
Germany, 6, 10, 13, 25, 34, 42, 44, 56, 58, 64, 69, 73, 80, 82–83, 85, 88, 96, 98, 117, 134, 137, 145, 149, 160
Gin, 72
Girls, 77, 79, 88, 103, 142, 176, 195
Global economy, 28, 152, 185, 189
Gold, 36, 78, 89, 129
Golf, 5
Goods, 1, 3, 5–9, 12–29, 31–41, 43–59, 61–63, 65, 67–68, 77, 79–82, 85–86, 93–94, 98–102, 105–10, 112, 114–17,

119–21, 124, 136, 138, 140, 144–49, 151–57, 159–62, 164–67, 169–72, 174–77, 179–81, 189, 192–93, 197–200; manufactured, 21, 26, 31, 33–34, 37–38, 47–48, 52, 54, 68, 72–73, 77, 82–83, 86, 93, 96–97, 149, 152–54, 156–57, 161, 165, 191, 199; used, 116, 172, 176. *See also* Households, goods; Western goods

Grain, 17–21, 26, 31, 33–34, 37–38, 47–48, 52, 54, 68, 72–73, 77, 82–83, 86, 89, 93, 96–97, 122, 149, 152–54, 156–57, 161, 165, 191, 199

Grapes, 13, 122–28, 130–31, 143–46, 149

Guano, 34–35, 38–39, 48, 64

Guatemala, 74

Gudeman, Stephen, 201

Guitars, 80, 85, 148

Gunpowder, 72

Habsburg Empire, 18, 20–21

Haciendas, 36–38, 41, 43–44, 50–51, 103, 105, 109, 143

Ham, 69–71

Hamilton, Gary, 22–23

Hammers, 56, 140

Hardware, 34–35, 37, 44, 51–52, 54, 58, 62, 65, 136, 140, 143. *See also* Appliances; Doorknobs; Hinges; Tools

Hats, 10–11, 25, 55, 75–77, 79, 85–86, 157

Heating, 157

Herbs, 14, 73

Herring, 69

Hides, 46, 68

Hinges, 86, 140–41

Hoes, 17, 145

Holland, 69, 72, 74

Home, 25, 27, 34, 54, 59, 87, 105, 114, 134, 155, 161, 165, 167, 181, 188–90, 196

Horses, 128, 142, 147–48, 160–61, 193

Households, 12, 20, 26–27, 47, 50, 67, 80–82, 85–86, 145, 151, 153–60, 164–68, 170–72, 174–76, 178, 180–82, 188–90, 192–95, 199, 201; goods, 67, 80–81, 85–86, 164. *See also* Families

Houses, 5, 13–16, 20, 35, 37, 40, 54, 57–58, 63, 80, 82–84, 98, 114, 117, 119, 121, 127–28, 137–44, 146–47, 160, 162–63, 167, 170–71, 173, 178, 181, 185–201; construction, 140, 162, 181, 192; improvements, 189–90; rooms, 139, 190. *See also* Adobe; Architecture; Balconies; Bathrooms; Bathtubs; Brick; Concrete; Curtains; Dishes; Doorknobs; Furniture; Gardens; Home; Mansions; Palaces; Patios; Roofs; Shacks; Windows

Hungary, 19–21

Identity, 7, 9, 12, 16, 18, 27, 114, 116, 118–19, 153, 171, 181, 185–86, 192, 199

Illness, 73

Immigration, 45, 49, 64, 117, 152, 165, 172, 179, 181. *See also* Migration

Imports, 1–3, 5–9, 11–17, 19–29, 32–38, 44–46, 48–62, 65, 68–69, 74, 77, 80–81, 83, 89, 94–99, 101, 105–6, 108, 110, 114–16, 120, 122–32, 136, 140, 143–46, 151–57, 159–65, 167–83, 185–87, 198–99

Incas, 36, 49, 117

Income, 3–4, 19, 23, 46, 50, 55, 57, 67, 83, 108, 144–46, 167, 170–71, 174, 176, 181, 183, 185, 188–90, 192–94, 199, 201

Independence, national 2–3, 7–8, 21, 25, 28, 31, 33, 37–38, 44, 48, 56, 64, 95, 99, 106, 110, 115–16, 123, 130, 135, 140, 144, 146–47, 196

Indians, 13, 16, 31–33, 40–41, 43, 48–52, 56, 62, 65, 93–95, 97–105, 107, 110, 112, 115, 117, 121, 124, 144; Indian communities, 32, 50–51, 56; Indian tribute, 49

Indonesia, 17

Industrialization, 3, 25–26, 54, 56, 58, 156
Industry, 1–2, 17, 20, 23, 49, 56, 63–64, 66, 88, 114, 153, 156, 164, 171. *See also* Factories
Ink, 85
Intellectuals, 49, 89, 116, 119, 160
Iran, 24
Iron, 34, 45, 50, 52, 83, 85–86, 89
Islam, 24
Italy, 44–45, 54–55, 97, 119, 128

Jackets, 76–78, 85
Jazz, 121
Jews, 6, 11
Justice, 151–53, 155, 157, 159, 161, 163–65, 167, 169–71, 173, 175, 177, 179–81, 183

Kerosene, 22
Kitchens, 54, 59, 137, 139, 158, 181, 190–91, 194–96

Labor, 3–4, 15–16, 49–51, 63, 98–99, 104–5, 109–10, 156, 159, 162, 164, 167, 171, 177–78, 180–83, 185–89, 193–94, 199–200; labor force, 3, 104, 171; labor markets, 180, 188, 199; labor relations, 98
Lace, 86, 114
Lamps, 59, 61, 70, 80, 158
Landscape, 51, 119, 186, 192, 200
Laundry, 158, 197
Leather, 40, 44, 54, 56, 59, 119, 156–57, 162
Lebanon, 24
Linen, 75, 77–78
Lingerie, 88
Linings, 23
Liquor, 5, 44–45, 67, 71–74, 80, 85. *See also* Aguardiente; Alcohol; Beer; Cognac; Gin; Pulque; Whisky; Wine
Luxury items, 35, 37, 44–45, 47, 50, 123

Machetes, 85, 158
Machinery, 2, 34, 36, 55–57, 68, 79

Machines, 6, 34, 56, 83, 88–89, 158–60, 165–68, 170, 173–76, 183, 197
Magazines, 9, 11, 88
Maize, 14, 52, 95, 101, 121–22, 187, 191, 193–94
Mansions, 5, 20, 114, 128, 138, 141, 145–49
Manufacturing, 21, 26, 31, 33–34, 37–38, 47–48, 52, 54, 68, 72–73, 77, 82–83, 86, 93, 96–97, 149, 152–54, 156–57, 161, 165, 191, 199
Maquiladoras, 170–72, 176, 183
Marble, 80–81, 128
Markets, 7, 12, 20, 22, 25, 28, 31–37, 39–40, 44–45, 48–49, 50–55, 57–63, 65–66, 68–70, 78, 81–83, 94, 97, 101–3, 108, 118, 124, 137, 140, 145–47, 149, 177–80, 182, 187–88, 191, 199–200; provincial, 32, 37, 53, 61–63
Mass media, 185
Material culture, 94, 152–53, 155–57, 161, 163–65, 167, 174, 180–81, 183
Mattresses, 80, 158, 165–66, 175, 191
Meat, 47, 89, 148, 166–67, 174, 181–82
Medicinal herbs, 73
Medicines, 67–68, 70, 72–75
Melanesia, 17
Men, 12, 16, 27, 41, 60, 76–78, 86, 97, 99, 103, 105, 109, 111, 116, 123, 133–34, 142–43, 151, 155–56, 158, 160, 165, 167, 170–71, 174, 177, 185, 188–89, 194–95; sons in families, 45, 159, 172
Merchandise, 22, 33, 45, 58, 68, 70, 81, 84–86, 88–89, 98, 172. *See also* Goods
Merchants, 13, 23, 32–36, 38, 44–45, 50–51, 53–58, 63, 69, 70–72, 74–79, 81–88, 95–97, 100–102, 110, 112, 115, 135, 156; wholesale, 36, 57. *See also* Peddlers; Retailers; Shopkeepers; Traders
Mestizos, 13, 43, 96–97, 103–8, 117, 120–21, 135
Metates, 157–58, 191

Mexico, 5–7, 13–16, 117, 120–22, 129, 138, 151, 153–79, 181, 183, 185–93, 195, 197–201; PAN, 129, 163, 178; PRI, 177–79. *See also* Braceros; Ejidos; Maquiladoras
Middle class, 12, 32–33, 36, 46–47, 62, 65, 145, 160, 170, 177, 191, 198
Migration, 15, 98, 103–5, 108, 110, 153–54, 156–57, 181–201. *See also* Immigration
Military, 25, 76–77, 86, 97–98, 100, 104, 110, 117. *See also* Soldiers
Mining, 8, 13, 15, 31, 35, 37, 39, 41, 51–52, 54, 97, 103, 108, 115, 127, 129, 133–34, 143–44, 149, 151, 154, 156, 159–65, 169–71, 174–75, 178–82
Mintz, Sidney, 152, 185–86
Mirrors, 54, 80, 82–83, 95, 158
Missions, 97, 101–4, 186
Modernism, 186
Modernity, 2, 8–9, 11, 13–14, 18, 20–23, 25, 28–29, 31, 33, 37–38, 42–43, 46–47, 49, 52, 56–58, 61, 118–21, 135–37, 143, 147, 149, 163, 181, 185, 187–88, 191, 195, 197, 199
Modernization, 6, 113, 119, 161–62, 185–86, 188
Moral evaluation, 157
Motorcycles, 158
Music, 13, 24, 121, 157, 167. *See also* Jazz
Musical instruments, 82, 159. *See also* Accordions; Guitars; Pianos
Muskets, 103

NAFTA, 153, 155, 176
Nationalism, 13, 18, 21, 23–25, 27–28, 57, 118, 120, 129, 148, 153–55, 164, 169–70
Neckties, 76
Newspapers, 6, 44, 47, 54, 57, 67–68, 73, 82, 87–88, 134
New York, 29, 65, 69, 84, 119
Nitrates, 113, 115, 117–18, 120, 143
Noodles, 71–72

Obrajes, 48, 96
Oil, 69, 80, 85, 158, 169
Olive oil, 69, 85
Olympics, 121
Opera, 8, 119
Orlove, Benjamin, 1, 13–14, 16, 32, 64, 113, 152, 186, 200
Ornaments, 77–78
Ottoman Empire, 18, 24–25, 28

Palaces, 141, 144, 146
Pants, 27, 97
Paper, 47, 81, 86, 95, 100, 111, 186, 200
Paris, 5, 9–11, 42, 76–77, 79, 84, 111–12, 118–19, 121, 124, 129, 144
Patios, 82, 137, 139, 146–47, 193, 195–97
Patriarchy, 195
Pearls, 68, 78
Peasants, 13–14, 18, 20, 25, 31, 33, 37, 40–41, 47–53, 61–62, 76, 80, 82, 128, 154, 159, 170, 177, 182, 188, 192
Peddlers, 35, 37, 42, 69, 139, 156, 165, 172
Pepper, 70, 136
Perfumes, 34, 45, 77, 86
Peru, 13, 15, 31–39, 41, 43–45, 47–49, 53–55, 58–66, 111, 117, 123, 149
Pesos, 70–73, 75–76, 81, 85–86, 96, 99, 101, 107, 112, 115–16, 120, 128, 137, 154, 169, 172–73, 175–76
Petroleum, 113
Photographs, 97, 140, 191
Pianos, 5, 13, 35, 37, 43, 45–46, 80–82, 114, 140, 148
Pickaxes, 86
Plantations, 2, 104–5, 108–10
Plows, 6, 17, 83, 193
Poland, 19–21
Poor, the, 3, 5–6, 16, 23, 26–27, 33, 45–48, 54–55, 58–59, 65, 77–78, 82, 86, 97, 104–5, 130, 134–35, 137, 139–48, 152, 160–62, 173, 175, 177, 185, 187, 198, 200. *See also* Poverty
Porcelain, 17, 22, 80–81

Postcoloniality, 7–9, 14, 18, 27, 116, 119–20
Postmodern, 8
Potatoes, 70, 89
Pots, 51, 85, 191, 194
Pottery, 2
Poverty, 19, 47, 52, 160, 162, 164
Power, 4, 17–19, 22, 26, 40–41, 43, 50, 55, 62, 78–79, 94, 98, 100–101, 106–8, 152, 159, 163, 167, 169–70, 172–77, 179, 183, 187, 192
Prices, 4, 23, 28, 34, 37, 44–47, 50, 52–53, 59, 63, 70–76, 78–79, 81, 86–89, 96, 104, 124, 137, 145, 171–72, 177–78; prices, low, 2, 35, 37, 43–44, 52, 70, 73, 75, 172
Privacy, 5, 17, 25, 46, 82, 84, 99, 112, 115, 130, 140, 147, 153, 171, 176, 192, 195–97
Production, 1–2, 4–5, 7, 9, 14, 19–20, 23, 28–29, 33, 40, 48–49, 51–55, 57–61, 63, 66–67, 89, 108, 113–14, 123–26, 128–29, 137, 145, 151, 156, 159–60, 170, 179–80, 185–86, 193–94, 196, 199, 201
Progress, 13, 32, 36–37, 39–40, 48, 52, 57, 88, 118, 147, 180. See also Development, economic
Proletariat, 152, 185, 199
Protest, 177–78
Pulque, 6, 121–22
Pumps, 27, 82
Purchasing power, 40, 170, 176

Race, 11, 16, 166–67, 178. See also Europe; Foreignness; Indians; Mestizos
Radio, 159, 165–66, 168, 175
Railroads, 9, 36–37, 45–47, 53, 58, 115
Ranching, 2, 95, 97–104, 106–10, 166, 182. See also Haciendas
Reciprocity, 41, 50, 107
Recreation, 174, 186, 194
Refrigerators, 27, 154, 156, 158, 168, 175, 181, 198

Reproduction, 27, 151, 191, 193–94, 199
Restaurants, 5, 21, 40, 124, 160
Retailers, 35, 44, 60
Ribbons, 52, 77, 85–86, 88
Rice, 69, 77, 131
Rituals, 17, 59, 121, 136, 146
Roofs, 14, 140, 162, 189, 192–94, 197
Rugs, 158
Rutz, Henry, 152, 186

Saints, 42–43, 64, 78, 83, 119, 139, 142
Sales, 34–35, 39, 42, 44–45, 62, 81, 88, 133
Salmon, 69
Salt, 69–71, 136
Sandals, 6
Servants, 20, 139
Sewing machines, 34, 56, 88, 158, 160, 165–68, 170, 175
Shacks, 139, 143, 146
Sharecropping, 188
Shawls, 78, 86
Shirts, 48, 75–76, 97
Shoes, 55–56. See also Sandals
Shopkeepers, 33, 42, 46, 51, 69
Shopping, 45, 142, 151, 171–72, 174, 176, 182–83
Shops, 24, 40, 45, 57–58, 60, 72–75, 77, 79, 81, 84–88, 133, 158, 171–72, 174–75, 177, 180. See also Stores
Silk, 22, 35, 46, 76–79, 85–86, 88
Silver, 20, 64, 82, 97, 103, 108, 135, 146–47
Sleep, 48, 157
Soap, 38, 44, 54, 56, 69, 74, 85
Soccer, 121
Social Darwinism, 94
Social identity, 7, 185
Social relations, 12, 14, 32, 41, 43, 59, 63, 153, 164, 182, 186–87, 191, 195, 199
Social structure, 153, 179–80, 186, 200
Sofas, 67, 69, 71, 73, 75, 77, 79–83, 85, 87, 89, 91, 140, 157–58, 168, 175, 178

Soldiers, 97, 100, 107. *See also* Military; Uniforms

Space, 2, 16, 68, 82, 85, 127, 139, 141–42, 186, 191, 193, 195–96

Spain, 5, 36, 42, 51, 68–69, 71, 95, 97, 107, 115–18, 121–23, 143, 146–47, 155

Spices, 17, 74, 137. *See also* Garlic; Herbs; Pepper; Salt

Standard of living, 109, 165–66, 171, 175

Statues, 82

Status, 7, 17, 22–23, 33, 38, 43–44, 46–47, 50, 62, 107–8, 116, 120, 122, 125, 128, 137, 147, 155, 163, 171–72

Steel, 86, 191

Stockings, 75, 77

Stone, 162, 189, 191–92

Stores, 34–36, 40, 45, 54, 60, 69, 73, 77, 79, 84–89, 142–43, 147, 151, 154, 156, 164–74, 177, 180, 182, 195, 199; company, 151, 154, 164–67, 169–71, 174, 180, 182. *See also* Shops; Warehouses.

Stoves, 153, 157–58, 160, 165–67, 175–76, 193–94, 196

Streets, 5, 9, 15, 34, 60, 74, 88–89, 139, 141, 144, 173, 195, 197

Style, 5, 14, 20, 41, 59, 76, 78–79, 121, 127, 157, 162, 170, 179, 188, 191–92, 196, 198. *See also* Fashions

Subsistence, 20, 49–51, 56, 71, 101, 156, 160, 185, 187–88, 193, 198–200

Sugar, 23, 35, 68, 72, 84, 86, 102, 104–5, 108–10, 131, 136, 185

Sweaters, 27

Tables, 20, 35, 70–71, 73, 75–77, 80–81, 83, 85–86, 88, 128, 133, 137, 156–59, 165–68, 174–75, 182–83, 190–91

Tailors, 9, 11, 34, 40, 42, 45, 55–58, 60, 72, 85, 137

Tango, 121

Tariffs, 38, 44, 130, 179

Tea, 4, 9, 14, 22, 27, 114, 121, 131, 133–38, 145–46

Television, 168, 175, 178, 191, 193, 196–98, 201

Textiles, 2, 34, 38, 44, 48, 52, 54, 58, 60, 62, 68–69, 77, 86, 93–94, 96–97, 100–103, 105–10, 112; factory, 36, 40, 54–56, 63. *See also* Cloth

Time, 10, 15, 20, 26, 32, 36, 38, 57, 68–69, 73–74, 81, 84, 87–88, 101, 103, 114, 116–17, 121, 123, 130, 133–34, 145, 148, 151, 154, 157, 159–60, 163–64, 166, 173, 176, 179, 182–83, 186, 189–91, 196–97, 199

Tobacco, 72, 107–8. *See also* Cigarettes; Cigars

Tools, 6, 14, 34, 41, 45, 52, 55–56, 61, 145, 158–60, 167, 181. *See also* Appliances; Axes; Hammers; Hoes; Machetes; Metates; Pickaxes; Plows; Pots; Pumps; Sewing machines; Typewriters; Utensils

Towels, 145

Toys, 42, 77, 85, 87–88, 159

Trade, 1–5, 13, 16–22, 25, 27, 32, 35–36, 45, 50, 53, 58 –60, 64–66, 68, 79, 82, 84, 86, 93, 96–102, 105, 111, 115, 133, 143, 153, 155–56, 172

Traders, 54, 96

Tradition, 6, 11, 41, 128, 179, 185–87, 195

Transportation, 22, 37, 45, 58–59, 115, 123, 157. *See also* Airplanes; Automobiles; Railroads; Trucks

Travelers, 33–34, 41, 51, 58–60, 63–64, 67, 72, 78–79, 94, 114, 119, 123, 134, 137, 139, 197

Trousers, 75–79

Trucks, 151, 158, 160, 165–68, 174–75, 179, 193–98

Turkey, 24–25, 27

Typewriters, 61, 159

Underwear, 75

Uniforms, 97, 107

United States, 2, 4, 8, 13–14, 16, 21, 53, 68, 88, 118, 129, 140, 143, 151,

United States (*continued*)
153–54, 156–62, 164–65, 169,
171–74, 176–77, 179–83, 185–201
Urban areas, 3, 6, 11–12, 14–15, 18–19,
21, 26–27, 31–33, 36, 42, 45–48, 52,
56, 61–62, 65, 68, 81–83, 89, 93, 115,
117–18, 120, 136–40, 143, 145–49,
154–55, 161, 163–64, 179–80, 185,
188, 191–92
Uruguay, 121
Utensils, 54, 158
Utility, 18, 178

Values, 40, 125, 131, 161–63, 188, 192,
198
Venezuela, 113
Vests, 76, 79
Villages, 15, 27, 41, 60, 62, 95, 98–99,
104, 106–7, 110, 144, 154, 163,
185–90, 192–94, 196–201; economy,
188, 200

Wages, 50–52, 99, 110, 116, 137, 156,
159, 164, 169–72, 178, 181, 188, 193,
199
Warehouses, 84, 85
Washing machines, 158, 173, 175, 183,
197
Wealth, 3–4, 18, 38, 40–41, 43, 50, 114,
121, 143, 151, 160, 178–79, 183,
201
Western goods, 22, 94
Whips, 85
Whisky, 3, 14, 43, 72
Wilk, Richard, 159, 192
Windows, 20, 83, 86, 141, 172, 177,
191–92, 196, 199
Wine, 5, 13, 20–21, 24, 43–44, 71–74,
114, 121–31, 138, 140, 144–48. *See
also* Chacolí; Champagne; Chicha
Women, 12, 16, 26–27, 40, 42, 45, 60,
76–79, 86, 97, 103, 105, 107–9, 112,
116, 134, 142, 151, 155, 158–61, 163,
165, 167, 170–71, 174–77, 185,
193–95; daughters in families, 15,
159, 167, 172, 196–97
Wood, 83, 87, 135, 139, 141, 156–57,
166–68, 193–94
Wool, 15, 32, 35–36, 45, 50, 75–76, 79,
86, 108
Working class, 116, 154, 156–57
World War I, 2, 65–66, 125, 128–29,
136, 140, 143, 145, 161, 201
World War II, 154, 160, 165–66,
169–70, 174, 182

Youth, 27, 82, 85, 101, 116, 142–43,
160, 165, 171, 183, 189, 198